To Karl

C000161108

To Karl
D...

...McClure...
OBE

To Karl,
Best Wishes,
John Bevan.

20 Legends

Warrington Wolves

Phil Hodgson

20 Legends

Warrington Wolves

Phil Hodgson

VERTICAL EDITIONS

www.verticaleditions.com

First published in the United Kingdom in 2012 by Vertical Editions, Unit 4a, Snaygill Industrial Estate, Skipton, North Yorkshire BD23 2QR

www.verticaleditions.com

ISBN 978-1-904091-64-6

A CIP catalogue record for this book is available from the British Library

Cover design by HBA, York

Printed and bound by MPG, Bodmin

Contents

Phil Hodgson has been involved in rugby league for almost 50 years, since first venturing down to Hunslet's venerated Parkside ground as a wide-eyed young fan in the early 1960s.

He went on to play at the ground for Hunslet Juniors and, on growing down, became a journalist with the *Rugby Leaguer*.

He was a founding editor, a decade ago, of *League Weekly*, before switching to *League Express*, where he covers all aspects of the sport, from Under 8s to World Cups.

The author of other books published by Vertical Editions such as *Headingley Heroes*, *Odsal Odysseys*, *High Ambitions* and *20 Legends: Castleford Rugby League*, Hodgson lives in Methley, West Yorkshire, where he is heavily involved with his local club, Methley Royals. He is also the chairman of the Castleford & Featherstone ARL.

Acknowledgements

For their help in compiling this book, the author would like to thank: Jack Bentley, Ian Bridge, David Burke, Simon Burke, Richard Coomber, Jonathan Doidge, Neil Dowson, Ray Fletcher, Ray French, Craig Garner, Paul Garrity, Robert Gate, Dave Hadfield, Glen Hudson, David Huitson, Lionel Hurst, *John Player Rugby League Yearbook*, John Huxley, Sig Kasatkin, *League Express*, *League Weekly*, Keith Macklin, Graham Morris, Mike Parsons, Bev Risman, Charlie Seeling, Gary Slater, George Thornton, *Warrington Guardian*, Alan Whiticker, Dave Williams, Jack Winstanley, George Woodhead, Larry Writer, Bob Young.

1

JE Warren

JAMES EDWARD WARREN was perhaps the first of many all-round sportsmen who have graced the Warrington club in nearly a century and a half of the club's existence. founded 1879

The man known to his friends and associates as Ted was a fine athlete and gymnast, in addition to being a rugby player – in both the union and the Northern Union codes – of some distinction. He also left a lasting legacy, for Warrington and for the Northern Union – which became the Rugby Football League in 1922, four years after his death – for his exemplary administration, underpinned by a strong moral philosophy, perhaps in the mould of the 'Victorian Gentleman'. That legacy arose through a singular sequence of events, given that JE Warren was born and raised many miles away from the strongholds of the Northern Union.

Warren, in fact, first viewed the world on 8 June 1860 in the rural confines of Braunston, a small village in Northamptonshire, situated between Daventry and (perhaps appropriately) Rugby. His family uprooted when he was still a young child to another rural village, Dunham Massey on the outskirts of Manchester, situated on the old Roman Road between Chester and York, two miles south west of Altrincham.

It was a move that was to have a significant impact on his life, possibly in two key respects. Historians have noted that while Dunham Massey may have been a highly desirable place to live, the school was a full six miles away. The young JE Warren walked (or perhaps ran) part of the 12-mile circular route, thereby laying the foundations for an ingrained athleticism which, in common with any fine African athletes who have been sustained by similar experiences and upbringing, was to stand him in good stead for his career in football. It also helped him acquire the physique and the fitness for successes, in his youth and early manhood, at athletics and gymnastics.

Having entered his teenage years in fine condition, Ted Warren turned initially to athletics, joining Orford Hare & Hounds at the age of 16. The Hare & Hounds were leading harriers and boasted in their ranks top runners of the era such as Andrews, Yeomans, Ratcliffe and Hough.

Ted Warren, despite – or perhaps because of – his youth, proved himself equal to the task of representing such a fine outfit. His first win (over an irregular distance; one lap, equal to about 730 yards) came at Moston the following spring. He went on to cross the line first at many events, thrilling the crowds from Chorley to Widnes, at Birmingham and Swinton, and to Blakeley, Blackburn, Preston and beyond, as he quickly established a reputation and a standing, based on results and times, as a quarter-miler and as a hurdler who was clearly threatening to seriously test the best.

JE Warren also somehow found time to develop, hone and refine his talents as a gymnast, and soon earned a reputation as being one of the finest in the north of England. Indeed, at the age of 30, he was a member of the Warrington team that threatened the various favourites in the National Physical Recreation Society's prestigious national competition.

As if athletics and gymnastics were not enough, the Fry-like figure also turned his hand to football, of the rugby variety, joining Padgate Excelsior, who were rated by many as being a superior club to the neighbouring Warrington outfit, perhaps partly – at least in time – because of his own involvement. He became captain and, with colleagues such as Secretary Harry Ashton and Treasurer C Leigh, went on to give a quarter of a century or more of service to the Warrington club after the two outfits merged in 1881.

The arrangement set JE Warren on a term of tenure which was to stretch well into the twentieth century, in a host of capacities which included office at the very head of the Northern Union.

JE Warren was linking up with a Warrington club that had played, following a merger of enthusiasts of Padgate RUFC and Zingari RUFC, on spare land off Sankey Street, opposite the Town Hall. The fledgling club's first game had been at Rice Lane, Liverpool, on Saturday 18 October 1879, against Walton, when the side, captained by WG Edwards, slipped to defeat against a team that registered three converted tries.

Before the month was out, however, Warrington had posted their first victory, accounting for Outrington, notching three converted tries to one after both teams had trekked from Warrington's base at the White Hart Hotel, Sankey Street, to the pitch, which was about

100 yards away.

The first season closed with a very decent record of seven wins and two draws from 11 fixtures. The 1880-81 campaign was highlighted by a move to Wilderspool Causeway, close to St James Church, following the purchase by the Warrington Guardian of the Sankey Street plot, Warrington celebrating the move with a victory over Fairfield Wanderers, of Liverpool, who went home empty-handed thanks to a drop goal by Lewis.

Warren gravitated to the Warrington side in 1881 following yet another change of ground, to Slutchers Lane, in the shadow of the British Aluminium factory at Arpley Meadows. What he brought to the cause, at the age of 21, was qualities of leadership, and no little skill. He also possessed, and had nurtured through his athletic pursuits, power, pace and courage. As such he became renowned as one of the most skilful half-backs in the county, proving to be a handful for opposing sides at, for the era, a handy 10st 10lb in his 5ft 8in frame in an age in which backs could often find themselves committed to involvement in perennially-rolling scrums.

Warren perhaps proved his value to the side in a concrete fashion, on one occasion scoring more than half the Wire's tries in a season. His game, however, involved much more than that, with credit often given for his powerful runs, his unselfish and intelligent passing, which benefited his threequarters in match after match and in season after season, and for his fearless defence.

As a very capable captain, he was judged to be 'genial, affable and courteous', earning due respect in return for the respect he unfailingly showed his players.

Despite his abilities and undoubted qualities, JE Warren was unable to force his way into the crack Lancashire team of the age, with his pathway obstructed by the Swinton duo of Mills and Bumby, and Broughton pair Payne and Deane. He did, however, captain the West Lancashire team against Cumberland.

Twelve months after the merger, in 1882, Warrington moved once more, this time to Sankey Street (opening with a 0-0 draw against St Helens) with changing facilities still at the White Hart Hotel, but playing in black jerseys. JE Warren was elected secretary, initially for two seasons, and Tom Pemberton was handed the role of treasurer, in which capacity he served the club for 37 years.

Warren and his committee facilitated a further move, a year later, to Wilderspool Road, a shade to the south of their previous pitch, and the continual switching may arguably have had an effect on stability on the field of play.

An inability to field a full side in a number of matches led to Warrington merging, in 1884, with Warrington Wanderers, and the input of fresh personnel led to an immediate improvement in fortunes, the Wirepullers registering 14 wins and five draws in 22 outings in 1884-85.

Folk in the town were beginning to sit up and take notice, and in 1885-86 a record 10,000 packed into Wilderspool Road for the Border Cup 'derby' with Widnes. That game, however, came close to providing an unwilling backdrop to tragedy, the wooden stand which was capable of housing only 200 spectators collapsing.

JE Warren had again become Secretary that season, replacing JR Calvert; he was to remain in the role until 1899.

Having opened the year by hosting the representative game between West Lancashire and Border Towns Union and West Cumberland, under Harry Ashton, who was captain in the absence of Warren through injury, picked up the 1885-86 South West Lancashire and Border Towns Trophy with a victory over Aspull in a final at Fairfield, in Liverpool, earned with a drop goal by Tommy Barnes and a try in response to a sole try by their opponents.

Warrington had accounted for St Helens and Runcorn en route to the final, with the game against Runcorn at the penultimate stage providing high drama. The referee sent off a player from each side following a fracas, and was then faced with a problem when Runcorn walked off when he refused to allow the dismissed man to replace an injured player. He opted to abandon the match and the authorities ruled that the game should be replayed, Warrington prevailing at Southport.

As the year entered its last month, Warrington ditched their black colours, opting for narrow primrose and blue stripes, celebrating their first outing in their new strip with a 5-0 home win over Wigan. The motivation behind the move was a bid to impress the wealthy Greenall family, which owned the local Greenall Whitley Brewery. Primrose was selected because Lady Greenall was President of the Primrose League, an organisation dedicated to boosting support for the Conservative Party; blue was selected through it being the official colour of the Conservatives.

The last year of the decade opened, on 17 January 1889, with a visit by the touring Maoris, perhaps Warrington's proudest moment up to that point, the New Zealanders prevailing by two goals and one try to one try and two minors (a minor being awarded on a defender touching down behind his own goal line). And, before 1890 arrived, Warrington, seen very much as a club on the rise, hosted their first county game.

In another accolade, Wirepullers captain W Dillon was selected seven times for Lancashire.

Warrington's near-nomadic existence continued with another switch of base, from the Roebuck Arms to the Norton Arms, on Wilderspool Road, amid concerns that the Derbyshire and East Coast Railway was poised to take over the ground.

As the battleground began to be prepared for the 'breakaway' of 1895, Warrington launched a third team, embracing their old rivals Warrington Excelsior in 1893. And, when Stockton Heath were disbanded in 1893-94, the Wirepullers picked up several fine players in the shape of Fair Barber, F Broady and G Cross. The subsequent addition of C Burton from St Mary's resulted in Warrington being able to select arguably their finest threequarter line up to that date.

That extra piece in the on-field jigsaw was timely.

Warrington were among the 21 Rugby Union clubs – and were in fact represented by JE Warren – that convened at the George Hotel, Huddersfield on 29 August 1895 to debate the issue of 'broken time' over loss of earnings incurred by players through playing on Saturday afternoons.

The delegates voted in favour of the decision that 'the clubs here represented decided to form a Northern Rugby Football Union, and pledge themselves to push forward without delay its establishment', on the principle of payment for bona fide 'broken time only', with full-time professionalism deemed to be illegal.

A little over a week later the Wire were, together with 19 others (Dewsbury having prevaricated on the basis that their committee, rather than their delegate, should decide on the historic move), played the first raft of fixtures – still entirely under Rugby Union rules – in the breakaway code.

Warrington were given a home game, on 7 September 1895, against the crack south Leeds side Hunslet who, sadly, were without a number of leading players, notably Albert Goldthorpe, who were missing because of cricket commitments and concerns that they could be 'professionalized' by taking part, thereby running the very real risk of being banned from sports such as cricket, athletics and cycling.

Memories of the severe frost at the turn of the year, which had led to no games being played for the best part of two months, were distant for a game played on a balmy late-summers day in conditions which, according to contemporary reports, were 'too genial for keen football' and (as if to salve the consciences of the Hunslet absentees) 'more fit for cricket than football'.

The teams that lined up at Wilderspool that historic day were:

Warrington: Boscow; Barber, O'Brien, Burton, Carey; Foden, Bate; Turner, Dakin, Taylor, Nevins, Berry, Sankey, Swift, Saunders.

Hunslet: W Goldthorpe; Hannah, Wright, Townsend, Mitchell; Lapping, Gillings; Barraclough, Deacon, Greenwood, Hill, Kaye, Mawson, Rubrey, Walsh.

Fullback Joe Boscow was an important figure in the early stages, helping Warrington survive a period of intense pressure in the oppressive heat by halting a threatening raid by Hunslet's dangerous threequarter line. Despite the conditions, and partly because of Boscow's heroics as Hunslet, aided by a couple of penalties, dominated territorially in that opening spell, neither side was able to score in the first half. Warrington winger Fair Barber came closest when, after a clearing dribble by forward Sankey, he crossed the visitors' tryline, only to be forced into touch-in-goal by several Hunslet defenders, headed by fullback Walter Goldthorpe.

Goldthorpe put the Parksiders ahead as the second period got under way, reminding spectators that Ahr Albert was not the only member of the clan blessed with specialist kicking skills. The fullback offered no threat when he collected the ball near touch but Goldthorpe turned a difficult position around by beating several men and slotting over a drop goal that was, at the time, worth four points.

Duly roused, Warrington wasted no time in responding, their pack 'rushing' to the visitors' line for stand-off Foden to cross the whitewash. Centre Burton added the conversion from close to the touchline, to edge Warrington 5-4 ahead, and that proved to be enough to seal a win which, Hunslet agreed, was deserved. Warrington went on to close the inaugural Northern Union campaign in 13th position, recording 17 victories and five draws in their 42 matches. To put their opening win in its context, Hunslet closed in seventh position, with 24 wins and two draws.

Surprisingly Hunslet, despite being something of a power in Rugby League until the mid-1960s, never came closer than that to winning at

Warrington, a 7-5 Challenge Cup quarter-final reverse at Wilderspool, when the Wire were in Division One and Hunslet in Division Two, in 1963 marking another near-miss. Ironically, Warrington's biggest defeat is the 68-14 loss at Hunslet on 10 April 1928.

The South Leeds side, incidentally, had more reasons than most to vote in favour of the launch of the Northern Union, as their Parkside ground had been closed by the Rugby Football Union until the first Saturday in December because of crowd trouble following a 3-0 home reverse at the hands of Brighouse the previous April. The Wirepullers themselves had fallen foul of the authorities three years earlier, their ground being 'suspended' after members of the crowd mobbed the referee, as he left the ground, disputing a number of decisions he had made during the 2-2 draw with Salford. 1892 had, in fact, been an eventful year, several fixtures and a club tour being cancelled because of a smallpox epidemic. Meanwhile, the fixture at Wakefield Trinity in April 1896 was switched to Warrington because of a similar ban on Belle Vue.

Twelve months later, in 1896-97, the Challenge Cup, a competition that was to prove dear to Warrington's heart, was launched. The Wirepullers enjoyed some success on their first taste of the world's greatest knockout competition, reaching the semi-finals before slipping 6-0 at Fartown to eventual winners Batley, who were to win the Challenge Cup three times in the first five years.

Warrington's opening tie was a scoreless draw at Broughton Rangers (who would become the first team to pull off the Cup and League 'double' four years later), the Wire duly winning the replay. Holbeck were beaten 24-0 in the second round, in a match played in four quarters of 20 minutes because of a gale force wind.

JE Warren, in another fillip for the club, was elected President of the Northern Union, perhaps in recognition of his drive and enthusiasm. That vision was a factor in Warrington moving to Wilderspool (the name derived from 'Wild Beasts' Pool') in time for the 1898-99 season, on a ten-year lease; the ground, previously used by Latchford Rovers, was to be their home for the next 105 years.

The Wirepullers celebrated their new move on 3 September 1898 with the visit of Swinton, 7,000 spectators witnessing a 3-3 draw in which Robert Bate scored the first try on the ground, for Warrington, with Morgan Bevan touching down for the visitors. Some fans may have been a shade too excited by the action; the club was ordered to post 200 notices in the town, warning of unruly conduct at games.

JE Warren was elected President of Warrington on 1906-07, and retained the position the following season. He continued to administrate with integrity and efficiency, having pointed the way for the Northern Union by overseeing such radical rule changes as the abolition of the line-out, and the decision to make all goals worth two points.

A Mason, who was inducted into the Lodge of Lights in 1902, he rose to the office of Worshipful Master.

He passed away, at the age of 58, as the First World War drew to a close, on 14 September 1918, following an illness lasting several months, and was buried in Warrington Cemetery.

2

Alf Boardman

ALF BOARDMAN, who signed for Warrington in 1898 – making his debut at the age of 18 on Saturday 3 September of that year, against the crack Swinton side of the era, in the first match played at Wilderspool – was a reliable, one-club prop forward, adept at the required skills of the era of scrimmaging, dribbling and marauding, who made 403 appearances from that date until his final game, in January 1914, at Hull.

His contribution, along with those of such as Jack Fish, Ernie Brookes and fellow ex-Latchford Rangers players Ted Hockenhull, Robert Bate, Jack Hallam and Elliott Harris, helped keep Warrington in the vanguard of the Northern Union at a time when the burgeoning sport of Association Football was threatening to take a grip in Lancashire and Yorkshire.

Various rugby teams, particularly in the county of the broad acres, switched to soccer at a time when there was relatively little difference between the Northern Union, Association and Rugby Union codes. Leeds side Holbeck, for example, were seriously miffed at their defeat at the hands of St Helens in 1903-04 in a play-off to determine which of the two sides that had finished joint second in Division Two would accompany champions Wakefield Trinity into the top flight. St Helens won 7-0, scoring a try and two goals at Huddersfield's Fartown in a season in which the Division One championship itself was also settled by a play-off, Bradford and Salford having finished joint top with 52 points each from 34 games. Bradford beat Salford 5-0 at Hanson Lane, Halifax, in the decider and Salford merely shrugged their shoulders and, bruised but unbowed, began to prepare for the following season. By contrast Holbeck, who had been just one of many of the subjects of blandishments by a Football Association concerned that it had no presence in the West Riding of Yorkshire, opted to switch to soccer, emerging for the 1904-5 season as Leeds City AFC and playing in the Football League's Division Two.

The defection may have been a huge blow for the Northern Union, but the saving grace was that the departing club would, on the evidence, have eventually brought disgrace on the fledgling code. Leeds City rose as high as fourth, in 1913-14, in Division Two, under Herbert Chapman, who would go on to earn lasting fame as the manager of Arsenal and Huddersfield Town. During the First World War, however, alleged financial irregularities included the flouting of rules preventing players from being paid during the period of conflict, and the Football League's concerns came to a head after only eight games of the 1919-20 season had been played, when City were expelled from the league in mid-season, largely because the club's directors flatly refused to aid officials in their inquiries, or to assist through the releasing of accounts for inspection.

Happily for the Northern Union, the Football League brought in a team from beyond the heartlands as a replacement in the shape of Staffordshire side Port Vale (who only escaped a similar fate to Leeds City, in 1968, on a vote of fellow clubs). Less fortuitously, perhaps, another soccer team stepped into City's shoes at Elland Road. That team was Leeds United, who would go on to become, in the late 1960s and 1970s, under manager Don Revie, one of the strongest teams in the world.

Even more worryingly for the Northern Union, who had Warrington's JE Warren at the helm in 1897-98, overtures by the Football League were accepted by teams other than Holbeck.

Manningham, the first champions of the Northern Union, in 1895-96, moved over to soccer at the end of the 1902-03 season, remaining at Valley Parade as Bradford City while a few years later, in 1907, their neighbours Bradford also embraced the round-ball code, becoming Bradford Park Avenue. Adherents of rugby in the area immediately launched Bradford Northern, based in the south of the textile city but dubbed 'Northern' in homage to their code of preference, the Northern Union version of football.

Manningham were tempted to leave the Northern Union because they had fallen some way from the heights of seven years earlier and had, in fact, been left out of what was in effect the first 'Super League' when 12 teams agreed, at a meeting in May 1901 at Huddersfield that in some ways echoed the gathering of 1895, to launch a 'Northern League'. Warrington were among that number, which also comprised Bradford, Batley, Broughton Rangers, Halifax, Huddersfield, Hull, Hunslet, Oldham, Runcorn, Salford and Swinton.

By contrast Warrington who had maintained a position as a

leading light of the Northern Union, were able to see off, at an early stage, the threat of soccer, aided perhaps by the fact that strong clubs such as Bolton Wanderers and Everton were already bestriding the Lancastrian sporting stage, leaving little room for another worthwhile addition to the Football League.

An Association Football team was, in fact, launched in the town in 1899, leading to very real worries among the rugby fraternity. The team, however, lasted no more than 12 months, and Rugby League has remained, and continues to remain, in the early years of the twenty-first century, the major sport in the area.

Within three years of having joined Warrington, Alf Boardman found himself playing in a Challenge Cup Final, with five Yorkshire sides being seen off on the way to the decider against another White Rose outfit in the shape of Batley.

Castleford, Leeds, Heckmondwike, Leeds Parish Church and Bradford were disposed of en route to the final, but there was to be disappointment for Boardman, and the rest of the Warrington side, which comprised: Hallam; Fish, Isherwood, Dickenson, Harris; Bate, Duckworth; Alf Boardman, Fell, Edmondson, Scholtze, Eden, Cunningham, Morrison, and Swift.

Batley won the cup for the third time with a 6-0 win, at Headingley, before a crowd of 29,563, with the following line-up: Garner; Davies, Fitzgerald, Goodall, Auty; Oakland, Midgley; Fisher, Judge, Rodgers, Stubley, Spurr, Maine, Fozzard, and Hollingworth.

The only highlights for Warrington were the brilliant runs of winger Jackie Fish, with referee Mr J Kidd of Millom allowing tries by the Gallant Youths' wingers Wattie Davies and Wilf Auty.

Only two days later Warrington had the chance to ease the anguish of the defeat at Leeds by appearing in the renamed South West Lancashire Cup against Leigh. The Wire were again nilled, although Leigh were also unable to get off the mark; Warrington's players, called on to step forward for a replay 24 hours later, could not comply. With the Wilderspool outfit unable to raise a team, the trophy was awarded to Leigh, with many observers reflecting that the side had very little left to offer physically after the exhausting experience of the Challenge Cup Final. None, though, can have been more drained than Boardman who, after having played in all 29 of the Wire's fixtures in 1899-00, had offered 60 successive outings from 3 April 1899 to 30 March 1901 in a sequence which took him some way to becoming the first player to turn out in 400 games for the

Wire.

Warrington's players, meanwhile, had nothing to show from what had been a generally successful 1900-01 campaign, with the Wire having finished sixth out of 14 sides in the Lancashire Senior competition; an identical spot to that which had been enjoyed the previous campaign.

Warrington had, after fetching up at thirteenth in the inaugural 1895-96 season (a little below halfway in the 22-team table), closed at seventh in the Lancashire Senior Competition in 1896-97.

When the 'Super League' of the Northern Rugby League was launched, in 1901-02, the Wire finished seventh, having – in common with Salford, Runcorn and Bradford – had two points deducted for 'breaches of professional rules'. Hunslet and Swinton meanwhile, had four points docked. There was some solace, however, with a 7-2 victory over Widnes in the South West Lancashire Cup Final in which Jack Fish scored a try and two goals, which also helped to atone for the disappointment of having defaulted on the previous season's decider.

The following season (1902-03) saw the formation of a Second Division. Included in the 18 teams in the bottom tier were Leeds who, having been runaway leaders of the Yorkshire Senior Competition, were aghast at not having been included in a top flight which had been enlarged from 14 to 18 teams. The Loiners had been excluded in favour of bottom side Brighouse Rangers, who had been re-elected, while Hull KR, St Helens, Wigan and Widnes were also admitted to Division One. Included in Division Two alongside Leeds were the likes of Keighley, Millom, Rochdale Hornets, Wakefield Trinity, Bramley, York, Castleford and Dewsbury.

The decision of the voting clubs to vote against Leeds was vindicated, up to a point, when the Loiners failed to come top of the section, finishing second, a point behind champions Keighley, but six points ahead of third-placed Millom.

Brighouse, meanwhile, again came bottom of Division 1 – and, this time, automatically tumbled through the trapdoor – while St Helens were also relegated, having finished six points shy of third-from-bottom Wigan. The Saints' demotion, and a similar experience for others over the ensuing century and more, has left Warrington as the only founding member of the Northern Union never to have been outside the top flight in British Rugby League.

A major rule change, aimed at opening up the game more, was

introduced in the 1902 close season, the punt out from touch being replaced by a 10-yard scrum, and it was perhaps no coincidence that Alf Boardman matured as a forward, and Warrington became more of a force.

The Wire, in addition to rising up the table in the mid 1900s, also reached successive Challenge Cup Finals.

The first of the two, in 1903-04, followed a busy spate of fixtures during which the Wire played 12 games in April. That, however, had little impact on enthusiastic Warrington, who booked a place in the final against Halifax at Salford on the last day of April. Warrington could so easily have slipped along the way, with draws against Swinton in the first round and against Bradford in the semi-final while, between-times, Wigan and Pontefract were disposed of. Halifax, though, had the better of the decider, winning 8-3 to retain the Challenge Cup after having beaten Salford 7-0 in the previous season's final, at Headingley, Leeds.

Boardman had, following that match, to come to terms with a major rule change introduced during the close season ahead of the 1904-05 campaign. Northern Union chiefs decreed that only three men could pack down in the front row of the scrum in an attempt to prevent 'wheeling' and barging. And, in a successful bid to create more open play, the knock on rule was amended, in that the non-offending side was allowed to secure possession even if the ball had touched the ground.

The rule changes seemed to have little adverse effect on the Wire, who rose from seventh to fifth in the table and, at the same time, once more forced their way through to the Challenge Cup Final.

It was, again, far from plain sailing. The side accounted for Morecambe in the first round and then, after Keighley had forced a draw at Wilderspool, had struggled to get to Lawkholme Lane for the replay, the train arriving at Keighley late.

The game kicked off at 5.00pm, but the Wire reacted to the delay better than did Keighley, having the upper hand in the encounter and going on to face Wigan successfully in the next round.

Warrington won the Challenge Cup for the first time, and also secured their first major piece of silverware, with Boardman snaring his first winner's medal, with a 6-0 victory over Hull Kingston Rovers, in which both tries were scored by Fish, before a 19,638 crowd at Headingley. Thousands also delighted in the following days in the sight of a tram, decorated by Warrington Borough Council, to celebrate the event.

Boardman's abilities were recognised with selection for the England team that played Other Nationalities at Bradford Park Avenue on 2 January 1905. England – who had lost what could be described as the sport's first-ever international, also against Other Nationalities, on 5 April 1904, having slipped 9-3 to Other Nationalities at Wigan – prevailed at Bradford 26-11.

It was to be Boardman's sole international cap, following six outings for Lancashire, with whom he had enjoyed a stop-start career.

He had first appeared in a Lancashire trial in October 1900, turning out for the Possibles against the Probables, and was finally selected to wear the famous Red & White shirt in October 1902, for the fixture against Cheshire.

The Northern Union had in place at the time, however, stringent rules – the `Working Clause' – stipulating, in a defence against rugby union's accusations that full-time professionalism was possibly on the agenda, that all players must have worked during the seven days preceding a game. Alf Boardman had not, and was therefore ruled ineligible. He was not allowed, either, to turn out for Warrington that day.

His wait, however, was brought to an end less than three months later, on 10 January 1903, when he made his county debut in the Lancashire side that beat Cumberland 21-3 at Millom.

The following season, 1903-04, he picked up two more caps, scoring a try in the 42-0 verdict over Durham & Northumberland at South Shields, and featuring in the 15-0 success over Cumberland at Wigan; he was selected for his county on three occasions in 1905-6.

Meanwhile the 1904-05 season was to be the last in which the Northern Union operated two divisions until the 1962-63 season, when the Rugby Football League launched a three-year experiment which was shelved after only two seasons, in the light of dwindling crowds among the 'lesser' teams.

The Northern Union insisted that sides from the same county played each other, but made no strict provision for cross-county games, with league positions settled on a percentage basis. The result was that there was a wide disparity in the number of matches played by clubs until the 1930-31 season, when the Rugby Football League at last stipulated that all teams should play 38 games, comprising home and away matches against the other 14 sides in its county competition (in Warrington's case, the Lancashire League), and home and away fixtures with five sides from across the Pennines of a similar standing.

A smallpox epidemic didn't aid fixture planning in the first season of the system (1905-06). Warrington played 38 games, winning 19 and drawing three for a percentage of 53.95, finishing fifteenth. Only Oldham, who played 40 games (winning 28 and drawing two to finish fourth, with a success rate of 72.50 per cent) played more. Halifax got through the same number of matches as the Wire, winning 20 and finishing all square in eight of their 38 outings for a percentage of 63.15.

By contrast some teams played far fewer games, notably Castleford, who only visited the washing machine on 20 occasions, prevailing in three games and drawing two for a 20 per cent record which saw them finish fourth-from-bottom, in twenty-eighth spot.

Oldham argued that they had paid a price for playing so many matches. Leigh secured the championship having taken to the pitch only 30 times, winning 23 and drawing two of their fixtures for an 80 per cent rating; crucially, it was noted that they had made few trips over the Pennines to face leading Yorkshire teams. Hunslet came second, 25 victories in 32 skirmishes securing a 78.12 percentage, and Leeds reached the unprecedented heights of third with 76.47 per cent from 25 wins and two draws in 34 games.

Hunslet led the many objectors to a system that it was felt had helped Leigh to the title. It was agreed that the championship would, in future seasons, be settled by a Top Four play-off, with the team finishing in pole position hosting the side finishing fourth and the third-placed team travelling to the side fetching up second. The survivors would meet in a Championship Final played on a neutral ground.

Warrington's last game of 15-a-side rugby was, perhaps appropriately, against Hunslet – their first opponents in the Northern Union – at Wilderspool. The Wire won the game 15-2, with Sammy Lees scoring the final try and the final goal.

It had been Warrington, in fact, who had put forward the idea of a reduction to 13-a-side. Their proposal had been seconded by Leigh (perhaps motivated by a liking for lower figures, the irascible could claim), while most clubs would no doubt have also been influenced by calculations which suggested that something in the order of £100 per annum in wage bills could be saved by eliminating two players. The Northern Union's AGM, held in June 1906, agreed to remove the spoiling flankers of the rugby union game, to make the sport yet more attractive.

The County Cups, meanwhile, had also been launched in 1905-06. Warrington enjoyed a 10-0 win at Rochdale Hornets in their first game in the competition, earned with tries by Bill Harmer and Danny Isherwood, with Jack Preston adding a couple of goals. The Wire, however, went out in the second round, being limited to a penalty by Preston in a 5-2 home defeat by Leigh in a game in which Warrington's players wore numbers for the first time.

Leigh went on to reach the inaugural Lancashire Cup Final, against Wigan, which went to a replay before being decided. The sides drew 0-0 at Broughton, Manchester, before 16,000 people in the first game; Wigan won 8-0 in the second encounter, also at Broughton, which attracted 10,000 folk. Warrington, meanwhile, had hosted a Challenge Cup semi-final for the first time, Salford and Keighley attracting a crowd of 8,500 to Wilderspool.

Twelve months later Warrington reached the Lancashire Cup Final themselves with Broughton Rangers, on this occasion, participants rather than hosts. The game, played at Central Park, Wigan, before a 14,048 crowd, was won by the Manchester outfit 15-6.

Any dismay at that reverse was eased by a rise up the table to eighth position, the side winning 21 and drawing one of its 34 games for a 63.23 percentage. And there was joy, for the second time in two years, when the Wire won the 1906-07 Challenge Cup.

Boardman was in the side that met Oldham at Broughton, winning 17-3 before 18,500 supporters, in the first season of 13-a-side rugby, a mode of football that suited his approach, as it did those of Jack Fish and Danny Isherwood, with whom he shared the distinction of having played in each of the club's four Challenge Cup Finals to date.

A fortnight after having hit the sporting heights, however, Boardman was faced with personal tragedy, discovering on his return home from work that his three-year old son Thomas had drowned in a clay pit at Latchford. It was a blow from which Alf Boardman would never quite recover, passing away on 12 November 1918 at the early age of 37.

Alf Boardman also packed down in the Wire's two games against the inaugural Australian tourists of 1908-09, having been outstanding the previous season in the 8-7 victory over the famous New Zealand All Golds. He played alongside his brother Peter in the first game against the Kangaroos, which Warrington won 10-3; the second match was drawn 8-8.

The Wire were quick to secure the services of Australian Tourists Lol O'Mally and Dan Frawley, and fellow countryman Jim Stuntz, being able to impress upon the Antipodeans the calibre of the team they would be joining by sweeping to a club record 78-6 victory over St Helens at Wilderspool on 12 April 1909. Welsh forward George Thomas – who would also, taking into account the 1912-13 decider, play in four Challenge Cup Finals for Warrington – led the way with five tries and eight goals; a personal haul of 31 points, while Boardman touched down twice.

Alf Boardman's forward partner Frank Shugars became Warrington's first tourist, being selected for the Northern Union's first tour, to Australia and New Zealand in 1910. Shugars played in 12 of the 18 games on the tour, scoring one try. He did not feature in either of the two Tests in Australia, which the Lions won 27-20 and 22-17 before crowds of 42,000 and 18,000. He was, however, selected for the one international in New Zealand, which was won 52-20.

Boardman, meanwhile, settled for `A' team football from the 1911-12 season, but was called back for a last moment in the spotlight for the game at Hull on 17 January 1914.

Warrington's regular players had gone on strike after discovering that their opponents in a fixture earlier that month – Huddersfield – had been on a bonus of £1 to win (a claim contested by the Fartown committee).

The Wire had prevailed 14-8 and, on learning of the incentive allegedly offered to the men from Fartown, their players had asked for the same bonus to be paid to them. The committee's response had been to turn down the request and suspend any player who refused to turn out.

Boardman stepped forward in the crisis, and duly closed his first-team career at Warrington on the receiving end of a 51-8 hammering at the Boulevard. Warrington's players then ended their strike, beating Runcorn the following week 27-7.

3

Jack Fish

The Cause of It
His look was pale, and weird, and wan
And damply did he greet
A melancholy Salford man
I met him in the street.
'I prithee tell – and tell me true –
How came thy sad condit-
Ion. Salford gent?' He sobbed 'Boo-hoo!
The cause of it is Fish!'
'Nay, nay,' quoth I, 'this is not Lent;
Roast turkey is the fare,
With sausages, thou Salford gent;
And pudding rich and rare.
And surely 'twas no fishy thing
That caused thy woe!' But 'Fish!'
The Borough boy said blubbering,
'I tell you it is Fish.'
'But was it whale or mackerel?
Or sole? Or plaice? Or eel?
Or lobster in its armoured shell?
Or sardines tinned a l'huile?
Or salmon, served with mayonnaise?
(Toothsome, dyspeptic dish).'
But still with dull, averted gaze,
The man said: 'No, just Fish!'
He turned and left me with a nod
And still quite in the dark
It may have been a piece of cod;
It may have been a shark.
Will someone make this dark tale clear?
It is my ardent wish.
My theory inclines to beer,
Super-induced by Fish.

THE poem, written after Warrington won at the Willows, Salford, for the first time, on Boxing Day 1903, first appeared in the *Athletic News* of Manchester several days later and was repeated in the *Warrington Observer* the following month.

The poet had been moved to pen the lines by Jack Fish's display, the winger scoring two tries, including one after intercepting a pass by the legendary Jim Lomas, and racing the length of the field.

A cult hero before the concept became fashionable, Fish was the ideal subject for such an poem, and was the jewel in the crown of the Warrington side that was a leading light in the early days of the Northern Union.

That Fish made a huge contribution to the cause of the Wirepullers is beyond dispute. As suggested by the above ode, however, bald statistics tell only part of the story; the manner in which the flier on the touchline obtained many of his touchdowns is another matter altogether, his input as a player of true star quality helping inspire Warrington to deeds of which they may not otherwise have aspired.

Charisma, a rare attribute, was there for all to see in the young Fish and it was that quality, as much as any other, that persuaded Warrington's directors to adopt a dramatic approach when they chased his signature in the early days of the Northern Union. £50 worth of silver no doubt weighed a fair amount, apart from having enormous value, in the later years of Queen Victoria's reign, and the haul will perhaps have made something of a noise when it was smashed down on the table when the young Fish met Warrington bosses in 1898. The ploy, however, had the required effect. The youngster took the bait and Warrington's first superstar was born.

Fish, born in Runcorn in 1878, had emerged as a winger of note with Lostock Gralam Rugby Union side of Northwich, Warrington taking the opportunity of arranging a match against the junior side so they could sample his talents at first hand and, perhaps, identify any deficiencies. Subsequent events suggest that they noted plenty of the former, and few of the latter.

Fish left the village of Lostock Gralam – noted, among other things, for a public house called the 'Slow and Easy' (neither term applying to the young flyer) – for the big time of Warrington, and immediately prospered in a career spanning almost 14 years.

He made his debut on 15 October 1898, electrifying the crowd in a home friendly with Barrow by sprinting in from halfway at Wilderspool. That was merely a taste of what was to come. Fish was, between that fixture with the Shipbuilders and his final match, in the late winter of 1911, destined to make a lasting, indeed unparalleled, mark on his adopted club.

The winger, signed not only for his try scoring prowess but for his accuracy with the boot, played 321 games for Warrington, scoring 214 tries and 263 goals, remaining the only man to achieve 'double century' notoriety in both aspects, and totalling 1,168 points. He became, on 2 December 1899, the first Warrington player to score a hat-trick, crossing three times in a 14-6 win at Leigh. For a shade over two years, he jointly held the record for points scored in a game, his 29 registered against Goole at Wilderspool on 24 March 1900 in a second round tie in the Challenge Cup equalling the total scored by Billy Jacques, of Hull, whose effort against Elland on 1 April 1899 had bettered the 27 points recorded by W Phillips, of Salford, in their fixture with Luddendenfoot on 18 March 1899.

Fish, in reaching that astounding total in the 44-0 win, had become the first Warrington player to register five tries in a game, seven goals taking him to the 29-point mark.

Fish's and Jacques' record would stand until 29 March 1902, and Goole were again on the receiving end, shipping 31 points to Salford's Jim Lomas. Almost three years later, on 4 March 1905, Hull KR's George 'Tich' West would shatter all records with his 53 points against Brookland Rangers.

Many of Fish's tries and goals had a major impact on Warrington's myriad successes in the era, although there were several disappointments in store for Fish and his team-mates before the major prize of the Challenge Cup was secured.

The Wirepullers' first appearance on the major stage in the early days of the Northern Union was in the 1900-01 Challenge Cup Final. Warrington progressed to the decider with Fish scoring at least one try and at least one goal in every game, against Leeds, Heckmondwike, Leeds Parish Church, Bradford and Castleford; he totalled 10 touchdowns and eight goals.

Mighty Batley represented the last hurdle, and a testing one at that. The Gallant Youths had been inaugural winners five years earlier, beating St Helens 10-3 at Headingley, and had backed up that success with a 7-0 victory over Bradford 12 months later.

After a two-year hiatus, Batley were back in the limelight and travelled to Leeds as strong favourites to see off Warrington, who were not happy that the venue was so close to their opponents' Mount Pleasant base.

A crowd of 29,563 – the biggest for a Challenge Cup Final up to that point, and almost 12,000 more than had paid to see the decider of 12 months earlier, between Salford and Swinton at Manchester, perhaps vindicating the Northern Union's choice of venue – gathered at Headingley to witness a match which ended in a narrow defeat for Warrington, despite the dismissal of Batley forward George Maine 10 minutes into the second period.

The trumpeted involvement of Batley's famous winger Wattie Davies and Fish was a key factor in that mammoth gate, and Fish offered plenty of thrills for the crowd to savour with a series of thrilling runs. None, however, resulted in a try. The Gallant Youths, by contrast, registered two, with Davies crossing the whitewash and Wilf Auty also touching down on the other wing.

Fish brightened the 1900-01 season with 22 tries, including three hat-tricks. In the 1901-02 campaign the Wire secured their first honour, beating Widnes 7-2 in the South West Lancashire and Border Trophy Final. Fish, typically, scored all his side's points with a try and two goals.

On 12 October 1903, a couple of months after having agreed a signing-on fee of £3 to take part in the 1903-04 season (with match pay increased to £1.00 – centre George Dickenson, intriguingly, was given £4.00 to sign on, but was paid only 17s 6d a win, and 12s 6d for a defeat or a draw) Jack Fish was perhaps involved in some kind of history being made by playing for both the Probables and the Possibles in a Lancashire county trial game staged at Wilderspool. Not only did he play for each team; he also scored for both. In the Probables ranks in the first half, he scored two tries and three goals to help leave the Possibles 28-0 adrift at the interval. The backs then changed sides for the second period, Fish scoring another try and landing another goal.

Warrington had the opportunity to go one better than in 1900-01 during the 1903-04 campaign, after having seen off Swinton in the first round of the Challenge Cup at the second time of asking, following up that edgy piece of progress by disposing of Wigan before what was then a record home crowd of 10,558.

The reward for the victory over the Pie Eaters was a trip to Pontefract, where the Liquorish Eaters were seen off in the quarter-final.

Bradford – in their original Park Avenue manifestation – provided the final stumbling block and, like Swinton, shared the spoils with

Warrington at the first time of asking, the sides finishing all-square at 3-3. Warrington, though, were not to be denied in the replay, and Fish was the central figure, claiming a try and a goal in an 8-0 success.

Halifax, the Wire's opponents in the 1903-04 final, were the holders of the Challenge Cup, having beaten Salford 7-0 at Headingley, Leeds, 12 months earlier before a 32,507 crowd. On this occasion, the match was brought back to Lancashire where, once again, the Northern Union was served with evidence that the code's blue riband day was a bigger attraction in the County of the Broad Acres than in the Red Rose shire.

Only 17,041 turned up at the Willows, Salford, for the game – albeit an improvement on the 15,006 that had paid to watch Broughton Rangers and Salford lock horns two years previously at Rochdale – and the absentees perhaps made the right choice, at least if the prospect of seeing Jack Fish in action was one of the main attractions of the contest.

Halifax, boasting a heavy pack and a fine tactical kicker in Cumbrian fullback Billy Little, managed to keep Warrington on the defensive for much of the contest and, in particular, succeeded in starving Fish of possession. A try by centre Joe Riley, plus a penalty from winger Herbert Hadwen, put Halifax (who had finished ninth in the league table) 5-0 up at the break against a Wire outfit that had closed at seventh. Warrington, despite being under the cosh, forced their way back into the issue when Fish hoisted a high kick, Welsh stand-off Dai Davies getting to the touchdown ahead of Little. The try, though, was scored too far out for Fish to convert, and the Yorkshire side sealed an 8-3 victory when captain Johnny Morley scampered over from the base of a scrum.

Third time lucky, so the saying goes, and that was exactly the experience of Warrington and Fish, who found themselves back on the big stage at the close of the following season. That the Wire were there at all was in no small measure due to Jack Fish, who pulled off a superb interception try in the semi-final against Bradford.

Hull Kingston Rovers, Warrington's adversaries this time, were making their first appearance in a Challenge Cup Final, and there was a feeling in some quarters that Warrington's big match experience, gained in the defeats in previous finals at the hands of Bradford and Halifax, was instrumental in their lifting the trophy for the first time. Certainly Warrington, and in particular Fish, were fully aware that they had to be at their best against Hull Kingston Rovers. The Robins had in their ranks – and directly opposite Fish – the winger George Henry 'Tich' West, who had set the record for points in a game in that season's first round by posting 53 points, with 11 tries and 10 goals in the era of the three-point try, against Cumbrian amateur side Brookland Rovers.

That record would remain in place for over a century, until 2011 in fact, when Chris Thorman scored 56 points for York City Knights in a Challenge Cup tie against Northumbria University, who were beaten 132-0.

West, all five feet four inches of him, was not going to get anywhere near his record against Fish who, at 5ft 7in, hardly towered over his opposite number. Tich West was, in all truth, not a player in the same class as Jack Fish. Although he had shattered the record books with his feat against Brookland, he never came close to again matching his performance that day, and did not subsequently feature among the game's leading seasonal scorers. Indeed, he scored nearly half his total for the 1904-05 season in that single game. And during his entire career at Craven Park, which was to come to an end four years later, he would register 98 tries and 44 goals, a total of 328 points; a respectable but hardly earth-shattering record. Sadly, he was to pass away too early, at the age of 44.

Fish, then, will not have been unduly concerned by the prospect of marking the sport's suddenly-famous record breaker extraordinaire, even though Hull KR had subsequently accounted for Leeds in the next round, followed by the era's giants in Hunslet, who were to win the Yorkshire Cup the following autumn and who were to become the first team, in 1907-08, to pull off the magnificent 'All Four Cups' feat. Broughton Rangers, who had achieved the 'double' in 1901-02, were seen off at the semi-final stage by the Robins.

Jack Fish had, the previous season, confirmed his consistency by scoring 28 tries in all matches, to finish third in the Northern Union's standings (Broughton Rangers' Andrew Hogg had headed the list in 1903-04 with 34) and third, also, in the goalkicking list with 37, behind pacesetter Jimmy Lomas, of Salford, who landed 65. His points' total of 158 was bettered only by Lomas' 214.

The 1904-05 final didn't start too propitiously for Jack Fish, who was wide of the target in the heavy conditions with an early penalty attempt. He also missed out on a try-scoring chance as half-time beckoned, racing clear and finding himself and the Warrington fans in the disappointing crowd of 19,638 frustrated when he slipped on the greasy surface, damaging his thigh. Many players may have retired from the fray following such an injury. Not Fish, who brushed the pain aside to help the Wire take control of the contest in the second period.

There was still no score when Fish, with only three minutes having passed, set off on a long run from a position which, from Hull KR's perspective, would have offered little threat in usual circumstances. Jack Fish, however, was no usual winger, leaving the opposition trailing and impotent in a surging, try-scoring race.

He was unable to add the extras, and it fell to Warrington's acclaimed defence to keep the Robins at bay as the East Riding of Yorkshire side responded with a spell of heavy pressure.

Having withstood the storm, the Wire replied with Fish's second score. On this occasion the try was very much a team effort, launched by scrum-half Dai Davies whose incisive break led to Danny Isherwood racing away, Fish popping up on the centre's shoulder for a vital try. Uncharacteristically, he was unable to add the goal, and he was also wide with a subsequent penalty. He had, however, at last picked up a Challenge Cup winners' medal after the disappointments of 1900-01 and 1903-04.

Fish, and Warrington, were back in the final again two years later, in 1906-07, and were to emerge once more as victors, the success helping ease the anguish of the Wire's superlative winger, who had missed half of the previous season with a broken leg but who had already vividly illustrated that his powers had not diminished by scoring four tries and kicking nine goals – a total of 30 points – in the 50-3 victory over Huddersfield on 20 October 1906; the first time the Wire had scored a half-century on their own Wilderspool patch.

Now captain, Fish guided Warrington to the final, which was held at Broughton Rangers' Wheater's Field Stadium on 27 April 1907, through the testing hurdles of Batley, Hull and Huddersfield, each side a major power, before accounting for Swinton, who disappointed their supporters in a 21-0 defeat in the semi-final.

Mighty Oldham provided the opposition, and were hungry for victory, having failed to reach the final since the 1898-99 season, when they had beaten Hunslet 19-9 at Fallowfield, Manchester. The Roughyeds had no reason to lack confidence, wins en route to Broughton over Runcorn, Halifax and Wakefield Trinity being followed by a notable victory over the previous year's runners-up Salford at the Athletic Grounds, the home of Rochdale Hornets.

Fish, perhaps more aware in his late twenties than he had been in his youth that time was possibly slipping away a little in a glorious career, enlisted the services of a sprint coach in the build-up to the final. An indicator of the supreme professionalism that had helped him, over the years, boost his income spectacularly, with leading athletes of the day often challenged, successfully, to races, with a £100 sidestake (a massive sum) usually the prize. The sprinter, in fact, once raced Wigan's Buckie Green for that figure which, in the early years of the twenty-first century, would equal nearly £40,000.

In the event, Jack Fish didn't quite get the chance to show his paces against Oldham, although he thrilled the 18,500 crowd – a healthy figure in a period of falling gates that had lead to a reduction to 13-a-side, given that sleet had fallen throughout the morning – with a stunning solo score in the second half which helped Warrington to a 17-3 verdict. Oldham, however, had the better of the opening period and, at the interval, looked eminently capable of winning a contest played in conditions described as 'heavy and slushy' in a game said to be 'all pack, possession and kick'.

The men from Watersheddings sucked on their lemons reflecting on a 3-2 lead earned with a try by second row Bert Avery, who was sent over by stand-off Arthur Lees, while Warrington had to settle for a sole penalty by Fish, who had seen a couple of other efforts awarded by referee Frank Renton, of Hunslet, drift wide.

A tactical masterstroke during the interval, inspired by Fish, resulted in a huge change of fortunes in the second half. Ernie Brookes was brought in from the wing to the stand-off position, with Ted Hockenhull moving out to the flank. The switch was inspired. Oldham rarely had a look-in during the last 40 minutes, while Warrington registered three tries. Stand-off Sammy Lees scored the first, courtesy of a break by centre Isherwood and Fish, who added a fine conversion. Fish added to that score with a long-range solo try, dribbling the ball over 50 yards from inside his own half, before touching down. And there was no way back for Oldham when Hockenhall crossed towards the close, Fish again adding the extras to help the side to a notable victory.

Warrington, as one of the leading sides in the Northern Union, were an obvious nomination to be one of the sides to host AH Baskerville's famous 1907-08 New Zealand All Golds, who were the first touring side to this country and who, through their vision and courage, set the scene for Rugby League to be established in the southern hemisphere. The Wire won 8-7 before 8,000 supporters and, 12 months later, on 14 November 1908, hosted the inaugural Australian tourists, who played 45 games in a six-month adventure which was hit by disappointing attendances, strikes in the cotton mills of the north having an adverse affect on the enthusiasm of spectators.

Jack Fish scored a try and a goal in the 10-3 win, with Ike Taylor also crossing and George Dickenson also landing a conversion before a 5,000 crowd.

Warrington's team on a historic day was: Jimmy Tilley; Jack Fish, George Dickenson, Ike Taylor, L. Treharne; Ernie Brookes, John Jenkins; Billy Dowell, Alf Boardman, Billy O'Neill, George Thomas, Peter Boardman and John Willie Chester.

The Kangaroos, back for a second bite at the cherry later in the tour, were held to an 8-8 draw, Fish and Jenkins claiming the Wire's tries. Dan Frawley and Larry O'Malley subsequently signed for Warrington and thrilled the Wilderspool crowd in 1909-10.

After closing his career with a try-scoring appearance against Coventry, on 18 February 1911, in the first round of the Challenge Cup, Jack Fish enjoyed a benefit season which earned him the handsome sum of £268 15s 11d.

4

Ernie Brookes

THERE are snips, there are bargains, and there are deals which almost amount to daylight robbery. In Rugby League – or, at the time, Northern Union – terms, the latter is epitomised by the signing by Warrington as the nineteenth century was left behind of Ernie Brookes.

The Wirepullers coughed up, in pursuit of the signature of the Bewsey product, a small lemonade, a cigar and a pat on the back. And that was it.

In return, Warrington were given 19 years of entirely committed service by a player who was equally effective on the wing or at halfback, who gained international honours, and who eventually captained his home-town club. It was a return on an investment that would startle the most optimistic of bankers, and the beginning of a relationship which opened with a debut against Hull Kingston Rovers on 22 November 1902, and closed with an emergency call-up at scrum-half in a game at Salford on 20 March 1920 which finished in a 14-12 defeat.

Along the way, Ernie Brookes, a product of the Monks Hall club, made 297 appearances for Warrington, scoring 81 tries and kicking 25 goals for an overall contribution of 293 points. A proven match-winner, Brookes was instrumental in helping the Wirepullers achieve victory in several of their major games, including his first Challenge Cup Final, when Warrington beat Hull Kingston Rovers 6-0 at Headingley, Leeds in 1904-05. The Robins were very much in the contest, at only 3-0 down, having conceded a try to winger Jack Fish, when Brookes took a hand in proceedings early in the second half, making a telling break. Fish are often found near Brookes and it was no different on this occasion, the winger popping up in support to steam in for his second score, a try that effectively clinched the game.

A speedy and elusive back, weighing in at 11st 8lbs in his prime, the 5ft 8ins Brookes was regularly used as a winger in the first half by Warrington, switching to stand-off or scrum-half in the second half, invariably to devastating effect. The strategy particularly paid off following the reduction in players from 15 to 13 in 1906, the Wire immediately stating their intent, given the extra space, by posting a 33-7 victory over Hull at Wilderspool in their first home fixture under the new rules; Brookes, on that occasion, helped himself to a hat-trick, while Warrington scored nine tries in total.

Ernie Brookes was able to add a second medal to his trophy cabinet in the autumn of 1906-07, albeit a loser's one. Warrington featured in the second Lancashire Cup Final, facing Broughton Rangers at Wigan, who had won the inaugural competition. Brookes scored a try, together with George Dickenson, but it wasn't enough to prevent a 15-6 defeat by a side that prevailed with a try and a goal by Jack Flynn, touchdowns by Bob Wilson and Charlie Darlison, and a couple of goals by Billy Harris, before 14,048 spectators.

He closed the 1906-07 season as Warrington's top scorer, crossing the whitewash 26 times. He didn't score, however, in arguably the most important game of the campaign – the 17-3 victory over Oldham in the Challenge Cup Final – but he was perhaps the pivotal figure, being switched inside at the interval, when the Roughyeds led 3-2, and helping turn around a previously attritional contest.

His impact, and perhaps his versatility, led to him being elevated to the fledgling international scene. He played for the Northern Rugby League side which lost 10-9 to Australia on 18 November 1908 and was duly selected for the Test team that faced the first Australian party to visit these shores. Warrington were honoured by also having centre George Dickenson in the line-up, while Ernie Brookes, at stand-off, would prove to be the hero of the hour.

The historic First Test against the Kangaroos was at the Park Royal, the home of Queens Park Rangers AFC, the sport's authorities showing an adventurous spirit in promoting not only the match but the code. The Northern Union, however, had failed to take note of what counter-attractions were on offer in the capital that day. The Varsity Rugby Union match between Oxford and Cambridge was also being played that afternoon while, down the road, Chelsea were entertaining Newcastle United in an important Association Football fixture. Consequently, only 2,200 turned up to watch the game; the majority, however, will have left the stadium singing the praises of the 13-a-side code, with neither side deserving to lose a game that finished in a 22-22 draw.

The teams for the historic clash were:

Northern Union: Harry Gifford (Barrow); Billy Batten (Hunslet), Bert Jenkins (Wigan), George Dickenson (Warrington), George Tyson (Oldham); Ernie Brookes (Warrington), Johnny Thomas (Wigan); Arthur Smith (Oldham), William Longworth (Oldham), Bill Jukes (Hunslet), Asa Robinson (Halifax), Arthur Mann (Bradford), John Higson (Hunslet).

Australia: Mark Bolewski; Bill Heidke, Jim Devereaux, Sid Deane, Herbert Henry 'Dally' Messenger; Arthur Butler, Arthur Halloway; Jim Abercrombie, Larry O'Malley, Alex Burdon, Patrick Walsh, Sandy Pearce, Tedda Courtney.

Dally Messenger, who had taken over as captain of Australia from Denis Lutge, who had not been in his best form, scored the first points in Ashes history with a penalty goal for the Kangaroos, who had acquired the nickname when manager James Giltinan, something of a showman, somehow produced a creature of that ilk (he proved to be evasive over whether it had travelled with the party from the Antipodes – in breach of quarantine regulations – or whether it had been purchased from an English zoo). Thus Australia had a nickname preferable to the 'Colonials' or, as had been used by an English report at York the 'Blues', to one which matched that of the Australian rugby union side, who were in the country at the same time and who had billed themselves as the Wallabies.

The Northern Union, however, hit back with tries by Wigan scrum-half George Thomas and the powerful Hunslet centre Billy Batten – the 'Forceful Youth from Kinsley' – who, at the turn of the decade, would transfer to Hull, who paid him the astronomical sum of £14 per week.

Centre Jim Devereux replied for the visitors, but a fine try for Brookes, which he duly converted, helped get the Northern Union clear, and the hosts went in at the break 14-5 ahead after Batten crashed over in the corner for his second score.

The Northern Union appeared to have the game wrapped up when left-winger George Tyson, of Oldham, crossed on the resumption to stretch the lead to 17-5. Australia, however, staged a superb recovery, sparked by a second touchdown for Devereux.

Hooker Larry O'Malley, who was destined to join the Wire, grabbed another score for Australia, dribbling his way over the try-line, and with Messenger improving both efforts the Kangaroos were only a couple of points behind.

As the game headed to a thrilling climax, Halifax second row Asa Robinson finished off a move launched from deep in Northern Union territory. Messenger, however, served notice of why he would become one of the sport's immortals by pulling off an interception which led to a hat-trick score for Devereux. Messenger's conversion restored parity at 20-20, and the same player then edged his side in front with a subsequent penalty.

The spoils appeared set to go to Australia but, in the final minute, the Northern Union were awarded a penalty. Up stepped Ernie Brookes who, calming his nerves, coolly slotted over the goal that ensured that the sides would finish on level terms, at 22-22.

A little over a fortnight after that game Brookes played for England against Wales at Broughton, on 28 December 1908, scoring a try in a 31-7 success. Meanwhile Australia, who had been somewhat out of sorts on their inaugural trip and who had generally failed to excite the interest of English crowds, were given a much-needed financial boost when 22,000 turned up at St James' Park, the home of Newcastle United AFC, for the Second Test on 23 January 1909.

Ernie Brookes was again in the home line-up, but the kicking duties went to the Salford centre and captain James Lomas, who was to go on to become one of the great figures of the British game.

The Northern Union won 15-5 after having successfully protected, on this occasion, an 11-point lead. Lomas scored a try and three goals, including a late drop goal, and there were touchdowns for Thomas and Tyson. Messenger offered the highlight of the game, however, with a memorable try in which, after fielding a towering kick, he raced through the entire home ranks for a wonderful score, which he himself converted.

Brookes was still at stand-off for the Third Test, played at Villa Park, the home of Aston Villa AFC, in Birmingham, as the Northern Union continued its policy of spreading the gospel.

A disappointing crowd of only 9,000 turned up for a game – played on Monday 15 February 1909 – which was dominated by forwards, but in which the rugby version of the Ashes was won by the host nation, thanks to a late try by Tyson which, after an earlier touchdown by Johnny Thomas, resulted in the Northern Union emerging as 6-5 winners. The Kangaroos were left regretting the absence of Messenger, who would have been likely to have converted a try by Dan Frawley which Devereux, who was successful with a penalty, missed.

That game was Brookes' last in the international arena. One of Warrington's nominations for the inaugural 1910-11 tour to Australia, he was, somewhat surprisingly, not selected. He did, however, add to six games for Lancashire with one more outing for the Red Rose county, making his last representative appearance in the 28-7 defeat at the hands of Cumberland on 9 October 1911. Happily, if ironically, the venue was his beloved Wilderspool.

That game brought the curtain down on a relationship with Lancashire which was launched on 2 November 1907 with a 15-11 defeat at the hands of Yorkshire at Thrum Hall, Halifax. Brookes scored two tries the following October when Lancashire accounted for Cumberland 15-8 at Workington, and was in the side which followed that success up with a 13-0 verdict over Yorkshire at Salford to lift the 1908-09 County Championship.

Towards the end of November, Brookes wore the red and white of his home county in the 20-6 reverse at the hands of Australia at Wigan, and was captain when Lancashire again faced the Kangaroos, on 8 March 1909, at Leigh; Australia won the game 14-9.

He scored a try in an 8-3 defeat by Cumberland at Barrow on 4 October 1909, a two-year gap then ensuing before his finale at Wilderspool.

Ernie Brookes' last game on the international stage was also the last for Mr Giltinan, the Kangaroos' tour manger. Australia had attracted average crowds of only 5,421, compared to the New Zealand All Golds' 8,877 of the previous year. The Australian tour manager left for home before the final match of the trip, the aforementioned 14-9 victory over Lancashire on Monday 8 March. Four years later, he was declared bankrupt, having been sued by an investor who had pumped £2,000 into the tour.

Ernie Brookes, meanwhile, continued to enjoy his club football with Warrington and was selected on the wing for the 1912-13 Challenge Cup Final against Huddersfield's great 'Team of All the Talents' which, two years later, would emulate Hunslet's feat of 1907-08 by winning All Four Cups.

A crowd of 22,754, the best for four years, made its way to Headingley, Leeds, for a game in which Huddersfield were rated as favourites by virtue of the fine free-flowing play they had shown in winning the Yorkshire League and which would also help them secure the Northern Rugby League Championship.

Fartown left-winger Stan Moorhouse has perhaps gone down in history as being some way behind Huddersfield right-winger Albert Rosenfeld who, in 1913-14, would establish a record which has yet to be broken of 80 tries in a season. Moorhouse, however, was no slouch and, in 1911-12, had set a record for an English-born winger of 55 tries in a season; a tally which was equalled in 1926-27 by St Helens' flyer Alf Ellaby.

Playing opposite Brookes on this occasion, and perhaps helped by the fact that he had the immortal Harold Wagstaff as his centre, Moorhouse scored two second half tries, neither of which was converted, to help his side to a 6-5 lead.

Warrington, who had gone in front with a try by left-winger Bert Bradshaw, converted from the touchline by fullback Ben Jolley, for a 5-0 interval lead, never quite recovered.

Moorhouse went on to eclipse Brookes – not to mention Rosenfeld and Bradshaw – with his third try, to complete the scoring at 9-5. He thus became only the second man to score a hat-trick in a Challenge Cup Final, the feat having first been achieved by Bob Wilson, in the 25-0 win over Salford in Broughton Rangers' double-winning season of 1901-02.

Twelve months later, in 1914, Warrington's players found it necessary to go on strike, claiming that they had not been paid a £1 bonus. However, Ernest Brookes perhaps confirmed his loyalty to Warrington by captaining the Wire in 1914-15.

During that season he scored what many observers of the era felt was his best try for the Wire, registered in the fixture against Leigh, at Mather Lane, on 5 September 1914. A contemporary report stated, 'When he received the ball he had a fair distance to travel to the line, and running here and there, scattering opponents right and left, he made a flying leap over Clarkson, the Leigh fullback, to touch down over the Leigh line, for a most spectacular try to win the first match of the season.'

Ernie Brookes played for Warrington in the following three seasons of wartime friendly matches. He featured in 13 games in 1916-17, contributing 10 points with two tries and two goals, and turned out just once in 1917-18. He had five outings in 1918-19, when he again did not score, and his commitment to the cause was vividly illustrated when he donned the primrose and blue for the last time, in an injury crisis, in the defeat at Salford in 1920. Including international and county appearances, he had played 310 games, scoring 86 tries and

27 goals for a points' tally of 312.

Ernest Brookes had scored a hat-trick for Warrington on four occasions, three of those coming in late 1906. He achieved the feat for the first time in the previously mentioned 33-7 win over Hull at Wilderspool on 8 September 1906. The following month he netted three tries again, this time at the expense of Barrow, also at Wilderspool, in a Lancashire Cup quarter-final in which Warrington prevailed 47-14. He was at it once more on 10 December, away from home in the 47-7 lashing of Liverpool, and his final hat-trick was against Ebbw Vale, at Wilderspool, on 21 March 1908, when the Welshmen were scuttled 40-9.

The Warrington 'great' passed away in 1940, at the age of 56, having suffered from septic broncho-pneumonia; he had been the landlord of the Gladstone Arms, Church Street, Warrington for 30 years, often modestly regaling regulars with tales of the great deeds in the days of the Northern Union.

5

Billy Cunliffe

BILLY CUNLIFFE was a loyal, one-club servant of Warrington whose career, while successful enough, would arguably have reached even greater heights were it not for the First World War. The front row forward was not the only sportsman, by any means, to have his ambitions thwarted by greater fields of conflict than those offered by football pitches or cricket arenas.

It may be viewed as crass to even consider the impact on the best years of their athletic lives as a loss when compared to the severe suffering of those (including, of course, many players) who incurred severe injuries or, all too often, laid down their lives. Among that number can be included Warrington's George Thomas, one of all too many who were lost in the Great War.

But the fact that the careers in the Northern Union of such as Billy Cunliffe were hit hard by matters entirely beyond their control is, nevertheless, one which gives some cause for reflection, despite the accident of timing of his birth leading Cunliffe, who was born shortly before the turn of the century, to make his debut for the Wire in October 1914, less than three months after the onset of hostilities.

Cunliffe was joining a Warrington outfit that was, perhaps, already slipping a shade from its eminent role in the early days of the Northern Union. The side finished in thirteenth position out of 25 teams in his debut campaign; not a disreputable rating but one which nevertheless mirrored the standings of eighteenth in both the 1911-12 and 1912-13 seasons, and eleventh position in 1913-14.

Nor had Warrington been amongst the silverware. Between 1900-01 and 1906-07 the Wire had featured in four Challenge Cup Finals, losing the first two and prevailing in each of the remaining deciders. The side had also, in that last season, been Lancashire Cup runners-up. In the intervening eight years, however, Warrington had tasted the big time only once; in 1912-13, when the side lost to Huddersfield in the Challenge Cup Final.

There was a feeling that the outbreak of war hit the Wire harder than most, and a resume of Warrington's record in the 1920s supports the view that, a false dawn or two apart, the Wire took some time to recover. The first campaign, after peace had been declared in November 1918, suggested that all would, perhaps, be well. The Wire closed the 1919-20 season in tenth position, with fifteen teams below them, but in the ensuing campaigns the men from Wilderspool experienced a slide down the ratings.

The team finished thirteenth in 1920-21 (when what was thought to be the first crowd of over 20,000 at Wilderspool was recorded, for the 16-5 victory over Hull in the first round replay in the Challenge Cup) and fifteenth in 1921-22; however, that season was relieved by success in the Lancashire Cup, in which the Wire overcame Oldham in the final, at Broughton, 7-5 before an 18,000 crowd. Bob Bradbury scored the Wire's try, while Ben Jolley landed two crucial goals, leaving adrift a Roughyeds outfit that posted a Joe Ferguson try and a goal by Reg Farrar. Warrington had perhaps, with that win, flattered to deceive, closing below halfway in the table.

The side also finished the 1922-23 campaign in fifteenth spot, this time out of twenty-seven teams, and then slipped to twentieth in 1923-24.

Happily, the next two seasons saw something of a revival. The Wire rose to ninth in 1924-25 and, in 1925-26, to a heady second; their highest rating since they came fifth in 1904-05.

Twenty-seven wins and a draw from their thirty-six fixtures gave Warrington a percentage of 76.38; enough to secure the runners-up spot at the expense of Swinton, who came third with twenty-six wins and two draws from the same number of games, for a 75.00 per cent return.

Table-toppers Wigan, who had won 80.26 per cent of their games, with twenty-nine wins and three draws in thirty-eight outings, hosted fourth-placed Hull in the play-offs, the Airlie Birds having prevailed in twenty-four of their thirty-eight matches (drawing three for a 67.10 return). Warrington, meanwhile, were at home to a Swinton side that would win the title 12 months later and which, in 1927-28, would become the third team, after Hunslet (1907-08) and Huddersfield (1914-15) to win All Four Cups.

The Wire booked a place in the final with an 11-8 victory over the Lions at Wilderspool; star-studded Wigan, meanwhile, accounted for Hull by an ominous scoreline of 34-0 in the other semi-final.

A crowd of 20,000 gathered at Knowsley Road, St Helens, for the final, which went the way of the Pie Eaters 22-10. Wigan perhaps won the game more comfortably than the scoreline would suggest, with the great winger Johnny Ring scoring a hat-trick to take his season's total to 63 in a campaign in which he topped the league's try-scoring list for the fourth year on the trot. Ring, who had scored 76 tries for Aberavon rugby union side in 1919-20, and who had also spent a couple of seasons as Swansea City's centre forward at soccer, had joined Wigan partly for the substantial cash sum which enabled him to pay for medical treatment for his sister, who was lame. It was remarkable, given his pre-eminence as a winger in the 1920s, that he was only selected twice for Great Britain, including just one Test on the 1924 tour of Australia and New Zealand. His centre, the undemonstrative Tommy Howley, also crossed the whitewash, while Attie Van Heerden bagged a brace and legendary fullback Jim Sullivan kicked a couple of goals. Alf Peacock and Fred Ryder replied for the Wire, with Ned Catterall kicking an early penalty to put Warrington ahead, and also improving Peacock's try.

Warrington slipped to sixteenth the following season, in which a highlight was the decision of the authorities to allocate Wilderspool – which had had a concrete wall built around the playing area – its first Lancashire Cup final. A crowd of 19,439, the highest for three years, turned out to watch St Helens beat St Helens Recreation 10-2.

The Wire dropped a further slot 12 months later, in 1927-28, when there was ample recompense with an appearance in the Challenge Cup Final.

Billy Cunliffe was at prop for an occasion which arguably represented the pinnacle of his career. The Wire, who had reached the final, at Central Park, Wigan, in the last season before Rugby League's showpiece occasion was moved to Wembley, faced the formidable challenge of Swinton, who had already claimed the Lancashire Cup on their way to immortality as All Four Cups heroes.

Warrington had reached the decider with a 43-2 win over amateur team Kinsley in the first round, and victories in difficult ties against leading sides of the era in the shape of Hull Kingston Rovers, Huddersfield and Leeds.

The Wire should, perhaps, have had little hope of success against a team that had headed the league table, a full sixteen places higher than the men from Wilderspool. But a strong mid-April wind at Central Park, Wigan, while chilling the 33,909 crowd, promised to be something of a levelling factor, aiding the Wire's heavier, workmanlike side against the more mercurial Lions.

Swinton went in front with a touchdown for winger Chris Brockbank – the man who would subsequently become the far-seeing Secretary of Warrington – which was hotly contested by the Wire.

Warrington's Welsh winger Dai Davies, brought in from the flank following an injury to Wire scrum-half Billy Kirk (the only Englishman in an otherwise all-Welsh back division) went on to transform the contest in a manner reminiscent of the way in which Northern Union hero Ernie Brookes, who was regularly switched in the same manner as a tactical ploy, had been used a couple of decades earlier.

The Wire were unfortunate to remain 3-0 in arrears at the interval; but it was Davies who sparked a move involving each of the threequarters, comprising winger Billy Rhodes and centres Jesse Meredith and Les Perkins, and finished off by loose forward Charlie Seeling, who had been switched to the wing following the loss of Kirk and whose All Black father – also Charlie – had played for Wigan in the 1910-11 Challenge Cup Final.

Billy Rhodes was unable to add the conversion and the game headed towards the final whistle with the teams on level terms before referee H Horsfall, of Batley, took a decisive hand.

A scrum five yards from Warrington's tryline, fed by Davies, was twice won by the Wire, who also had the head. Each time, however, Mr Horsfall insisted on a repeat feed. On the third occasion, the ball came out behind the Swinton pack; the Lions' Welsh scrum-half Billo Rees fired a pass back to centre Jack Evans, who was hovering in position to land a match-winning drop goal.

Warrington were dismayed not only by the refusal of the match official to allow play to continue when the ball emerged behind their pack; they were disconcerted by Mr Horsfall's decision to award a scrum in the first place.

Fullback Arthur Frowen, Warrington's best player on the day, had touched dead a high kick by Brockbank behind his own goal line. Mr Horsfall, however, ruled that Frowen – who Wire coach Jack Fish and the supporters felt had allowed the kick to go over his head – had, in fact, touched the ball in the field of play, duly awarding a five-yard scrum instead of a 25-yard drop out.

As if news of the 5-3 defeat, and it's manner, wasn't bad enough for those Warrington supporters who hadn't made the trip to Wigan, there was – so it seemed – even worse to come.

Kirk, when injured, had been attended to by two people from

the crowd who, according to radio commentators, were thought for some reason to be clergymen, with some observers later suggesting that they may have had their collars reversed. The scrum-half was lifted onto a stretcher and, covered completely by a blanket, carried off the field. The same radio commentators who had identified the attendants as clergyman made the assumption that Kirk was dead, relaying the news to the listening thousands. Happily, Kirk was in (more or less) rude health, if not at that particular moment, and enjoyed life for many more years.

Billy Cunliffe and his team-mates responded to that disappointing defeat by rising to seventh in the league the following season. In his final year, in 1929-30, Cunliffe picked up his second Lancashire Cup winners' medal in a season in which the Wire closed at eighth. The opposition in the final, at Central Park, Wigan, was Salford.

The two sides attracted a crowd of 21,012 to the game, which was won convincingly by Warrington, Kirk serving concrete evidence that he was alive and kicking with a try that supported touchdowns from Meredith and Tommy Blinkhorn, with Billy Holding landing three goals.

Billy Cunliffe was in his last full season, and retired in September 1930, making his final appearance that month in a 10-4 defeat to Wigan at Wilderspool. He had enjoyed a superb career as a hard-working, reliable cornerstone of Warrington's pack; attributes that had helped him gain 11 caps for Great Britain, between 1920 and 1926, and 10 caps for England, between 1921 and 1926.

Cunliffe's international career began with Great Britain's tour of Australia and New Zealand in 1920. Called up with fellow Warrington packman Arthur Skelhorn, he played in 15 of the 25 games on the trip, scoring one try. Skelhorn made 13 appearances, touching down on four occasions. The most arresting statistic, however, applied to John Wilson of Hull Kingston Rovers, who accompanied the party as Tour Manager but turned out in three games, kicking one goal. A happy summer for Wilson was made even more memorable by his election in England, despite his absence, as successor to Mr J Platt, who had been in the post for twenty-five years, as Secretary of the Northern Union. Mr Wilson was to go a shade better than Mr Platt, remaining at the helm for 26 years, until 1946, when Mr Bill Fallowfield took over the reins in a term of tenure that would last until 1973.

Billy Cunliffe and Skelhorn missed out on the first two Tests in Australia, each of which the Kangaroos won to regain the Ashes secured by Great Britain in the famous Rorke's Drift Test of 1914. There was some solace for the Lions, however, in a healthy profit from tour takings of £28,000, a surplus that looked likely when a world record attendance of 67,859 turned up for the opening game of the trip, when the Lions accounted for Metropolis 27-20 at Sydney. Crowds of 60,000, meanwhile, were recorded for successive games against New South Wales, also at Sydney; Britain lost the first one 42-6 but turned the tables in the return, prevailing 18-10.

Tries by stand-off Charles 'Chook' Fraser and loose forward Frank Burge, with legendary winger Harold Horder adding a goal, helped the Kangaroos to an 8-4 win in the First Test at Brisbane, after the Lions had gone in front with two goals by Huddersfield prop Ben Gronow.

The Ashes were lost when the Lions went down 21-8 in the Second Test at Sydney, where 40,000 witnessed British tries by Widnes prop Arthur Johnson and Dewsbury loose forward Frank Gallagher, with Gronow kicking a goal. Australia dominated the contest in the forwards and their pacey backs wreaked havoc, Horder scoring a try and a goal. His fellow threequarters, Viv Farnsworth, Herb Gilbert and Dick Vest also swept in, with second row Norm Potter also ploughing over. Fraser – at fullback – and Burge, operating in the second row this time, each kicked a goal.

The pride of the Lions was restored following the introduction of Cunliffe and Skelhorn, Great Britain pooping the party for Australians in the 32,000 crowd at Sydney's Royal Agricultural Ground, winning an entertaining clash 23-13. The success was arguably built on the platform established by props Skelhorn and Cunliffe, leading to a brace apiece for Oldham second row Herman Hilton and Hull centre Billy Stone. Leeds centre Jim Bacon also touched down, while Huddersfield winger Johnny Rogers landed three goals and there was one goal for Stone. Australia, in contrast to their earlier experiences, had to settle for a try and two goals by Burge, a touchdown for his second row partner Bert Gray, and a try by scrum-half Duncan Thompson.

A record 34,000 crowd for a British Test in New Zealand amassed for the First Test in Auckland which the Lions, with Cunliffe and Skelhorn in the front row, won 31-7 in a game in which Wakefield Trinity scrum-half Jonty Parkin and Stone (this time on the wing) excelled with hat-tricks. Bacon claimed the Lions' other try and Gronow, in the second row to help accommodate the Warrington duo, chipped in with five goals. Prop Bill Scott got the Kiwis' only try and fullback Bill Davidson and centre Karl Ifwerson each kicked a goal.

The attendance dropped to 10,000 for the Second Test, at Christchurch, and from the perspective of home sensibilities the stay-aways perhaps took the right option. Great Britain saw off the Kiwis 19-3 with two tries by Stone, touchdowns for Bacon, Parkin and Hilton, and a couple of goals for Gronow. New Zealand, meanwhile, were limited to a try for winger Bill Guiney.

Cunliffe missed out on the Third Test, at Wellington, but Skelhorn was still in the front row as the Lions won 11-10, registering tries by Rochdale Hornets' prop Joe Bowers (who had stepped in for the Wire packman), Bacon and Huddersfield second row Duggy Clark. Fartowner Gronow landed a goal, while Ifwerson (on the wing in this game and, intriguingly, substituted by Stan Dobson), scored a try and two goals, and loose forward Stan Walters also popped over.

The party returned to England without the Ashes, but after their success as joint props Down Under, Cunliffe and Skelhorn were retained for Australia's tour of England the following year. Great Britain's hooker for the 1921-22 Kangaroo tour was Leigh's Joe Cartwright, and the front row set the platform for a 2-1 Series win.

The First Test, at Headingley, Leeds, was a tense affair in which Great Britain edged the issue 6-5 before 32,000 fans – the same figure registered for the previous meeting between the two countries in Sydney a little over 15 months earlier. The 'Northern Union', still the operating name of the founding country's national side, were trailing 5-3 as time began to run out, but a piece of magic from the veteran Huddersfield centre Harold Wagstaff, who had been the captain of the heroic 'Rorke's Drift' side of 1914, undermined the tourists' cause. With only three minutes left, Wagstaff broke through in a move maintained by Huddersfield's Rogers (in his usual position of scrum-half after having been obliged to play on the wing in the Third Test in Sydney), Parkin and Bacon. Leeds winger Squire Stockwell finished the raid sweetly, ducking under the arm of Horder to snatch a dramatic try that secured a win that had looked unlikely when Australia responded to an interception try in the tenth minute by Stone with a touchdown for Cec Blinkorne, off a pass from Vest with centre Jim Craig adding the extras.

Great Britain's hopes of retrieving the Ashes after two games were dashed at the Boulevard, Hull. A 'gate' of 21,504 convened at the home of Hull FC aware that the Kangaroos had lost several games against club sides, but a hand injury to Stockwell in the opening minute was a blow from which the Northern Union never recovered.

Thompson and Rogers traded penalties in the first 40 minutes, but the hosts fell away in the second period. Vest intercepted a pass by Bacon intended for his Leeds club-mate Stockwell, and that touchdown was followed by a stunning solo effort by Horder. Blinkhorn added a couple of late tries, and Thompson kicked his second goal; and the Test Series was all square following Australia's 16-2 verdict.

The pendulum had swung towards the tourists but, just as the injury to Stockwell had hampered the Northern Union's cause at Hull, so an injury to an Australian – fullback and captain 'Chook' Fraser – wrecked the Kangaroos' prospects, at the turn of the year, at Salford. The injury, in this instance, was rather more serious, Fraser sustaining a broken leg in the thirty-fifth minute before being carried from the field before 21,000 chastened observers.

Billy Cunliffe, together with Hilton and Hull second row Bob Taylor, had worked a move which Hilton finished off in the twentieth minute and the hosts were only prevented from stretching their lead by magnificent Australian defence. Great Britain were in no mood to allow the one-man advantage to go to waste. The Kangaroos were unable to withstand the second-half pressure indefinitely, and the clinching score came when a heavy tackle by Dewsbury loose forward, Frank Gallagher, on Thompson, led to the latter spilling possession, Gallagher pouncing for an opportunist try that sealed the Ashes.

Cunliffe was called up for the return tour to the Antipodes, in 1924, as Warrington's only representative. He played in 17 of the Lions' 27 matches, including all three Tests in Australia and the first of the three Tests in New Zealand, scoring three tries in other games.

There were 50,000 witnesses, in the early stages of the First Test at Sydney on Monday 23 June 1924, to an incredible start to the international career of Wigan's great Welsh fullback Jim Sullivan who, with his first touch of the ball, landed a penalty over a reported distance of 60 metres.

Another goal by Sullivan got Great Britain – the 'proper' title, now, of the tourists following the decision in 1922 to change the name of the sport from Northern Union to Rugby League Football – in the right frame of mind, but Australia were back in contention by the break after winger Cec Aynsley (the 'Red Flyer') crossed.

The dismissal of Australian prop Norm Potter five minutes into the second period, however, gave the Lions the chance to take control;

with captain Jonty Parkin at his incisive best, Great Britain took that opportunity with assurance and aplomb, adding four more tries in a 22-3 win. Two of those touchdowns went to Parkin; Wigan second row Jack Price and Oldham winger Sidney Rix crossed, and Sullivan totalled five goals.

There was a drop in the crowd for the Second Test, also at the Sydney Cricket Ground, demoralised Australians perhaps not helped by heavy rain, or by the fact that there were only five days between the games. A crowd of 33,842 turned up for a mud-bound match in which Great Britain were obliged to switch Gallagher from loose forward to stand-off.

Australia went in front with a try by Aynsley; a score that, in the conditions, could perhaps have been enough to secure victory. The brilliant Parkin, however, was both patient and perspicacious and, ten minutes from time, made the most of a gap in the Kangaroos' defence for a try which Sullivan converted for a 5-3 win that secured the Ashes. Part of the credit for that score went to manager Harry Dannatt who when informed before the game by Parkin, who had both ankles bandaged, that he could hardly walk, simply replied 'go out there and run, then.'

The good folk of Brisbane, or 36,000 of them, turned out for the Third Test, which Australia won 21-11. Britain's cause wasn't helped by the dismissal of loose forward Gallagher, who became the first Lion to be sent off in a Test match Down Under. Britain led 5-4 at the interval, having posted a try by Swinton winger Frank Evans, which Sullivan converted, in response to two goals by Aynsley. The Kangaroos, however, took control in the second half with a long-range try by Arthur Oxford, who also kicked a goal, together with touchdowns by winger Bill Paten and second row Vic Armbruster, two goals by Thompson and a goal by centre Jim Craig. Britain rallied bravely through tries by Parkin and Evans to hint at what could have been achieved with a full complement.

Billy Cunliffe played in the First Test in New Zealand, which was lost at Auckland 16-8 before 22,000 spectators. A factor in the defeat was his own dismissal, leaving the Lions unable to register more than a try and a goal by Leeds second row Joe Thompson and a touchdown by Broughton Rangers winger Billy Bentham. New Zealand inflicted a surprise win, after Great Britain had cruised through their opening four games on that leg of the tour, with tries by centres Bill Stuart and Terry Gilroy, stand-off Maurice Wetherill and prop Ernie Herring, with substitute winger Frank Delgrosso kicking two goals.

Suspended, Cunliffe could only watch as the Kiwis thrilled a 6,000 Wellington crowd by recovering from 11-0 down to win the Second Test only four days later. The Lions had appeared to be in control after producing tries by Barrow centre Charlie Carr, Wigan centre Tommy Howley and Oldham flying winger Rix, plus a Thompson goal. The Kiwis, though, blasted back to beat a Great Britain side that also lacked Sullivan and Parkin, who had both gone down with diphtheria, to win 13-11 with tries by winger Harry Mullins, centre Hec Brisbane and prop Jim O'Brien, with fullback Craddock Dufty adding two goals.

Great Britain, still without Cunliffe, won the Third Test, at Dunedin, 31-18, despite having been forced to play three internationals in seven days, disappointing 14,000 New Zealand residents with a brace for Oldham second row Albert Brough and tries by Wigan stand-off Danny Hurcombe, Carr, Howley, Evans and Price; Sullivan totalled five goals. The Kiwis' Dufty converted three of the tries by Brisbane, Delgrosso, O'Brien and Herring.

Those displays by New Zealand prompted the Rugby Football League to invite the Kiwis, rather than the Kangaroos, to Great Britain for the incoming 1926 tour. Cunliffe was in the side for the First Test, at Wigan, which was won 28-20 before 14,500. The Lions, however, had to withstand a strong rally by the visitors after New Zealand had gone in at the break 20-5 adrift, and had to seal their win with tries by Hull second row Bob Taylor and Carr. Carr, Rix, Taylor and Gallagher had crossed for Britain in the opening period, with Sullivan kicking the first four of his five goals, while New Zealand closed with tries by second row Bert Avery, centre Brisbane, second row Len Mason and centre Bill Davidson, with loose forward Neil Mouat adding four goals.

Billy Cunliffe was not selected for the Second Test and had, in fact, played his last game for Great Britain, who went on to win the last two games in the Series 21-11 at Hull, and 32-17 at Headingley, Leeds.

Cunliffe, meanwhile, went in to give four more distinguished years of service to Warrington, for whom he had scored 38 tries in his 438 games.

6

Bill Shankland

THE Australian CB Fry. That's a description that could be ascribed to Bill Shankland, the Australian who set off to tour Great Britain with the 1929-30 Kangaroos – and who, on being attracted to Warrington, never returned.

Shankland, who was born in Sydney in 1907, is arguably Australia's finest all-round sportsman, turning his hand, foot and eye to many and varied disciplines, and enjoying a degree of success in each. Whether swimming, boxing or playing cricket – or operating in the threequarters or at fullback at Rugby League – Shankland was a top performer from an early age.

On his retirement from Rugby League in 1937 – after steering Warrington to success over Barrow in the Lancashire Cup Final – he switched his attentions fully to golf; a diversion in which he perhaps excelled more than in any other, appearing in every British Open between 1937 and 1955. And, speaking shortly before his death, he admitted that golf, as much as Rugby League, had persuaded him to leave his native land. He said: 'I decided I wanted to come to England not only because I'd enjoyed the 1929 tour, but because I wanted to get into professional golf, and I reasoned that would be easier over here.

'I opted for Warrington because I got on very well with their Secretary, Bob Anderton. The only worry was that I'd been told it would be terribly wet.'

His exploits as a speedy winger had already brought him distinction on the rugby field, initially with Sydney side Glebe, for whom he played 14 games in the 1927 and 1928 seasons, scoring three tries and kicking four goals. Even within the confines of Rugby League he illustrated that he possessed wide-ranging qualities, impressing the selectors enough from the wing position to earn a call-up for New South Wales at stand-off in 1928, before reverting to the wing for the Sky Blues the following year, by which time he had moved on to Eastern Suburbs.

It was while with Easts that he was picked for Australia's tour of England in 1929 – a trip that remains unique for having four Tests matches played, an extra game being arranged at short notice when the Third Test finished in a 0-0 draw after the teams had each won one of the previous two games. Shankland played in each of the matches, and in 23 of the Kangaroos' 35 fixtures, a figure beaten by only two men – Jack Kingston and Fred McMillan, who both turned out in 26. Shankland was the top try-scorer on the tour, with 24 (one more than Bill Spencer), and the second-highest points scorer, his 17 goals taking his tally to 106 points, behind Eric Weissel's 127 from five tries and 56 goals.

The Aussie's abilities were all too evident, at least for British sensibilities, in the First Test, at Hull Kingston Rovers' Craven Park, where 20,000 east coast folk witnessed the Eastern Suburbs flyer claim two sparkling tries. His first closed a sweeping movement by the tourists, helping them, with tries by second row George Treweeke, loose forward Wally Prigg and hooker George Bishop, plus three goals by stand-off Weissell, to an 18-2 interval lead, and his second, after Great Britain had responded with an unconverted touchdown by Salford second row Alf Middleton, ended home hopes of a revival. It was, fittingly, a classic winger's effort in which he contrived, with a mesmerising blend of pace and elusive guile, to leave four defenders sprawling in his wake, Australia going on to prevail 31-8 with tries by Spencer and Weissell, who closed with five goals. The Kangaroos had finished only a couple of points shy of their previous best Test win in England, the 33-8 success in the Third Test at Birmingham in 1911-12.

Great Britain, mindful of the need to starve Shankland and his co-winger, Spencer, of possession, adopted spoiling tactics for the Second Test, at Headingley, and the strategy was successful, to the delight of the majority of the 31,402 crowd. Not that Shankland could be kept at bay entirely. The winger made the most of a slim chance to squeeze in at the corner after Wigan fullback Jim Sullivan had opened the scoring with a penalty goal, but that try was to be the Kangaroos' only acquaintance with the scoreboard.

Wakefield Trinity halfback Jonty Parkin and Swinton scrum-half Billy Rees worked space for Castleford centre Arthur Atkinson – who had been brought in solely to mark Australia's centre and captain Tom Gorman – to race in, Sullivan adding the extras and a penalty to secure a 9-3 Series-levelling victory.

The Third Test, played at Swinton on Saturday 4 January 1930, offered one of the most controversial incidents in Rugby League history. A fiercely contested affair kept a 33,809 crowd on tenterhooks throughout, despite the fact that, with time ticking away, there was no score.

With 15 minutes remaining the Kangaroos scrum-half Joe 'Chimpy' Busch broke clear from the base of a scrum, on the opposite side of the pitch to Frankland's wing, and headed for the corner. Great Britain loose forward Fred Butters, of Swinton, was in hot pursuit and, having already denied Australia twice with wonderful last-ditch tackles, was the man the home side wanted to represent them in that situation. The chase went to the line, Busch diving for the winning touchdown and Butters propelling himself in the same instant, taking the Kangaroos legs from under him and forcing him into touch-in-goal.

Busch and his team-mates felt that he had got the ball down before he had gone dead; the touchjudge, supported by referee Bob Robinson of Bradford, felt otherwise.

The game closed in a 0-0 draw, leading to immediate calls by Australia's visionary manager Harry Sunderland, backed by the press, for a Fourth Test, to settle the stalemate. The Rugby League Council concurred, by a 13-11 vote, and a game was hastily arranged for the Athletic Grounds, Rochdale, on the afternoon of Wednesday 15 January 1930.

A healthy crowd, given working commitments, of 16,743 turned up to witness another match dominated by defences. The result, and the destiny of the Ashes, hinged on an injury to Australian centre Cec Fifield, who broke his ankle in the second half at a time when there had, as in the Third Test, been no score. Australia, reduced to 12 men, battled on bravely until five minutes from time, when Huddersfield's Stanley Brogden sent Wakefield Trinity winger Stan Smith over for the winning try of a series in which, after 39 points had been registered in the opening Test, only 15 were scored in the next three games.

The Kangaroos closed their tour with a match against Wales at Wembley on 18 January, winning 26-10 before 16,000 spectators in only the second Rugby League game to be staged at the Twin Towers, after the successful experiment the previous season of taking the Challenge Cup Final to the stadium, Shankland kicking four goals.

Shankland subsequently agreed terms with Warrington of a £1,000 fee up-front, followed by payments of £8 a match and £6 a week in wages. His signing, in July 1931, attracted huge interest and several thousand supporters gathered at Bank Quay railway station to welcome him to Warrington; a moment that, perhaps, helped persuade him to never return to his native land.

Those terms, incidentally, caused him one or two problems initially with less well remunerated colleagues; even though he scored a try on his debut, against St Helens Recreation on 29 August 1931, the touchdown helping the Wire to a 16-6 home win, and another try the following week in the clash with Swinton. He admitted later: 'Miners on 50 bob a week didn't always think too much of me getting 14 quid just for playing rugby. One refused to pass to me; he used to throw it over my head all the time. I talked him round in the end by persuading him that he'd get a lot more winning pay if he'd pass to me properly.'

His 23 touchdowns in his inaugural season at Wilderspool made him the Wire's leading tryscorer for the campaign. Promoted to captain the following season, he went on to serve the Wire with great distinction for the next seven years, during which he skippered the side in two Challenge Cup Finals. The first, in 1932-33, followed Warrington's success a few months earlier in the Lancashire Cup Final, in which St Helens had been beaten 10-9 at Wigan before a 28,500 crowd.

Shankland, now playing mostly in the centre, introduced his players to HRH The Prince of Wales, who had stepped forward because of the ill-health of his father, King George V, before the kick-off. The players were under strict instructions not to speak to his Royal Highness unless addressed first; the Prince, however, picked out Shankland in particular, enquiring how his golf was going. 'Fine, sir', replied Shankland, 'how's yours?'

None of those involved were aware at that time that, within three years, the Prince would be at the centre of the abdication crisis. Nor was Shankland aware that his team would lose 21-17 to Huddersfield in one of the best finals of all time, albeit a game in which the Wire missed their freescoring winger Tom Blinkhorn, who became sidelined when a leg injury turned septic.

Warrington had much the better of the opening quarter, testing the Fartown defence repeatedly with the help of astute tactical kicking by fullback Billy Holding, only to be unable to register the score their efforts arguably deserved. Instead, Huddersfield went in front in the 20th minute with a penalty by captain Len Bowkett, a capture from Coventry Rugby Union club, Bowkett extending the lead in similar fashion five minutes later.

Prospects deteriorated for the Wire when Bowkett converted a try by loose forward Fred Brindle, whose signing from Hull KR at the turn of the year had been a major factor in their march on Wembley. Warrington, though, hit back when centre Billy Dingsdale forced his way over, and the Wire went in at the break 10-9 up after scrum-half Dai Davies popped over direct from a scrum, Holding – who had been wide with three attempted penalties – converting both scores.

Bowkett nosed Huddersfield back in front four minutes after the resumption with a coolly taken penalty and, in a repeat of the pattern of the first half, Warrington again laid siege on Fartown for the next 20 minutes or so. Huddersfield, however, again held out, and went on to turn the tables in the closing quarter. Scrum-half Leslie Adams, who had been involved in Brindle's try, made the break that led to Aussie winger Ernie Mills flying in.

Holding pulled Warrington back to only four points adrift with his first successful penalty, but a poor clearing kick by Wire stand-off Jack Oster gave his opposite number Gwyn Richards the chance to pounce, Bowkett's conversion helping establish a nine-point lead.

With four minutes remaining Davies grabbed his second touchdown, Holding's goal bringing Warrington to within a converted score of victory. Time, however, ran out for Shankland and his troops, whose 17 points represented the highest losing score in a Challenge Cup Final until Hull lost 28-24 to Wigan in 1984-85.

There was disappointment for Shankland two seasons later, when Warrington lost 14-3 to Swinton at Wigan, before 27,700 fans, in the Championship Final. And, in 1935-36, the Wire missed out to a Leeds side that equalled Huddersfield's record of four Challenge Cup Final victories in a game remembered chiefly for a controversial try scored in the eighth minute by the Loiners' loose forward Ike Isaac.

Isaac was first to the ball after Leeds winger Eric Harris – the 'Toowoomba Ghost' – hoisted a high cross-field kick after breaking clear. Warrington's players, however, merely stood and watched, feeling that the loose forward was clearly offside. Referee AS Dobson, of Featherstone, felt differently, allowing a try which scrum-half Evan Williams converted.

Warrington failed to make the most of a couple of opportunities which could have got them back into serious contention, right winger Jack Garrett spilling a pass with a try begging and Welsh centre Ben

Hawker letting a similar chance go astray. Shankland, playing at fullback, got his side off the mark with a penalty awarded against centre Fred Harris, who responded in style by crossing after a well-worked scissors move with namesake Eric, Fred dummying and, after kicking over Shankland's head, winning the race to the touchdown. Williams was wide with the conversion attempt, but made no mistake with a penalty just before the break to help put Leeds 10-2 ahead.

Eric Harris helped Leeds get a real grip on the Cup with a fine solo touchdown in which he swept past three opponents, kicked on, and left a couple more defenders trailing for arguably the best try seen at Wembley to date. Williams added the extras and Leeds sealed an 18-2 verdict, and the biggest winning margin at Wembley up to that point, with a late touchdown by centre Gwyn Parker, who crossed after fullback Jim Brough had helped create an overlap.

Warrington reached the Championship Final for the second time in three seasons in 1936-37, missing out to Salford, 13-11, at Wigan, before a 31,500 crowd. The Wire, despite having finished two points behind the table-topping Red Devils in the final table, were viewed as slight favourites to prevail at Central Park, particularly as Salford had been beaten 10-4 on their own midden in the first round of the Challenge Cup some three months earlier. That billing was justified at the break when a 6-4 lead had been established and Warrington, who had successfully snuffed out their opponents' much-vaunted back line, looked poised to ratify the bookies' ratings when, with 11 minutes left, an 8-8 deadlock was broken when hooker Dave Cotton bustled over for the first try of the contest.

Salford, though, hit back only four minutes later with a stunning touchdown at the corner-flag by Great Britain winger Barney Hudson. And up stepped the immortal Gus Risman to land a wonderful touchline conversion that turned out to be the match-winner. Shankland had kicked a goal in the earlier exchanges, with fullback Billy Holding having two successes and second row Eric Welsby landing a penalty.

Bill Shankland closed his career at Warrington, however, with a couple of winners' medals. The Wire came top of the Lancashire League, for the first time, in 1937-38, a season in which they also lifted the Lancashire Cup, beating Barrow 8-4 at Wigan before a 14,000 crowd.

His last match for Warrington was the 8-4 'derby' defeat at the hands of Widnes on 15 April 1938.

Turning fully to golf, Shankland became the professional at Haydock Park, subsequently succeeding Percy Alliss at Temple Newsam, Leeds, in 1938. In 1939, with war clouds gathering, he was third, in the British Open at St Andrews, four strokes behind champion Dick Burton, who marked 290, and in 1947, at the Royal Liverpool Golf Club, Hoylake, he finished fourth, on 295, only two shots behind the winner Fred Daly, with Reg Horne and amateur Frank Stranahan closing on 294.

His best subsequent finish was in 1951, at Royal Portrush, County Antrim, when he came seventh, his 293 comparing favourably with the 285 recorded by champion Max Faulkner, while in 1949 he had finished twelfth, just six strokes adrift of Bobby Lock at Royal St George, Sandwich.

Between those tournaments he became the professional at Potters Bar, a Jewish-owned course. He later recalled:

> JB Reubens was one of the richest men in the country, but many Jews had difficulty in gaining membership of golf clubs. His solution was to buy one.
>
> He asked me if I would like to work for him. My response was that I was one of the highest paid golf players in the country, to which he inquired how much I earned. When I told him I was paid £650 a month, he said they would pay me £1,500. I spent 25 years at Potters Bar; the people there were wonderful, and I enjoyed every minute.

Shankland even relished the difficult task of honing the unquestioned talents of a young Tony Jacklin, who paid full tribute in later years to his mentor's contribution to his subsequent success. The 16-year-old was brash and Shankland admitted:

> I loved Tony's mother and father, but the boy himself was a shocker. He was a cheeky devil and it took a lot of work to get him into shape. I had to keep him under my thumb but he had great talent and worked hard, even though he always thought he was right about everything. I doubt if he would have become the player he was if I hadn't sorted him out.

Bill Shankland retired to Parkstone, in Dorset, in the 1960s, becoming a revered member, his qualities being recognised in exactly the way they had been at Wilderspool. He played exhibition matches, and helped raise money for charity, until 1996, when he was obliged to give golf up after injuring his shoulders in a fall.

It was on a return to Warrington that he passed away, on 8 September 1998, having helped the Wire celebrate the centenary of the Wilderspool stadium.

After several days of reminiscence with his many old friends, in which he recounted playing cricket with Don Bradman, swimming against Johnny Weissmuller and beating a leading American baseball pitcher in a throwing contest, he spearheaded the celebrations, at the age of 91, by leading out the past players in the centenary game against Huddersfield on 6 September 1998.

Two days later he slipped on the stairs in his hotel, banging his head. He never recovered consciousness.

It is, however, as a wonderful all-round sportsman, particularly at golf and Rugby League, that he will be remembered. He reasoned, without false humility:

I was lucky with my sport. I could do anything. I was a very athletic chap.

He will also be remembered as one of the Wire's all-time greats, and as a man who embraced the folk of Warrington. He said:

Wilderspool was a wonderful ground to me, and I have nothing but happy memories of the place. We used to get crowds of 10,000 to 12,000, and the people were always very friendly. I was involved with golf for a lot longer than rugby, but it was playing for Warrington that gave me the chance to come to this country and make my home here. I will never forget the good times I had there.

7

Gerry Helme

GERRY HELME has a rare claim to fame in the annals of Rugby League folklore. The scrum-half is, with Halifax prop John Thorley, one of only a couple of men to have direct connections with possibly the two most evocative events in British Rugby League, at least in the post-war period.

Helme, a product of the Culcheth amateur club, rose from those relatively humble origins to play a central role, in a single year, in the most revered episodes in our past. The first occasion was the Challenge Cup Final replay of 1954, when an estimated 130,000 crowd packed Odsal Stadium on the evening of Wednesday 5 May to watch Warrington dispose of Halifax. And the second, on Saturday 13 November in the same year, was the first World Cup Final in Rugby League, when Great Britain beat France 16-12 in Paris, to lift the trophy for the first time.

Gerry Helme and Thorley played in both matches, the first as opponents and the second as team-mates, and Helme was arguably the most influential figure on the pitch in each game. That assertion could perhaps be contested; but not the fact that, in each match, he scored the decisive try.

His touchdown in Paris sealed the Lions' victory; one which, it has to be said, had been very much unexpected when Great Britain set off for France for a tournament that had not attracted universal favour. Indeed, the leading British players of the era were generally against the idea, although a motivating factor in their antipathy may have been the fact that many of them had only just returned from Great Britain's gruelling tour of Australia, losing the Test Series 2-1, before winning 2-1 in New Zealand. Terms of £25 for the three weeks of World Cup duty also caused some to reflect on the value of taking part. With Wigan winger Billy Boston and Hunslet second row Geoff Gunney pulling out after being selected because of injury, and Barrow's legendary stand-off Willie Horne withdrawing because of business commitments, the British side certainly had a new look about it.

Helme, who had played in five of the six Tests on tour, was happy to accept the invitation to play for Great Britain in the inaugural World Cup, but only two others from the party that had played Down Under a few months earlier chose, in the end, to join him. They were Phil Jackson, the fine Barrow centre, and Dave Valentine, the former Hawick and Scotland Rugby Union man, who had switched codes to join Huddersfield and who was named captain of a pioneering squad that comprised, in addition to the loyalists from Australia, Helme's Warrington team-mate, centre Albert Naughton. The rest of the squad numbered stalwarts Jimmy Ledgard and Frank Kitchen (Leigh), David Rose, Gordon Brown (Leeds), Mick Sullivan, Billy Banks, Harry Bradshaw, Ron Rylance (Huddersfield), John Thorley (Halifax), Stan Smith (Hunslet), Bob Coverdale, Johnny Whiteley (Hull), Don Robinson (Wakefield Trinity) and Basil Watts (York).

The party was to make history, and Helme was to play in each of the four games, with Naughton appearing in two, including the final.

Given no chance at the outset, Great Britain got off to the best start possible in the bid to finish top of the table above Australia, France and New Zealand with a 28-13 success over the Kangaroos, before 10,250 spectators at Lyon, in which Jackson, perhaps the Lions' man of the series, scored two tries, together with Leeds stand-off Gordon Brown.

Winger David Rose, also of Leeds, added a touchdown, together with Leigh winger Frank Kitchen; Leigh fullback Jimmy Ledgard kicked five goals. Australia posted a brace for centre Harry Wells, a try by hooker Ken Kearney, and a couple of goals by winger Noel Pidding.

France, meanwhile, led by the incomparable XIII Catalan fullback Puig Aubert (a chain-smoker who it was rumoured wore shorts with pockets, wherein to house his cigarettes and matches for a quick 'puff' during quiet passages of play) beat New Zealand 22-13 before 13,240 folk at the Parc des Princes in Paris.

Australia had to dispose of New Zealand to make certain of remaining in World Cup contention, and that they did; 34-15 at Marseilles, where 20,000 turned out. Further north, at Toulouse, Great Britain and France fought out a 13-13 thriller. Helme, Brown and Rose claimed Britain's tries, and Ledgard landed two goals; the Tricolors' response in front of a 37,471 'gate' involved a brace for Bordeaux winger Raymond Contrastin, a touchdown for prop Joseph

Krawzyk, and a couple of goals by Puig-Aubert.

Great Britain, therefore, went into their final game, against a New Zealand side that had lost its first two matches, aware that they would finish top of the table if they won. France could finish level top if they managed to beat Australia and would, in fact, overhaul the Lions and take the World Cup if they could account for the Kangaroos (or even draw) and Britain lost.

France – an exciting and flamboyant outfit throughout the 1950s – duly disposed of the Kangaroos 15-5 with tries by Contrastin, centre Jacques Merquey and winger Vincent Cantoni, of Toulouse. Second row Kel O'Shea replied for the Kangaroos and Pidding landed a goal. The crowd at Nantes, a little surprisingly, was only 13,000. Great Britain, meanwhile, recorded the biggest winning margin of the competition with the 26-6 verdict over the Kiwis, the match attracting 14,000 at Bordeaux to watch Ledgard get a try and four goals, Kitchen bag a brace, and Rose, Jackson and Brown shoot over. Taranaki centre Ron McKay landed three goals for the Kiwis.

Great Britain and France therefore had to play off to determine the destiny of the inaugural World Cup.

The rivals duly descended on Paris, together with 30,368 excited observers, for a contest which ended with Valentine hoisting the World Cup aloft; thereby becoming the first British captain in a major sport to achieve such an honour. That Valentine did so was, apart from his own efforts, in no small measure due to the input of Jackson, who continued his fine form of the tour, and Helme, who grabbed the clinching try. His halfback partner, Brown, bagged a brace and Rose, too, maintained his record of crossing in each game; Ledgard landed two goals, while the entertaining French posted tries by wingers Cantoni and Contrastin, with Puig Aubert kicking three goals.

Helme and his colleagues returned home to a heroes' welcome, and everlasting fame, completing a heady year for the wily halfback.

The previous May, he had played a full part in the game with Halifax at Wembley which was the first Challenge Cup Final at the Twin Towers to finish in a draw. And it got even better for Helme in the replay. In his book *There were a lot more than that*, Robert Gate offers a copy of a match report by Bernard Ingham, who was then a sports journalist with the *Halifax Courier* before eventually gravitating to be Press Officer to HM Government during Margaret Thatcher's term as Prime Minister. Reflecting initially on the size of the crowd, Ingham wrote:

> Odsal Stadium lacked the splendour of Wembley but none of its excitement, Cup Final replays are very rare and the Odsal scene was unique.
>
> As thousands poured into the bowl, cramming every vantage point, one wondered how many would not see the match. Many did not – and hundreds must have caught only fleeting glimpses as they strained to peep. Some did not bother and one elderly woman made herself comfortable on the bank and calmly read a newspaper.
>
> As the players strode down the hillside on to the turf Halifax people, jovial and confident, made their greater numbers heard. The Warrington supporters were more serious in this predominantly Yorkshire crowd, but it may have been an indication of Lancashire purpose.
>
> Try as Kielty and Clarkson did to carve an opening in the initial assault, Warrington, looking formidable even in defence, weathered the storm. Too many dropped passes lost Halifax ground and then, in a flash, the Lancastrians were jubilant and Halifax stunned by Challinor's early try. In only eight minutes Warrington had succeeded in doing what they failed to do in 80 minutes at Wembley.
>
> Now the blue and white rosetted Halifax people were in a doubting mood. But they die hard at Thrum Hall and back they came, the forwards taking hold of the game. Warrington always had their measure, however, and were superior at halfback. Helme was a dangerous and brilliant tactician, and Price a valiant partner.

What Ingham didn't mention was that Helme scored the try – courtesy of an audacious dummy to winger Stan McCormick that bamboozled Halifax fullback Tyssull Griffiths, following a dazzling solo run – that clinched the Wire's victory. Halifax, who had replied to centre Jim Challinor's touchdown with a penalty a minute before the break by Welshman Griffiths, were only a point behind as the game went into the closing stages, Warrington second row Bath and Griffiths having traded further penalties.

Observing journalist Allan Cave reported:

> The issue turned on one of the best tries that Gerry Helme, the Warrington scrum-half, who was their Wembley hero in 1950, has scored. He was on the ball like a sweeping hawk when it came from a scrum.
>
> Two Halifax players bought a dummy and away went Gerry, finally

to double somersault over the line for a try, which made it 8-4 for Warrington, after Halifax had been striving desperately to get in front.

No wonder Helme won the Lance Todd Trophy for the best player afield, as he did in 1950.

Helme, and his co-halfback Price, ruled the middle.

Cave referred to Helme's fine performance in the 1950 Challenge Cup Final in his report, but of more interest perhaps to the scrum-half, at that moment at least, was the fact that Warrington were on course for the acquisition of three trophies in a single season, with only the Lancashire Cup eluding the Wilderspool outfit.

The Wire had already won the Lancashire League by the time the Challenge Cup Final came around, and it was Halifax who offered the only resistance to the coveted 'Cup and League double'. The sides met at Maine Road, Manchester, where Helme picked up his second Championship winners medal.

A man obviously made for the big occasion, Helme had won the Lance Todd Trophy in 1950 for his sublime display in the victory over arch-rivals Widnes. The 19-0 scoreline sounds emphatic enough, and the Wire did go into the contest as firm favourites. Widnes, however, exerted some early pressure in response to a raid in which winger Brian Bevan was only denied a try by a forward pass ruling, and it took several fine touch-finding kicks by Helme to ease Warrington's nerves. Warrington edged ahead through a drop goal by loose forward Harold Palin in the 15th minute, and the same player stretched the advantage three minutes later with a penalty. Palin then converted a try by second row Harry Bath, and Warrington took a real grip on the issue with a try seven minutes before the interval for centre Ron Ryder, followed by a Palin penalty as the half-time whistle beckoned.

The attritional nature of the early stages of the contest resurfaced on the resumption, with no further score until the 58th minute, when Palin kicked his fifth goal – including his early drop goal – to put himself in contention for the Lance Todd Trophy, which had been introduced four years earlier. The honour, though, went to Helme, partly for his efforts in the testing early stages, and also for the manner in which he carved out a try 13 minutes from time, with the neatest of reverse passes, for his halfback partner Bryn Knowelden.

Gerry Helme became the first player from a Lancashire club to take the coveted award, following in the footsteps of Billy Stott

(Wakefield Trinity) in 1946, Willie Davies (Bradford Northern) 1947, Frank Whitcombe, also of Bradford Northern, in 1948, and yet another Northern man, Ernest Ward, in 1949.

During his career with the Wire, which spanned the years 1945 to 1957, Gerry Helme collected every major honour available; not that, according to veteran Wire supporter George Woodhead, who was interviewed by the author of this book for the Rugby Leaguer in 2001, he particularly cared for the momentoes of his deeds,

Woodhead said, 'Gerry Helme was a close neighbour and a good friend. He sold us an easy chair once and we found one of his trophies down the side. It was a gold cigarette lighter that I think had been presented to him as the winner of the Lance Todd Trophy. When he next called round and took out a cigarette I lit it for him with his own lighter!'

Helme was a member of the side that won the championship for the first time for Warrington in 1947-48, the Wire accounting for a Bradford Northern team 15-5 that, seven days earlier, had lost to Wigan in the Challenge Cup Final. Brian Bevan, Stan Powell and Albert Pimblett scored the Wire's tries, and Palin landed three goals. Northern had to settle for a Des Case try and an Ernest Ward conversion.

In the same season, Warrington secured the Lancashire League title, exactly 10 seasons on from their inaugural success.

The coveted Red Rose championship was retained in 1948-49, while the Wire were runners-up in the Championship and Lancashire Cup Finals. The power of the side did not go unnoticed, with huge crowds being attracted to Wilderspool, headed by the club record of 34,304 that convened for the league game with Wigan – who won 8-4 – for a league fixture on 22 January 1949.

Following the tremendous 1953-54 season, and the wonderful experience of the World Cup in the autumn of 1954, Helme enjoyed the remainder of the 1954-55 season by helping the Wire keep their grip on both the Rugby League Championship and the Lancashire League championship. The title was retained in heavy rain at Maine Road, although the adverse weather had little affect on the attendance, which at 49,434 was significantly up on the 36,519 that had shown up for the previous year's meeting of the Wire and Halifax (that low figure being, in all probability, a reaction to the scenes at Odsal only days earlier).

Opponents Oldham were on level terms when Frank Pitchford

crashed over in response to Brian Bevan's touchdown, but a couple of Warrington penalties by Harry Bath settled one of the season's major issues.

Gerry Helme, who made 12 appearances for Great Britain, retired as a Warrington player in 1957. His international career stretched from the home series against Australia in 1948-49, in which he appeared in all three Tests, and climaxed with the World Cup Final of 1954.

Helme's debut for Great Britain was at Headingley, Leeds, in the opening game of the 1948 Ashes, when Great Britain prevailed 23-21 through tries by his club colleague, centre Albert Pimblett, who bagged a brace, while Belle Vue Rangers winger Stan McCormick, who would transfer to Warrington five years or so later, also crossed twice, together with Bradford Northern second row Trevor Foster, Huddersfield's Valentine registering one. Great Britain, in fact, scored seven tries to Australia's five, but Bradford Northern centre Ernest Ward was only able to convert one effort. The Kangaroos, who were 17-6 adrift at one stage, mounted a strong rally, forcing Britain to hang on in a desperate last 10 minutes which stretched the nerves of the 36,529 crowd.

A remarkably similar 'gate' – 36,354 – gathered at Station Road, Swinton, for the Second Test, enthused by the drama of the Headingley opener. They left the Manchester ground still enthused, and buoyed by a 16-7 victory. Helme, at the hub of activity, helped create the platform for Pimblett to grab two tries in the first half, Ward converting one and claiming a penalty for a 10-2 interval lead. The Kangaroos bounced back through centre Jack Horrigan, winger Johnny Graves adding his second goal to bring the tourists to within three points. But a couple of unconverted tries by Wigan winger Johnny Lawrenson in the second period saw Great Britain home, and ensured that the Ashes were retained after the Series success Down Under in 1946 by the famous 'Indomitables'.

Helme had to wait a little longer than expected for his next international appearance. The Third Test, which had been scheduled for Saturday 18 December at Odsal Stadium, Bradford, was postponed because of fog, and was rearranged for the end of January.

Australia looked capable at the interval, when they were 6-5 ahead, of staking a morale-boosting victory. Great Britain, though, upped the tempo in the second period, forging a 23-9 win which involved two tries by Salford prop George Curran, a try and four goals by Ernest Ward, and touchdowns for McCormick (who had transferred from Belle Vue to St Helens) and Leeds stand-off Dickie Williams.

Helme missed out on the 1950 tour to Australia and New Zealand, and on the home series of 1951 and 1952 against New Zealand and Australia respectively. He was, however, back in the line-up for the 1954 tour Down Under. The First Test was inauspicious for the Lions, who were on level terms at 12-12 on the hour mark, having posted a try by Barrow centre Phil Jackson and three goals by Leeds' Welsh wonder Lewis Jones, who played on the wing. Great Britain, however, inexplicably collapsed to a 37-12 defeat in which the hosts, before 65,884 fans at the Sydney Cricket Ground, registered a try and eight goals by Ben Pidding and tries by Ken McCaffrey (2), Norm Provan, Kel O'Shea, Duncan Hall and Brian Carlson.

Helme was held not to be at fault for the reverse, which had followed criticism of the decision of the tour management to bring in an Australian, the former Test player Ross McKinnon, to help with coaching. Happily the Lions, who had made five changes for the game, were utterly transformed, winning the Brisbane clash 38-21 to send the Aussies in the 45,000 crowd home disgruntled.

Wigan winger Billy Boston was in top form with two blockbusting tries, and Lewis Jones – at fullback this time – set a new Test record with 10 goals. Helme was among a list of tryscorers that also included Charlie Pawsey, Williams and Jackson. Australia replied with tries by Carlson (2), Keith Holman, Hall and Provan, with Pidding contributing three goals.

The deciding Third Test drew 67,577 to the Sydney Cricket Ground, some perhaps anticipating a torrid encounter after the previous tour match, against New South Wales, had been abandoned by the referee when tempers got out of control.

The Lions enjoyed the best of starts, and were 8-0 up before the Kangaroos recovered to lead 10-8 at half-time. Australia eventually won 20-16 to take the Ashes, with Great Britain reflecting on what might have been after notching a brace by Williams, touchdowns by Valentine and Wigan centre Ernie Ashcroft, and two goals from Jones. Pidding scored a try and four goals for the Green & Golds, whose other touchdowns went to Harry Wells, Alex Watson and Peter Diversi.

With the Ashes relinquished, Great Britain headed to New Zealand for a three-Test tour, after the 1946 Lions had played only one Test in that country and the 1950 tourists two, of which both were lost.

Gerry Helme played in the first two on the 1954 trip. Britain won the first, at Auckland, 27-7, before 22,097 fans. Boston was close to unstoppable, crashing over for four tries, while Ashcroft grabbed a couple, and Hull hooker Tommy Harris bustled over on his debut; Jones contributed three goals.

The Kiwis turned the tables in the Second Test, before only 4,240 folk at Greymouth, winning 20-14 through seven goals by Des White, plus touchdowns for Jock Butterfield and Frank Mulcare. Oldham winger Terry O'Grady and Halifax prop Jack Wilkinson replied for the Lions, and Jones offered four goals.

Helme missed out on the Third Test, which Great Britain won through tries by O'Grady and Warrington stand-off Ray Price, Jones adding both conversions and a penalty, with Des White kicking three goals for the Kiwis. He was, however, back in action for the World Cup, his stunning display in the final completing a heady rise from the obscurity of a number of trials staged at Wilderspool prior to the 1945-46 season, as the Wire sought to rebuild after the cessation of hostilities.

He went on to make 442 appearances for Warrington, scoring 101 tries (topping the club's list with 14 in that 1945-46 campaign), kicking 19 goals, totalling 341 points, and also impressing with his defence, notably the Cumberland throw which involved grabbing an attacking player's wrist and tossing him over his shoulder; an invaluable technique for a player who stood at 5ft 6in tall and generally weighed in at 10 or 11 stones.

His last game for Warrington was at Workington Town on 2 February 1957 and, after a brief spell at Keighley, he then went on to coach Leigh and Oldham before having a spell with amateur club Culcheth, who made him President, in the 1970s.

Gerry Helme passed away in 1981, shortly before Christmas, at the age of 58.

8

Brian Bevan

'IF he had only the fullback to beat, he had no one to beat.'

That was just one of many observations (not all of them as kind, given the often abrasive jealousy of notoriously partisan Rugby League supporters) made about the legendary Brian Bevan.

The commonly held image of a Rugby League player, at least among those who have no real interest in the sport, is that it's contested by man-mountains, with cauliflower ears, broken noses and pot bellies. Brian Bevan was the very antithesis of that profile – to the degree that he was allowed to slip through the net by two of the major outfits of the era although, in fairness to Leeds and Hunslet, neither club (contrary to myth, which insists that both turned him away as not being up to the job of being a professional Rugby League player) ever set eyes on the future legend. The rivals were simply too busy, in the turmoil of the post-war year of 1945, to follow up the recommendation of former Warrington and Loiners 'great' Bill Shankland, who was then the golf professional at Temple Newsam, Leeds.

Hunslet and Leeds, through their understandable but costly inattentiveness, missed out on a man who, in retirement, could reflect on a career in which he totalled 796 tries in all games, a record which far outstrips the number registered by another immortal (Wigan's Billy Boston) of 571, and a figure which included 740 in 620 games for Warrington which helped the Wire amass a horde of trophies during his 16 years at Wilderspool.

The Australian, who was keen to try his hand at Rugby League in England after completing his national service with the Australian Royal Navy at the end of World War Two, would perhaps have raised, in any event, the collective eyebrows at clubs other than Hunslet – who had won the Rugby League championship in the penultimate season prior to hostilities breaking out – and the Loiners.

Skinny, knobbly-kneed, prematurely bald and with few teeth to speak of, his slightly wizened appearance hardly boded well for the rough and tumble of Rugby League. Impressions, however, can never have been more misleading. Even Shankland was bemused by his initial sight of Bryan Eyrl Bevan. The great Australian later admitted:

> Brian Bevan just turned up at my home one day and asked whether I could help get him a game with someone. I might have turned him away, because he didn't quite look the part. But I knew his father, Rick, who had played for Eastern Suburbs, and that persuaded me to try to help him out. So, after my initial hesitation, I nodded, said I thought I might be able to do something – and it went from there.

Warrington, whose acting Secretary Jack Knowles acted on Shankland's recommendation, were more painstaking than either of their Yorkshire rivals and gave the spindly rookie a run-out with their A team in a Lancashire Combination fixture with Widnes at Wilderspool on Saturday 10 November 1945. The Wire won 23-8 and, in his book *The Great Bev*, Robert Gate quotes from the *Warrington Examiner's* match report:

> (Bevan) proceeded to give one of the most promising displays on the part of a newcomer ever seen at Warrington, capping it with a grand try from halfway for which the crowd gave him an ovation which must have made him blush!
>   Accepting a pass from his centre he sped down the wing with head up and shoulders back and at a speed which amazed the onlookers. At various intervals were no fewer than four opponents and it seemed they were all in a position successfully to challenge him. But sweeping past them in a straight dash he simply left them standing and went on to score in the corner without a finger having been laid on him. This was the last of a number of fine things he did. He frequently came inside and cut down the middle in a manner most disconcerting to the opposition and, what is more, he used a deceptive sidestep.

That display turned the derisive laughter of fans who had found Bevan's appearance, with his long shorts hanging down to his spindly knees, amusing when the sides ran out, into cheers of admiration. Those cheers, and the style of the *Warrington Examiner's* report of the winger's debut, would be replicated time without number over the best part of the next two decades, starting seven days later when Brian Bevan made his first team debut against Oldham in a fixture involving sides that would finish the campaign around mid-table, the Wire closing in 10th spot and the Roughyeds fetching up as 15th in the 27-team standings.

The *Warrington Examiner's* reporter reflected of a 12-3 victory in which Bevan was unable to score:

> The crowd rose to him in the second half when from a standing start he flashed past three opponents with as neat a sidestep as one could wish to see and, dashing into the middle of the field, started the movement which resulted in L Jones scoring after the ball had passed through several pairs of hands. Everything he did went to confirm the impression I gained when I first saw him – that he has real football skill. He combines pace with the ability to beat a man and he has the gift of being able to cut inside and do the unexpected, which is so disconcerting to a defender.

Warrington, suitably impressed, offered the young Aussie £300 to sign a three–year deal, and the maestro would reward their faith by proving himself, over a sustained period of time, to be arguably the greatest winger in Rugby League; a status that continues to pertain and which could remain the case for evermore.

Brian Bevan owes that rating to the possession of all the skills required of a winger. He boasted, in addition to the attributes spotted by the local scribe, tremendous acceleration, combined with an uncanny ability to stop on a sixpence. The flyer was as fast as any around and, in fact, took part in professional sprint competitions such as the famous Powderhall Sprint in the early 1950s. He was able to swerve his way past defenders, sidestep off either foot, jink and shuffle; in fact he could bring almost anything out of his armoury in the bid to reach the opposing tryline.

One tactic he did not use was the 'Batten Leap', the method used by Leeds winger Eric Batten and by his father Billy (Hunslet and Hull) before him, whereby fullbacks would be bypassed by the simple expedient of leaping over them. Nor did Bevan – not the heaviest of players, at 11st 8lbs in his 5ft 8in frame through most of his career – utilise the hand-off very often, although the skill was brought into play on occasion.

It has to be said, too, that Brian Bevan was not noted for his defensive prowess, nor that he was overwilling to take unnecessary punishment. The latter characteristic was, perhaps, linked to the first. As many of his coaches and team-mates – who picked up winning pay more often than they may have done otherwise because of Bevan's contribution with ball in hand – attested, there was no need for the Australian to pick up knocks in defence, or when totally cornered in attack, if the likely result would be that his attacking prowess would be blunted. For those reasons it was not unknown for Bevan to run the ball directly into touch on occasion; possibly a wise move in the circumstances.

Another skill, less remarked upon, that Brian Bevan possessed was the ability to kick goals, and he did in fact land 34 in 1946-47, his first full season with the Wire, after having had to return to Australia to complete his national service.

The winger, playing outside Glyn Williams initially, scored 48 tries in 1946-47 – his first full season – standing comparison with the previous best by a Wire player of 34, set by Welsh winger Islwyn Davies in 1938-39. Bevan eclipsed Davies' tally with his hat-trick against St Helens on 22 March 1947 in a second round Challenge Cup tie played before 23,500.

Brian Bevan crossed on 57 occasions the following season, including seven touchdowns in a 28-8 victory over Leigh at Wilderspool in March 1948 before a 20,000 crowd; a feat he was to repeat against Bramley a little over five years later. Earlier that month a club record crowd of 30,000 had turned up for the Challenge Cup quarter-final tie with Wigan as he proved to be a true crowd-puller.

He bagged 56 tries in 1948-49, before scoring 'only' 33 in 1949-50 in a season in which he was sidelined for six weeks with a leg injury.

He set a new benchmark as the 1950s arrived, however, with 68 touchdowns in 1950-51, a season in which he eclipsed Jack Fish's career record of 215 tries, with 51 recorded 12 months later.

The 72 he totalled in 1952-53, including 66 in the famous Primrose and Blue, topped the 71 registered by his arch-adversary Lionel Cooper, of Huddersfield, 12 months earlier. Bevan going on to register 67 and 63 respectively in each of the next two seasons, as his partnership with centre Jim Challinor, with whom he was paired on the right flank on 181 occasions, proved to be highly productive.

He became the highest try-scorer in history during the 1953-54 campaign, overhauling the 446 scored by Alf Ellaby, of St Helens, between 1926 and 1939. The maestro breached the half-century barrier in 1955-56 (with 57) and in 1958-59, when he chalked up 54 tries. 1956-57, when he was ruled out, through injury, in 18 of Warrington's fixtures, brought only 17 touchdowns, the only occasion on which he was unable to top Warrington's try scoring list, that accolade going to Laurie Gilfedder, and there were by his standards comparatively meagre returns (albeit ones that many other wingers would have given their eye-teeth for) in 1957-58 and 1959-60, when his tallies were 46 and 40 respectively.

As the clock began to wind down on his time at the top of the tree, he scored 35 and 15 tries in successive seasons before moving on to Blackpool for a couple of years, registering 10 touchdowns in his first campaign and seven tries in the second.

His above mentioned talley embraces 39 tries in various representative games, including Other Nationalities, the star-studded side that regularly took on England, Wales and France during the period of his career.

In addition, while it's often stated that Bevan never played first grade football in his native Australia, he did in fact make a handful of appearances for Eastern Suburbs. *The Encyclopaedia of Australian Rugby League Players* records: 'BEVAN, Brian. (Easts 1942) 7 games – 1g (2pts). While Brian Bevan was to play only a handful of games for Easts, the spindly winger was to become a legend in English Club football. After leaving Easts to serve in the Navy during the war, he played 18 seasons with Warrington (1946-1962) and Blackpool Borough (1962-1964), establishing many long-standing records – an incredible 796 tries in 695 games amid numerous Cup successes. Rated as the greatest winger English club football has ever seen, Bevan died in 1991.'

The 'spindly winger' would surely, had he stayed in his homeland, have been rated as the best winger Australian club football has ever seen, and he would certainly have amassed a host of caps for the Kangaroos who, during the period he was with Warrington, lost 17 and drew one of 27 Tests against Great Britain, winning only nine. He would, arguably, have been the catalyst that could have transformed these figures; Australia's loss was undoubtedly English club football's gain.

In an era in which a healthy number of truly great wingers graced the British game, Bevan reigned supreme, finishing on top of the try scoring list on five separate occasions, with a host of rivals including Wigan's Boston, Mick Sullivan and Brian Nordgren, his own Warrington team-mate Stan McCormick, Lionel Hunter (Huddersfield) and Tom van Vollenhoven (St Helens) among the chasing pack.

Statistics, it can be argued, can often mean little or nothing in sport. In Brian Bevan's case they mean a great deal, confirming as they do his phenomenal pre-eminence, as a record of having scored seven tries in a match twice, six tries in a match four times, five tries in a match six times and four tries in a match 20 times testifies; not to mention having registered 66 hat-tricks. For all that, they still fail to do justice to his crowd-pleasing displays, and cannot convey the sheer artistry with which he scored so many of his tries; artistry which not only boosted Warrington's prospects, but which also served opposing clubs well, the general feeling being that his presence added 5,000 or so to the attendance when the Wire came visiting.

One game in particular is seen as vividly showcasing his talents – the pre-season Ward Cup game against Wigan. Such matches are often described as friendlies, but there has rarely if ever been anything friendly about meetings involving the Wire and the Pie Eaters. That was the case in 1948, when the pair convened at Wigan for a game in which the players of each side were not only aiming to win, but to stake a claim for a place in their own club's line-ups as and when the season proper got underway. The 31,960 crowd was treated to a score by Brian Bevan that came to be described as 'the try of the century'.

Warrington, under the cosh early in the second half, secured possession close to their own line, thanks to a good heel at the scrum by hooker Dave Cotton. Audaciously, the Wire moved the ball wide through scrum-half Gerry Helme, loose forward Harold Palin and centre Albert Pimblett, who drew Wigan winger Jack Hilton to free Bevan. Rather than shooting down the touchline, however, Bevan raced towards the centre of the pitch, confounding the cover defence, where he confronted home fullback Martin Ryan on the Warrington 25-yard line. Ryan had centre Ernie Ashcroft and stand-off Cec Mountford, both of whom would subsequently coach the Wire, in close proximity but Bevan foxed them all with a heavenly swerve, leaving Ryan adrift and sprinting away from Mountford and the trailing Hilton to complete a 125-yard run by touching down midway between the posts and corner flag. He later added another try to help Warrington to an 18-8 victory.

The vast majority of Brian Bevan's touchdowns were, of course, notched in games in which something more than mere local pride was at stake: matches in which two league points were the prize, or progress in the Challenge Cup or the Lancashire Cup. A particularly outstanding effort helped the Wire to Wembley in 1953-54, Warrington winning 7-4 at Oldham in the second round thanks largely to Bevan's contribution. The Roughyeds were 4-2 ahead early in the second period, and looking likely to hold on to that lead on a mud-bound Watersheddings pitch, when Bevan took a decisive hand. Oldham, mounting strong pressure in Warrington's 25, looked likely to extend their advantage when Bevan seemingly popped out of nowhere to intercept a pass meant for Roughyeds left winger Terry O'Grady. The Australian had a long way to go in the heavy conditions, and faced Oldham's revered fullback Bernard Ganley. Most of the 21,000 observers expected Bev to seek to outpace Ganley down the touchline. Instead he headed straight for the fullback before belying the boggy ground to execute a dazzling sidestep, leaving Ganley behind as he crossed under the posts to shatter the hopes of the home fans in the 20,000 crowd.

Years later, Ganley would joke of suffering nightmares in which Bevan was running away from him.

Bevan had, in fact, gone against his own advice in intercepting with Ganley still at the rear. Following his retirement, in an interview published in one of Bev Risman's annuals, he said:

From the start of my footballing career I found that I was inclined to be unorthodox. It paid off in some games, although if I missed an interception and the opposition scored on my wing, my manager, team-mates and the press made a whole chapter of the miss. It was like a soccer marksman missing a penalty – and a vital one at that.

So I have always tried to keep my direct opposite and his friends puzzled. I learned not to try to steal a pass until I was correctly positioned and the fullback was attempting a link-up. This enabled me to have a clear run to the line, providing I took the ball cleanly. It looked ever so easy, ever so cheeky, but I tried it once or twice in a match, and my 796 tries include quite a lot from stolen passes.

He added:

Some people watching me at practice may have thought that I didn't follow my own rules. They were wrong. Even if I did not take the ball correctly I was often at full speed, and a change of pace and direction before I rejoined the game gave me confidence. Side-stepping is not an easy matter; you have got to try it off the right as well as the left foot.

Fullbacks will try to edge you over into touch, but don't be fooled into that move. If they think you are fooled, take the narrow gap and you can kid them by following that route and then catching them on the wrong foot.

It's possibly no coincidence that, with Brian Bevan in their ranks, Warrington secured the one major trophy that had previously eluded them. The Wire had won the Challenge Cup twice (in 1904-05 and 1906-07) and had prevailed in the Lancashire Cup in 1921-22, 1929-30, 1932-33 and 1937-38. Warrington had also claimed the Lancashire League title in the penultimate season before Word War Two; but one trophy, seen by many as the greatest prize of all, had eluded them. The Wire had come close to winning the Championship on four occasions, only to be beaten in the final in 1925-26, 1934-35, and 1936-37. Having acquired the services of Brian Bevan, that omission was about to be rectified.

Rising from that 10th position in Bev's first season to fifth the following year, Warrington made the Top Four Play-offs in 1947-48, finishing second in the standings behind Wigan. That secured Bevan and his team-mates a home semi-final against third-placed Huddersfield, who were beaten 17-5 at Wilderspool. The winger scored two tries, as did his centre Albert Pimblett, while Bevan rubbished any notion that he may have been little more than a 'greedy tryscorer' by handing a touchdown to veteran hooker Dave Cotton after he had torn open the Fartown defence in a game in which he also had the better of his personal duel with Huddersfield's fine Australian winger Lionel Cooper, with whom he had been a team-mate at Eastern Suburbs.

Fartown having been seen off, Warrington now had Bradford Northern (who had won 15-3 at Wigan) in their sights; and there was to be no escape for the men from Odsal.

A crowd of 69,143 – marginally short of the previous highest, the 69,504 who had gathered at the same venue for the 1938-39 decider between Salford and Castleford – amassed at Maine Road, the home of Manchester City AFC, for a game which Warrington won 15-5. Bevan scored his 57th try of the campaign in the victory, with other touchdowns going to Stan Powell and Pimblett, with Harold Palin adding three goals. Ernest Ward converted a try by Des Case, who was playing his last game for Northern, in response.

Brian Bevan's last appearance in a major final came in 1960-61, when the Wire appeared in the Championship Final against a Leeds side that had never collected that particular piece of silverware. That was to change as the Wire succumbed 25-10 before a 52,177 crowd at Odsal Stadium, Bradford. The Loiners, making the most of a 3-1 scrum-count secured by hooker Barry Simms, were never behind once Jack Fairbank powered over off a pass by his second row partner Dennis Goodwin, with Welsh stand-off Lewis Jones landing the first of his five goals. Warrington, not helped by a couple of missed penalty attempts by fullback Eric Fraser, were unable to force their way into serious contention on a disappointing afternoon on which Bevan had few running opportunities.

Leeds led 10-0 at the interval after scrum-half Colin Evans burrowed over from dummy-half, Jones having gone close following a raid involving Australian fullback Ken Thornett and centres Vince Hattee and Derek Hallas. Hallas added two touchdowns in the second period to put paid to the Wire's challenge, although Warrington offered a gallant response with a brace for centre Jim Challinor, Laurie Gilfedder improving each score.

The Loiners, though, had the last word with a try and goal by Jones, ensuring that Brian Bevan's last appearance on the major stage was to end in disappointment, his only real contribution being a superb try-saving tackle on Hattee.

Almost 12 months later, the curtain was to come down on his Warrington career. Men and women who had not seen a game of rugby for many years, yet who remembered with gratification the speed, craft and superlative tries, were there to pay homage on Easter Monday, 1962, to Brian Bevan in his last game for the Wire.

Warrington won 29-17, with Bevan scoring the opening try and narrowly missing with a shot at goal from the touchline in the closing seconds, to deny Leigh the chance of booking a place in Division One in the build-up to what was to be a doomed experiment with two divisions, the notion being abandoned two-thirds of the way through its three-year trial period.

The Leigh players were fulsome in their applause of the maestro, both before and after the game, when they joined in the call for three cheers, some perhaps mindful of the Easter Monday encounter in March 1948 in which he had raced in for seven tries against them. Brian Bevan, appointed captain for the historic occasion, lost the toss – meaning that he would spend the last 40 minutes of his career at Wilderspool playing towards the crowded Spion Kop end, a fitting finale to a wonderful era.

Leigh went in front with a penalty in the ninth minute by Bev

Risman. A minute later, Bevan claimed the try he and his army of supporters so fervently wanted. In his *The Rugby League Football Book* Risman himself relates:

> Warrington's brilliant scrum-half Jackie Edwards veered out towards Bevan's wing. With his quicksilver partner Bobby Greenough flashing up from behind, Edwards dropped the ball into the stand-off's hands as he went streaking by for the line. Ten yards from the line things looked desperate for Leigh. Risman, playing at fullback, was forced to move away from Bevan's wing to cover Greenough.
>
> This left Bevan and his 'shadow' Ian Hodgkiss alone as the two wingers raced neck and neck after the Warrington stand-off. This was a situation in which the great Bev excelled. His long experience at beating a man even before he got the ball was put into effect. He slowed down noticeably as Greenough's five-yard pass shot out. Hodgkiss hesitated, and Bev seized his chance to burst onto the pass at top speed, leaving the Leigh youngster grasping an armful of thin air as Bev spurted the five yards to the corner flag to touch down without having a finger laid on his famous no. 2 jersey.
>
> The crowd went wild. This was the try they had come to see.
>
> Warrington's tourist forward Laurie Gilfedder made it 5-2 with a glorious kick from the touchline, but the fans were still cheering Bev's brilliant effort as the ball was kicked off to restart play.

In a seesaw contest, Leigh were only 18-17 behind as the game drifted towards the close, having posted tries by Brian Brooks, Mick Martyn and Gordon Lewis, plus three more Risman goals. But the Wire, who had responded with an Edwards brace, ensured that Bevan's career at Warrington finished on a winning note with touchdowns for his centre Malcolm Thomas, Eric Fraser and Greenough, Gilfedder closing with four goals.

The last act of the match went to Bevan. Gilfedder tossed him the ball after Greenough's try, and the Australian duly took his first shot at goal since he had scored 34 in his first season at Wilderspool. He made a gallant effort from the touchline, the ball sailing high towards the posts before drifting wide.

The final whistle blew and spectators swarmed into the pitch to pay tribute to the all-time great, for whom the two sets of players formed a guard of honour as Brian Bevan was chaired from the field. The mass of supporters simply refused to come off the field until Bevan, with his wife Doreen and daughters Jennifer (11) and

Jeanette (10), reappeared in the directors' box, to be seen off to the strains of 'Waltzing Matilda'. Brian Bevan's total of 620 appearances for Warrington put him third in the list of most outings for a club, behind Jim Sullivan (774 for Wigan, from 1921 to 1946) and Oldham's Joe Ferguson (627, from 1899 to 1923).

Following that game Brian Bevan, perhaps mindful of how people – at least in the early stages of his career in England – had underestimated him because of his appearance, had some pertinent advice, even if it came a little late to be of much use to those who had struggled to contain him over the years. He said:

Never underestimate your opponent. He may look small, he may be making his debut, he may be playing his last-ever game and he may be having a bad spell. Moreover, first impressions may be awfully wrong and you may get the surprise of your life and leave the field of play knowing full well that you will not be on the team sheet next week.

I should know that appearances can be deceptive because when I came to England and sought out a new club, I got the brush-off by two Yorkshire clubs, who didn't think I was worth giving one trial game, even in the reserves.

I was not blessed with good looks by Mother Nature and even before I was 30 the hair on my head was not getting in my eyes. They have called me 'Knobbly Knees'. I'm referring to the critics, who have never been slow to follow the example of their Australian brethren and dole out all kinds of nicknames for me. But there is a saying among English youngsters about sticks and stones breaking bones, but names never hurting anyone. It is very important that you should never let the crowd get you down. Several times I have been annoyed by remarks by certain spectators. The only way to reply effectively to the rowdy ones who attempt to unsettle you is to keep your tricks ready for when the opportunity arises. Then the cheers for your effort, even if you don't get a try, will drown the shouts of the know-alls.

9

Harry Bath

WHEN Harry Bath moved south from Barrow to Warrington, having failed to settle in Furness, he was to set in motion a 10-year sojourn in which he was to give the Wire superb service and help the club achieve unprecedented success.

Bath, a Queenslander with an exceptional turn of speed for a second row or prop, made 346 appearances for his adopted club, bringing the curtain down on his time in England in a Challenge Cup tie against Bramley at Wilderspool in February 1957 (kicking four goals in a 14-2 victory), before returning to Australia, where he coached St George to two Grand Final successes and also guided Australia to two World Cup victories, in 1968 and 1970.

He quickly rose to the role of captain at Warrington, and led the side to Challenge Cup success in 1949-50 and was a member of the 1953-54 side on the occasion of the famous replayed final at Odsal Stadium, Bradford.

Warrington, with Bath, also secured the Championship in 1953-54 and 1954-55.

Those details are the mere skeleton of Harry Bath's contribution to Warrington's cause, and offer scant indication of his input as a man who gave equally remarkable service to his clubs in Australia. In his five seasons as a player Down Under, with Balmain in 1946 and 1947, and with St George from 1957 to 1959, he appeared in five Grand Finals, picking up a winner's medal each time; a phenomenal record which contributed to his being inducted into the Australian Hall of Fame in 2004. Four years later he was named as one of the '100 Greatest Players' when the ARL celebrated its centenary.

His deeds on the field of play were, moreover, matched by his accomplishments from the sidelines. His early venture into coaching didn't perhaps meet with unadulterated success, with Balmain missing out to the all-conquering St George side of the era in the 1964 and 1966 Grand Finals, 11-6 and 23-4 respectively. Harry Bath, however, learned his lessons well from those reverses – and from a spell with

Newton between 1969 and 1972 – before he joined St George, leading the Saints to the 1977 Grand Final, in which Parramatta were beaten 22-0 in a replay after the sides had finished all-square at 9-9.

St George were back, successfully, for the 1979 decider, when 'Bath's Babes' accounted for Canterbury-Bankstown 17-13.

Bath also achieved perhaps the greatest honour available, that of coaching his country.

He was given total control – as manager, coach and sole selector – of Australia for the home series against Great Britain in 1962; something of a poisoned chalice, perhaps, with the Lions only being denied a clean sweep, after victories in the first two Tests, through a contested try by winger Ken Irvine which the same player converted from the touchline to secure an 18-17 victory which prevented a whitewash.

It was a different matter towards the end of the decade when Bath guided Australia to World Cup success in 1968 and 1970; the side came close to retaining the trophy in 1972, only to be denied by Great Britain through the 10-10 draw at Lyons.

Between-times, in 1969 and 1971, the 'Old Fox' took Australia to New Zealand where the first series was drawn 1-1 and the second lost 1-0. He finally retired as a coach in 1981, 41 years after having signed for Brisbane club Southern Suburbs as a 16-year-old, bringing a close to a glittering career in every respect. He passed away on 6 October 2008, to be mourned in Australia as perhaps the greatest forward never to have worn the Green & Gold, and in England as one of the finest recruits from the Antipodes.

Harry Bath would, without doubt, have played many times for his country had he opted to remain in his homeland. After playing for Queensland in 1954 he headed south, to Balmain, where he was selected for New South Wales in the period before the launch of State of Origin, when players turned out for the state in which they played. It was with Balmain that he came closest to earning an Australian cap, against the Great Britain 'Indomitables' of 1946.

Selection for New South Wales against the tourists was welcome for its own sake, and also as a stepping stone for inclusion in the Kangaroos side for the First Test. A bad leg injury, however, not only ruled him out of contention for the opener at the Sydney Cricket Ground; it left him sidelined for the entire series, a setback that would, in the light of his subsequent career, leave him without an Australian cap to celebrate in his old age.

There was domestic comfort, with Balmain, in successive Grand Final victories. St George were beaten 13-12 in the controversial 1946 decider in which the general view was that Balmain had been allowed two tries which involved forward passes, while St George had a perfectly good touchdown ruled out. Twelve months later, Canterbury-Bankstown were accounted for 13-9 thanks to centre Jorgenson, who scored all his side's points with a try and five goals, including a penalty and a converted touchdown which helped Balmain recover from 9-6 down with only 10 minutes left.

Bath's contribution to those successes hadn't escaped the attention of leading Rugby League clubs in the northern hemisphere. Barrow, eager to maintain the impetus shown in the seasons before World War II, when they had been Challenge Cup and Lancashire Cup runners-up in 1937-38, tempted him to England with an offer of £1,000, and he crossed the globe eager to make his name in the premier competition in the world.

Harry Bath, however, was unable to settle in south Cumbria and, within six months, moved on to Warrington for a £1,500 fee; something of a bargain, considering that in 1947-48 a record transfer fee of £2,650 was set when Dewsbury fullback Jim Ledgard moved to Leigh.

Bath made his debut for the Wire on 17 March 1948, taking a second row slot in the 43-2 victory over Featherstone Rovers at Wilderspool. He set the benchmark for his future career with the Wire with two tries and a goal, although pride of place on the day went to Albert Johnson, who registered four tries. Remarkably, Brian Bevan failed to score on a day in which Warrington notched 11 touchdowns.

The Wire immediately took Harry Bath to their hearts, even if the Aussie had arrived too late to qualify for that season's Championship play-offs. He was, however, an effective off-field talisman, Warrington winning their first Championship with a 15-5 victory over Bradford Northern at Maine Road, Manchester.

In the same 1947-48 campaign, Warrington won the Lancashire League.

The following season, the side were runners-up to Huddersfield in the championship, losing 13-12 at Maine Road before 75,194. The Wire also lost to Wigan in the Lancashire Cup Final, missing out 14-8 before 39,015 (a record 'gate' for the competition at that time) at Swinton.

Warrington, however, were consoled by the retention of the

Lancashire League title and, the following season, the Wire hit the heights, reaching Wembley after beating Leeds in the semi-final before a record crowd at the penultimate stage of 69,898 at Odsal Stadium, Bradford, and duly lifting the Challenge Cup for the first time since 1906-07. That was a particularly proud moment for Albert Henry Bath who, in collecting the precious trophy from the Prime Minister, Clement Atlee, was the first captain of a winning side at Wembley to hail from overseas. Bath, moreover, had played a full part in his side's 19-0 win over neighbours Widnes, despite having to have a pain-killing injection prior to kick off to enable him to take part.

Warrington were four points ahead midway through the first half, thanks to a drop goal and a penalty by loose forward Harold Palin, who at that time was the Wire's regular kicker, and who closed the campaign level at the top of the kicking charts with Wigan's Ken Gee, on 133, in the process topping the points-scoring charts with 290. Palin's drop goal was highly unusual in that he landed it with his 'wrong' left foot, an incident that was, to the best of the knowledge of Warrington fans, without precedent or repetition. Any hopes Widnes had of forcing their way back into the contest were hit by Bath, who crashed over in the 22nd minute, Palin's goal extending the Wire's advantage to nine points.

Warrington went on to delight their supporters in the 94,249 crowd when centre Ron Ryder steamed in seven minutes before the interval, and there was clearly no way back for the Chemics once Palin landed a penalty as the half-time whistle beckoned, the Wire traipsing off to the changing rooms 14-0 ahead.

Palin, who – like Bath – pushed scrum-half Gerry Helme close for the Lance Todd Trophy, stretched the lead with a penalty as the hour approached, and victory was sealed when Helme sent stand-off Bryn Knowelden over the whitewash with a neat back-pass.

The success also delighted coach Chris Brockbank, who had been in the Swinton side that had beaten Warrington in the 1927-28 Challenge Cup Final – the last before the Wembley era.

Warrington (after finishing as runners-up in the Championship and Lancashire Cup Finals of 1950-51 – losing to Gus Risman's Workington Town 26-11 before 61,618 fans at Maine Road, Manchester, in the former, and to Wigan 28-5 in the latter, with 42,541 showing up for the contest at Station Road, Swinton) were back at Wembley in 1953-54, in a season in which they came close to emulating Hunslet,

Huddersfield and Swinton by achieving the 'All Four Cups' feat.

The Lancashire Cup had eluded the Wire, but Warrington secured the Lancashire League and headed to the Twin Towers intent on a Cup and League 'double' that would ultimately be achieved. Not, however, until after high drama in the Challenge Cup Final replay, preceded by a dull affair at Wembley.

Warrington had trailed 4-0 at half-time in that game, Halifax having landed a couple of penalties by their Welsh fullback Tyssul Griffiths.

It was a different story after the break, though, Bath restoring parity with penalties in the 51st and 66th minutes in a match in which, of 13 shots at goal, only four were successful in the sole Challenge Cup Final at Wembley in which not a single try was scored. Halifax, too, paid the price for not making the most of the lion's share of possession from a 16-4 second-half scrum count.

By contrast, two tries were registered in the replay – both by Warrington, in an 8-4 victory, in a match which has entered the annals of Rugby League, and sporting, folklore.

Incredible scenes surrounded the game, with the 81,841 who had turned up at Wembley eclipsed by the 102,569 – with an estimated 30,000 more simply charging through the perimeter fences – who descended on Odsal Stadium, Bradford, on Wednesday 5 May 1954.

Warrington were never behind at Odsal, despite Halifax hooker Alvin Ackerley's dominance of the scrums. Centre Jim Challinor crossed in the ninth minute, and that was how it stayed until the closing seconds of the opening period when Griffiths kicked a penalty in response to reduce the deficit to 3-2. Bath nosed the Wire 5-2 in front with a penalty as the hour approached, Griffiths responding in kind some four minutes later. Scrum-half Gerry Helme went some way to clinching his second Lance Todd Trophy with a scampering try 12 minutes from the close.

Only three days later the sides met again, this time in the Championship Final at Maine Road, Manchester. The attendance, this time, was a disappointing 36,519 – many of those caught up in the Odsal crush perhaps not relishing the danger of a repeat of that experience – but there was no disappointment for Harry Bath. Halifax appeared to be on the way to exacting revenge for the disappointment of defeat in the Challenge Cup when prop John Thorley forced his way over, Griffiths adding the conversion. Bath, though, clawed his side back into contention with two penalties, a similar effort by Griffiths bringing up a 7-4 half-time lead for Halifax. Bath added a penalty and with time running out, edged the Wire in front when it mattered with another successful shot, completing an 8-7 win for his side which would undoubtedly have put him firmly in the running for the Harry Sunderland Trophy as Man of the Match if that award had been in existence at the time, to round off a momentous season and close with 153 goals for the campaign.

Harry Bath had topped the league standings for the second successive season after having hit the mark 170 times in the previous campaign.

The championship was retained 12 months later, Oldham being beaten 7-3 at the same venue, before 49,434 supporters – a gate that was considered disappointing, with heavy rain deemed to be a contributory factor.

Bath was once again a central figure, with another display that would have put him in the frame for any man of the match awards, had such existed for the Championship Final. A try by Brian Bevan got the Wire in front, before Oldham equalised through Frank Pitchford. Bath, though, ensured that Warrington remained champions with a couple of well-taken penalties.

Harry Bath closed his career in England with a Lancashire League champions medal, Warrington heading the table in 1955-56, before heading back home to the adulation of British fans, especially those in Warrington.

During his time in England, although denied the chance to play for Australia, he had picked up representative honours with Other Nationalities, often packing down alongside fellow Aussie Arthur Clues, of Leeds and Hunslet, in the second row, in 12 appearances in which he scored 15 goals and two tries. He also appeared in the British Empire XIII that took on New Zealand at Stamford Bridge, Chelsea, in January 1952.

Returning to his homeland at the age of 33, Harry Bath set about proving that Indian Summers can apply to Rugby League careers as well as to the weather, helping St George to successive – and successful – Grand Finals, in 1957, 1958 and 1959. He brought back to Australia skills honed in England, where ball-handling forwards were far more common than Down Under, where members of the pack habitually adopted a more 'up and at em' approach.

His performance in the opening clash of the triumvirate was outstanding, his eight goals helping the Saints brush aside Manly-

Warringah 31-9.

The following year, in which his 225 points from 108 goals and three tries represented the most scored by a second row forward, St George retained the title with a 20-9 verdict over Western Suburbs. And, in 1959 (a season in which, having switched to the front row, his 205 points set a record for a prop), he was impressive in a 20-0 win over Manly-Warringah, even if he closed his interest early after being sent off, with Manly's Rex Mossop, for fighting.

Larry Writer, in his book *Never Before, Never Again*, in which he recounts St George's incredible 11 successive championships between 1956 and 1966, wrote:

> There is a famous photo of that incident, taken seconds after Bath and Mossop had been hauled apart by team-mates after slugging it out for nearly a minute.
>
> Darcy Lawler, his back to the camera, is about to send the combatants, deadly enemies for years, from the field. Dragons and Seagulls players – Kearney, Norm Provan, Roy Bull, Monty Porter, Geoff Weeks – mill about, seemingly stunned by the ferocity of the fight. At the far right of the photo is Mossop, dishevelled, cut and bruised, looking like a man who has just been rescued from a bad car smash. Bath, for his part, roly-poly, tousle-haired, his babyface the image of offended innocence, seems to be enquiring of the ref what all the fuss is about.

Mossop, with Norm Provan, was one of two men who kept Bath out of the Australian side during this period; but for that duo he could, perhaps, have set a record as the oldest Kangaroo. That early exit from the Sydney Cricket Ground also represented his retirement as a player. It was, however, far from the end of his involvement in the game.

A catalyst in the inaugural New South Wales Coaching Panel in 1961, he went on to have sole charge of Australia for the visit of the crack Great Britain side the following year. That series was lost 2-1, but Bath stayed in his post for much of the decade, during a period in which Australia, having for so long been on the back foot against the mother country, had got themselves on an equal footing. That they had got themselves in a state of parity at all was, in no small part, due to Bath, who had absorbed the handling skills of British forwards such as Bradford Northern's Ken Traill, and the Wigan threesome of Brian McTigue, Joe Egan and Ken Gee, and introduced them to the

Australian game.

In *Never Before, Never Again* Bath explained:

> I played at Warrington behind props such as Dave Cotton, who was nearly 40 and as hard as they came but who knew all about Rugby League.
>
> They could use the ball beautifully and, for me, a running forward at that time, playing with them was a revelation.
>
> They put me into open space 10 or 15 times a match. They'd scheme around the rucks until they found a gap, then pop a beautiful ball out of nowhere.
>
> I watched them, learned how to do what they did, and when eventually they retired and I got older and a bit slower I graduated to the front row and provided the same service for the young tearaway forwards coming through the ranks.

The usual war of attrition up front in the Australian game, with forwards charging into each other intent on making individual yardage and no more, was to become a thing of the past as Bath, spraying passes around which put team-mates into countless gaps as bemused opponents found themselves stretched, set new standards for the domestic game in Australia – those standards ultimately being carried on to the international arena.

Bath, in *Never Before, Never Again*, recalled of his return to club football in Australia: 'I taught blokes how to read what I was doing and run off me. Bob Bugden, who was very fast, couldn't believe his luck and scored a heap of tries.'

Bath also got them to cut out silly kicking – an Australian trait, including in their own 25, that flew in the face of required tactics in the unlimited tackle era – and focussed on one player in particular as an example of what he could bring to the team.

> Billy Wilson had a ton of guts and energy when we first played together, but no finesse. So I did for him what those wise old English props did for me. I'd have him trail me, and put him into gaps. Then, in turn, when he moved to the front row later in his career he carried on the tradition. When he was selected for the 1959 Kangaroos he thanked me for what I'd taught him. In England, I'd worked out that one doesn't beat one; two beat one. You draw a man, suck him in, and put your team-mate into the gap the defender you've drawn has left.
>
> It's simple. In attack you have to change the angles, stand deep and

have a man either side of you and behind you, backing you up, so you can create indecision in the opposition and give yourself options.

I'd never run far or get out too wide, I'd set it all up from in close.

Bath was also a believer in turning defence into attack, often seeking to batter the opposing forwards in the early stages of a game. 'Sometimes we'd let the opposition have the ball for the first 10 minutes, and just belt them.'

The great Australian admitted:

I went to England to make some money. Ray Stehr, an agent for English clubs, said Barrow wanted me and I would go to England for £1,000. '£1,000,' I said. 'For £1,000 I'd go anywhere.'

But Barrow proved to be a disappointment. The accommodation they arranged for us was lousy so I asked to be put on the transfer list. Warrington snapped me up and I played for the Wire for the next dozen seasons, the best years of my career.

I'll never forget my Warrington days, wonderful memories of friends and football, long coach trips to Hull and other northern towns, going to London shows, and running our pub, the Britannia, with my wife Gwen.

10

Parry Gordon

THERE was a time (a period which, perhaps, spanned much of the history of Rugby League, from the fledgling days of the Northern Union through to the launch of Super League) when every team seemed to boast a scrum-half of high quality. It was, from 1895 until the end of the 20th century, rare to see a halfback of indifferent standards, and it was almost unheard of for a number 7 to lack ability of some kind. Throughout the history of the code, it's fair to say, Rugby League in this country was blessed with an embarrassment of riches; to the point that many regular club scrum-halves could have quite easily been called up for international selection by Great Britain and at least done their job, while not perhaps quite setting the world alight in the manner of an Alex Murphy or an Andy Gregory.

Men of top calibre who come readily to mind during the 1960s and 1970s who rarely, if ever, got a sniff of an international cap, but who operated at top level in the domestic game, included the likes of Allan Agar (Dewsbury, Hunslet, Hull KR, Wakefield Trinity, Carlisle and Featherstone Rovers), Reg Bowden (Widnes and Fulham), Paul Harkin (Bradford Northern, Halifax, Hull KR, Hunslet, Leeds and Wakefield Trinity), Paul Daley (Halifax), Alan Marchant (Halifax and Hunslet) and Barney Ward (Bramley and Wakefield Trinity).

The list is, in fact, close to endless; but no litany of talented scrum-halves who missed out on the highest of honours between 1960 and the close of the 1970s would be complete without more than a passing reference to Parry Gordon. The diminutive halfback, who signed for the Wire as a 16-year-old from Wigan St Patrick's, went on to give glorious service to his adopted club for almost a quarter of a century.

Gordon made his first team debut for Warrington in October 1963 against Barrow in a fixture in the Western Division – a competition introduced, following the launch of two divisions, to offer 'derby' and localised matches lost through the loss of the Lancashire League. And the curtain was brought down on a glittering career on 13

September 1981 in a game against Castleford which Warrington, fittingly, won 14-7.

Between-times, including something of a lull in Warrington's perennially high standards in the late 1960s, Parry Gordon made 543 appearances for Warrington, scoring 167 tries and kicking one goal for a haul of 503 points in the Wire's cause. As such, he represents one of the club's best signings, certainly from the junior game, fully vindicating the decision of Cec Mountford, Warrington's coach at the turn of the 1960s, to splash out £400 for the promising youngster.

The capture of John Parry Gordon was Mountford's last for the Wire, and quite possibly his best. Also, possibly, his most confusing.

Signed on his sixteenth birthday, on 17 February 1961, the youngster opted to use his mother's maiden name as his Christian name throughout his career, prompting the thought that it's fortunate she had not been called Flash. John – or Parry – Gordon was joining a team that was riding high in the upper echelons of the Rugby League and which, less than three months later, was to reach the Championship Final, losing to Leeds – who had never previously lifted the title – at Odsal Stadium, Bradford.

He was also joining a side that, after having enjoyed heady success throughout the late 1940s and 1950s, was to slip a little from its previous high standards during the 1960s; not, however, through any fault of his own, as an era in which Brian Bevan bestrode the sport drew to a close. His debut, on 26 October 1963, was memorable for events on a wider stage than merely those, momentous as they were, at Wilderspool.

Following the game the young Gordon and his new team-mates may have helped ease the pain of a 25-12 defeat by sitting down together in the Wilderspool tearoom to watch an odd TV programme in which a police box, making strange noises, appeared as if from nowhere in a scrap yard. That was an event that changed the world – Dr Who would save the universe – and it was certainly a day that changed the life of John Parry Gordon.

He reflected, speaking to the *Warrington Guardian* following his retirement:

> I remember very clearly walking into the dressing room as it was then and looking at the number seven peg, which was straight in front of you when you went in.
>
> There had been times when I had looked around at the good

quality half backs at the club and wondered if I was ever going to get a chance but there I was and the peg was mine. It was such a great feeling.

Not one, however, that will have been totally unexpected. Parry Gordon had been hot property as his sixteenth birthday beckoned, and Warrington were determined to beat off all opposition for his signature. The fashion of the era was for clubs in such circumstances to effectively camp on a youngster's doorstep until the clock struck midnight, the player in question putting pen to paper within seconds of attaining the age of majority, thus rendering the deal legitimate and legal. So it was with Parry Gordon, who admitted to his local paper:

I was a Wigan lad but there was limited opportunity at the younger age groups. So I came to Warrington when I was only 15, and I felt at home immediately. There was a great feel about the place. They had so many fine players battling for their positions, and the excitement was tangible. And I loved Wilderspool straight away – what a ground!

I never had any qualms at all about wanting to be a Warrington player, but I must admit I didn't expect to be around for a generation! I always felt right at Warrington, though. Whenever I had a bad game, I knew I wouldn't get any stick off the fans; they were superb, and very supportive. They took a shine to me and I certainly took a shine to them.

So did the players alongside him during his lengthy spell with the Wire, notably the forwards – often a hardbitten bunch – who unfailingly protected a diminutive halfback who stood five feet six inches tall and who tipped the scales at 10 or 11 stones throughout his playing career.

'They protected me well,' he said. 'I always felt part of a close team; Other clubs came along with offers but I was never really tempted.'

The Welsh wing wonder John Bevan, perhaps grateful for the many scoring opportunities that came his way as a result of Gordon's guile and vision, rated him as 'the best scrum half I've ever seen' and there may have been a few fans in the ground on New Year's Day, 1964, who presaged that kind of assessment when Parry Gordon scored a superb solo try against Challenge Cup holders Wakefield Trinity, one of the real glamour sides of the age.

The 18-year old showed fine pace, and no little audacity, to romp over from 50 yards in his side's 21-12 Wilderspool success over the Yorkshire giants. A young star had arrived, and Warrington supporters continued to hold him in high esteem for the remainder of his career, getting behind two testimonials.

They did so in recognition of his commitment to the cause, to his input as a player of high ability, and to his loyalty. In addition, they did so in the belief, shared by many supporters throughout the game who could not be accused of any vested interest in Gordon's case, that he was the best uncapped scrum-half in the sport.

At the end of his career Parry Gordon had not a single Great Britain cap to his name, although he came tantalisingly close when, on 6 July 1975, he played for England in the 40-12 victory over Papua New Guinea in the World Cup warm-up match at Port Moresby. That game, which took place a little over four years before the Kumuls, having become full members of the International Board in 1978, played their first bona fide Test match, against France in Albi in October 1979, didn't count as a 'full' international, and the only representative caps Parry Gordon had to show for his undoubted abilities at the end of his playing days were the seven he gained with Lancashire, scoring one try in the process. He also picked up a Great Britain Under 24s cap, while making his mark for Warrington in the early stages of his term of tenure at Wilderspool.

Parry Gordon's first taste of silverware in the famous primrose and blue came in 1967-68, when the Wire won the Lancashire League. Success in that competition made up for the disappointment of missing out on the 16-5 victory over Rochdale Hornets in the 1965-66 Lancashire Cup Final, a game in which John Smith wore the number 7 shirt.

Gordon was in the side that met St Helens at Wigan in the Red Rose decider of 1967-68, finishing all-square, at 2-2 before a 15,000 crowd, Parry Gordon's halfback partner, Billy Aspinall, kicking a penalty in response to Kel Coslett's goal.

Warrington missed out in the replay, at Swinton, Parry Gordon scored a try in the 13-10 reverse, with centre Jackie Melling also crossing and centre Bill Allen landing a couple of goals; but it wasn't enough against a Saints side that prevailed through tries by winger Les Jones, prop John Warlow and second row Eric Chisnall, with substitute John Houghton getting a couple of goals.

The 1960s closed with Warrington having achieved a highest position in the league of second, in 1960-61, and a lowest rating of seventeenth in 1968-69. All that was about to change with the arrival, at the end of the 1970-71 season, of Alex Murphy, enticed from Challenge Cup Final wonders Leigh by chairman Ossie Davies.

The 1972-73 season was one in which all clubs were vying, first and foremost, for a place in the top flight, which could comprise the leading 16 sides in the 30-team league following the reintroduction of two divisions. Warrington made the cut easily; more than easily, in fact, coming top of the standings with 27 victories, and only five defeats – plus a couple of draws – from their 34 fixtures. Featherstone Rovers, the Challenge Cup winners, finished second, two points adrift of the Wire on 54 points, with Leeds a point shy of the men from Post Office Road. Dewsbury closed 10 points adrift of Warrington, in eighth position; and went on to eclipse the feat of Halifax, in the first season of the top 16 play-off format in 1964-65, of winning the championship from seventh spot.

Much is made of Dewsbury's victory over Leeds in the final at Odsal, and perhaps rightly so. A compelling case, however, can be made that their 12-7 win over Warrington at Wilderspool in the semi-final was even more impressive. The Wire, who had beaten Wigan (30-15) and Rochdale Hornets (16-9) in previous rounds were stunned by a fine Dewsbury side.

That disappointment was eased to a large degree in the next couple of seasons by a five-try romp for Gordon in 1973-74 (his teammates, upset by his being overlooked by the Great Britain selectors, making sure that he was on the receiving end of each closing pass) and, more importantly, by successive visits to Wembley, one of which was highly successful, at least in terms of the result, the other less so.

Gordon stepped gladly onto the biggest stage of all on Saturday 11 May 1974, ready and willing to lock horns with Featherstone Rovers, who were aiming to retain the Challenge Cup after having overwhelmed Bradford Northern 12 months earlier. Warrington denied them in their ambition, in a game which will be remembered as a hard-bitten affair, with some of Rugby League's less attractive traits, including an element of gamesmanship and, in the opinion of many, an overly physical approach by both sides too much to the fore.

Both Gordon and his halfback partner, skipper and coach Alex Murphy, had to withdraw, the latter 10 minutes before the break with rib trouble, and Gordon at the interval. The Wire, at that stage, were 9-8 down, stand-off John Newlove having scored a try with only seconds remaining – Gordon getting injured in the process – and fullback Harold Box tagging on the conversion. Murphy, however, was able to return with the help of a pain-killing injection and the Wire recovered to win 24-9.

Parry Gordon had a disappointing experience, both on a personal level and in terms of the result, in the following season's Challenge Cup Final. He went down with a throat infection only 48 hours before the game, leading to wild speculation that Murphy, who had retired as a player, would step forward. That didn't happen. Parry Gordon, operating behind a beaten pack on the day, wasn't at his mercurial best and he and halfback partner Alan Whittle, together with loose forward Barry Philbin, had to concede second billing to the Widnes trio of Eric Hughes, Reg Bowden and Doug Laughton. The Chemics flew their Australian winger Chris Anderson – a man who would earn lasting glory a decade later as player/coach with Halifax, whom he would steer to Championship and Challenge Cup success – back from his homeland for the game, and Anderson was able, as on so many occasions, to offer the magic his team needed.

Despite Gordon's tireless promptings, Warrington were unable to add to the John Bevan try that, converted by fullback Derek Whitehead, gave them an early lead, until three minutes into the second period, when Whitehead landed a penalty. Widnes, though, had gone in at the break 11-5 up and, for the second successive final, a low-key second half was dominated by kicking, the Chemics cementing their grip on the piece of prize silverware with a drop goal by fullback Ray Dutton and, in the 53rd minute, a Dutton penalty that proved to be the final score of the contest.

That also proved to be Parry Gordon's finale at Wembley, although he wasn't to know that at the time. Nor was he to know just how long his career would continue, or what further successes – and tribulations – lay ahead.

The tribulations, or one at least, came soon enough following that Wembley appearance. The following December he sustained a ruptured medial ligament injury that threatened to put him out of the game. Indeed, the following February he was interviewed by the veteran scribe Jack Bentley for the *John Player Rugby League Yearbook*, on his 31st birthday, against a backdrop of his career possibly being at an end. Gordon, it is true, had been assured by the club doctor that he would be able to play again – but, after a month or so of concern that he would have to hang up his boots, he was quite afraid of taking that message on board with too much confidence. Unaware, at that time, that his active involvement, on the pitch, in Rugby League was destined to continue for another five years, he confided to Bentley:

> I want to play again. It's just that I didn't think it would ever happen; that it would ever be possible. I want to get 100 per cent fit and then decide about my knee. If it's good then I shall carry on. I want so much to go on – I feel I have a year or two left. I just didn't want to finish my career going off on a stretcher.

He admitted,

> This medial ligament thing has been the worst injury I've had in the whole of my career which is funny, because my knees have always seemed to be the strongest part of me. The injury was particularly sickening because it came just when I'd begun to feel that at last some people in the game really believed in me. I'd been Down Under with the England World Championship squad during the summer and it seemed I'd really got somewhere and become something in Rugby League.

On the long reluctance to give him an opportunity at international level, he said,

> It's been a long road, I can tell you. So many times in the past the press and leading Rugby League officials have told me, 'You're up for international honours this season, Parry.' Then up popped somebody else, and I didn't get them.

That tendency was vividly illustrated in 1966 when, after only a couple of seasons in Warrington's first team, he was generally seen as firmly in the running for a seat on the plane when the Great Britain party flew out for the tour of Australia and New Zealand. The word was that Parry Gordon was in line for one of the two scrum-half slots, especially as it was understood that his stand-off partner at Wilderspool, Willie Aspinall, had been selected. The understanding was that the tour selectors, seen at the game between Featherstone Rovers and Warrington towards the end of the 1965-66 season, were monitoring the head-to-head battle between Gordon and his rival for a Great Britain shirt, Rovers' halfback Carl Dooler.

'I thought I played pretty well,' Gordon told Bentley. 'When Dooler was chosen and I wasn't, I thought I mustn't have played as well as I imagined.'

Parry Gordon did earn a Great Britain Under 24s cap, against France in that same year, and set out on his county career with Lancashire. A full international cap, however, was to elude him in an era in which Great Britain suffered from an embarrassment of riches in both halfback positions. The likes of Murphy, Tommy Bishop (St Helens), Keith Hepworth (Castleford and Leeds), Roger Millward (Castleford and Hull KR), Steve Nash (Featherstone Rovers and Salford) and Barry Seabourne (Leeds) all got the nod ahead of him, and his turn never came.

> I used to wonder what I was doing wrong. Didn't I run enough with the ball? Perhaps I wasn't very good around the scrums. Was my tackling up to scratch, and did I vary my play sufficiently? Something had to be wrong, but I just kept playing as best I could.
>
> It's funny that the selectors never seemed to get around to me, although I seemed to be in line for an international spot. But I never lost heart. I never went to pieces or anything like that. All I've ever really wanted to do was play the game.

Having missed out on earning a cap for his appearance against Papua New Guinea, on the basis that it wasn't a fixture in the World Championship, he reflected:

> I've set my mind on it now that I shall never get one – but I did play half a game against Papua in the first English side to play in that country, and that is something.
>
> When I came back from that trip I felt tremendous. People were at last recognising me, saying that I deserved to go. I felt great and was really looking forward to carrying on for a number of years.

The man who signed Parry Gordon for Warrington had his own thoughts on his mysterious exclusion from the international scene. Cec Mountford said:

> In the early days after the war, the selectors looked for certain qualities in a footballer. Parry Gordon had them. But from 1960 onwards, or perhaps a few years before, the selection pattern changed and the game altered. The great potential of Parry Gordon was never recognised in my view.

Gordon, in turn, recognised the abilities of Mountford, and of those who followed him into the Warrington dugout. He said:

I was always lucky with coaches at Wilderspool. They saw something in me that they thought they could develop and took the time to encourage me when I was starting out. There are great players that don't get the chances they need but I was one of the few who got the luck when I needed it. Perhaps I missed that when it came to Great Britain but there were plenty of good halfbacks out there.'

Parry Gordon, assuredly, was one of them, and proved it by skippering Warrington, at almost 33 years of age, to victory in the 1977-78 Players No. 6 Trophy, the Wire beating old rivals and neighbours Widnes 9-4 in the final at St Helens, before a then-record crowd for the decider of a competition similar in format to the Challenge Cup of 10,258. Widnes, on that occasion, could only muster a couple of penalties by centre Paul Woods, while Gordon lifted the trophy through a try by winger John Bevan and three goals by high-scoring centre Steve Hesford.

The Chemics turned the tables 12 months later, in what was to be Parry Gordon's last major final – the renamed John Player Trophy Final of 1978-79. There was a slight improvement on the previous year's attendance (to 10,743) although the 485 extra fans at the same venue somehow helped the gate receipts shoot up by around a third from £8,429 to £11,709. They either paid a hefty entrance fee each, or inflation may have hit a high in the so-called winter of discontent.

In the intervening years following the injury that had so concerned Parry Gordon, he had helped the side to the four-trophy successes of 1973-74 (Challenge Cup, Club Championship, Players' No. 6 Trophy and Captain Morgan Trophy), and appeared in the BBC2 Floodlit Trophy Final of 1974-75, won 10-5 by Salford in a replay at Wilderspool after the sides had fought out a scoreless draw at the Willows in the original game.

Parry Gordon, who coached briefly at Warrington before opting to leave following the departure of incumbent Billy Benyon in March 1982, Kevin Ashcroft coming on board, said of his career:

Despite not getting that piece of cloth I wanted so much, I've done well in the game. There have been compensations – two Wembley finals and lots of other medals. Missing selection never altered my approach. I don't think chances of international selection make a man play any better. At least they shouldn't. I've just tended to play for the love of the game, and Rugby League has been good to me.

11

Derek Whitehead

DEREK WHITEHEAD was the epitome of the archetypal goal-kicking fullback, and starred for Warrington during the heady decade of the 1970s having first spent six seasons with, initially, Swinton and latterly Oldham. The fact that he became a Warrington player at all, however, was an event that wasn't particularly of his choosing and certainly a move, from Oldham, that he didn't especially relish. That was understandable. Whitehead had been involved, in Swinton and Oldham, with two of the most successful sides in the history of the game, each having proud traditions stretching back to the launch of the Northern Union and beyond.

Warrington, too, enjoyed a pedigree of some substance, but the Wire were, at the time of his move to Wilderspool in 1969, in something of a lull, having finished the campaign in seventeenth position, thereby missing out on the Top 16 championship play-offs. Oldham, who Whitehead joined in 1968, were not in an immeasurably superior state. The Roughyeds closed the 1968-69 season one position higher, losing 32-12 at League Leaders Leeds in the first round of the play-offs.

Nevertheless, there was no obvious reason, at that stage, for Whitehead to up sticks and head west to Wilderspool. He was leaving a club that, while not overly successful in the 1960s, had won the Rugby League championship on four occasions, in 1904-05, 1909-10, 1910-11 and, more recently, in 1956-57. The men from the Watersheddings had, in fact, been among the leading lights of the Rugby League for much of its history, with particular success in the Northern Union era (it was said that if Hunslet hadn't become the first team to win All Four Cups in 1907-08, Oldham would have done so) and in the 1950s.

Prior to winning the Championship title in 1956-57, the Roughyeds had been runners-up in 1954-55. And, in the decade before Whitehead joined them, Oldham had all but taken out a mortgage on the Lancashire Cup, winning the Red Rose event in successive seasons in

1956-57, 1957-58 and 1958-59. The only missing link in the litany of achievements related to the Challenge Cup, at least in the Wembley era.

Prior to the Challenge Cup Final moving to Wembley in 1928-29, Oldham had appeared in seven of the twenty-eight finals – exactly a quarter – winning three and losing four. Since the decision to take the sport's red letter day south, however, the Roughyeds had enjoyed little good fortune in the Challenge Cup, reaching the semi-finals on seven occasions without being able to register the victory that counts more than most. Most memorably, Oldham came as close as any team has ever done to appearing at the Twin Towers, only to miss out, in 1963-64, the season of the replay, when a host of ties failed to be settled at the first attempt. The Roughyeds, drawn against Hull KR in the semi-final, drew the first game, at Headingley, Leeds, 5-5. The replay, at Station Road, Swinton, finished 14-14 after 80 minutes and headed into extra time. Oldham were 17-14 ahead, and set for their Wembley debut, when bad light stopped play. The regulations stipulated that the score after 80 minutes would stand, and that the Robins and the Roughyeds would have to meet again. This time, at Fartown, Huddersfield, Hull KR settled the issue convincingly with a 12-2 win, subsequently losing 13-5 to Widnes in the final.

Whitehead had only been at Oldham 12 months, scoring two tries and 139 goals for a total of 284 points in his 49 appearances, but he was already fully aware of the club's great traditions; a pedigree illustrated by the fact that a total of 84,755 folk had watched those three semi-finals in the spring of 1964. At that time, Whitehead had been a Swinton player, having joined a club, at the age of 17 from crack Manchester amateur outfit Folly Lane in 1961, that was about to register two successive Championships under the legendary captain Albert Blan.

The Lions set about winning the Division One title twice on the trot before the young Derek Whitehead made his debut, putting three successive opening defeats behind them in 1962-63 to come top of the pile in a three-year experiment with two divisions which would be aborted after the second term because of concern over falling crowds.

Swinton came close to reaching the Challenge Cup Final in the 1964-65 season, reaching the semi-finals before losing 25-10 to Wigan at St Helens before a 26,658 crowd, Wigan going on to beat Hunslet at Wembley in a classic.

The Manchester outfit had been as unlucky as Oldham, albeit in a different way, on missing out on an appearance at the Twin Towers. Prior to 1929, the Lions had appeared in four finals, including in the successive seasons of 1925-26, 1926-27 and 1927-28, losing only one. Even worse, Swinton did appear in the Challenge Cup Final a couple of years after the Wembley adventure had begun, in 1931-32; but the final was played, that year, at Wigan, the Rugby Football League having to return the game to the north because the selected date of 9 April clashed with an England v Scotland soccer international at the Twin Towers.

Swinton lost 11-8 to Leeds and have been destined not to reach the final since. Not that it would have felt that way on 3 October 1964 when Whitehead deputised for Great Britain fullback Ken Gowers at Rochdale Hornets, making an immediate and real contribution with four goals in a 14-4 success.

Despite having made a healthy enough, if belated, start to his first team career at Station Road, Whitehead had to wait another four months, until Saturday 6 February, for his second outing, on this occasion against leading amateur side Dewsbury Celtic in the first round of the Challenge Cup. This time Gowers was also in the side, operating at stand-off. Whitehead, at fullback again, was handed the goalkicking duties ahead of Gowers, landing nine goals and adding a try for a personal haul of 21 points in a 48-5 verdict. He made two further appearances that season (one on the wing, the other at fullback), totalling a try and 14 goals.

From that point on he became something of a regular, in an illustration of how a player who had had to wait four years in the 'A' team could, given an opportunity, make a real mark. In 1965-66, he was in the starting line-up on 23 occasions (20 times in the wing, and three at fullback), with a further three outings as substitute, scoring 170 points with six tries and 76 goals.

The following season, 1966-67, saw him at his most heavily involved at Station Road. He made 36 full appearances, with another five off the bench, and fell agonisingly short of his first century of goals in a season, landing 99, with eight tries bringing his points' tally to 222. He was selected, during that campaign, 26 times on the wing and 10 times at fullback as Swinton continued to give the impression that they didn't know quite what to do with him; understandably, perhaps, given that he was attempting to displace Gowers at fullback.

That uncertainty continued in his last season in Manchester, in

1967-68, when he was in the starting line-up in each of his 28 games, but vacillated between fullback (18 games) and wing (10 games). He kept up his scoring rate, though, with 71 goals and seven tries; a total of 163 points, verifying his rating as the club's main kicker since around halfway through the 1965-66 campaign.

His career record at Swinton read 91 appearances, plus eight as a substitute, in which he totalled 22 tries and 260 goals, for a grand tally of 586 points; a highlight of his time at Station Road was undoubtedly during the 1966-67 season, when he appeared in the BBC2 Floodlit Trophy Final against Castleford (at Wheldon Road) only a few days before Christmas. Not hindered by home advantage, Castleford prevailed 7-2. Whitehead, playing on the wing opposite the redoubtable and aggressive Jack Austin, kicked Swinton's penalty but it wasn't enough against a Glassblowers side that posted an Austin try, a goal by Ron Willett, and a drop goal by Keith Hepworth.

His last match for Swinton was in the home fixture with Leigh on 9 March 1968, operating on the wing and kicking a goal in an 8-5 win.

Oldham were hovering and, to the surprise and consternation of the Station Road faithful, Derek Whitehead headed west for the 1968-69 campaign. The Lions were very much a major club during Derek Whitehead's term at Station Road and that understanding, and the similar feeling around Watersheddings as to Oldham's status, perhaps underpinned his desire not to particularly want to switch to Warrington in a deal brokered largely because the Roughyeds – who under coach Gerry Helme, the former Warrington ace, had paid Swinton a transfer fee of £4,000 – needed the cash.

Whitehead went to Warrington in September 1969 and, despite any reservations he may have harboured, never looked back. He made his debut the following month, on 4 October, at St Helens, when he landed a goal (Willie Aspinall dropping a goal and Brian Glover grabbing a try) in an 11-7 defeat, quickly endearing himself to the Wilderspool faithful with his electric attacking style and his accurate goalkicking; not to mention a solid defence.

A straight-on kicker in an era increasingly dominated by the 'round the corner' stylists, he topped the club's scoring charts in each of the next seven seasons, with his best tally coming in 1973-74, when he hit the target on 162 occasions, matching the previous record set by Harry Bath in 1952-53. Steve Hesford eclipsed both efforts in 1978-79 when he kicked 170 goals; a record which, by 2011, remained unbroken.

The 1973-74 season turned out to one of Warrington's finest, with the Wire securing the Challenge Cup, the Club Championship (the equivalent of the Championship Final), the Players' No. 6 Trophy and the Captain Morgan Trophy. Derek Whitehead's contribution to the cause was immense, in terms of substance and of style. His 46 appearances were more than those made by any other player and he was the man of the match in both the Challenge Cup and Captain Morgan Finals.

The Captain Morgan Trophy – contested by the survivors of the first rounds of the County Cups – was a short-lived competition which was shelved after only one season. But it was there to be won, and the Wire won it largely through their strong defence, which kept Featherstone Rovers at bay throughout the final and through Whitehead's goal-kicking; two penalties each landed from 45 yards ensuring a 4-0 victory for Warrington.

He contributed a try and six goals in the Players' No. 6 Trophy Final against Rochdale Hornets, in which Warrington prevailed 27-16, and was a seminal figure in the 13-12 success over St Helens in the Club Championship Final at Central Park, Wigan.

It is, however, for his display in the Challenge Cup Final against Featherstone Rovers that he is perhaps best remembered at Wilderspool. In an ill-tempered contest, Derek Whitehead landed seven goals to have a major say in the 24-9 margin of victory in a game in which, despite the scoreline, only three tries were scored, two of them by Warrington, by hooker Kevin Ashcroft and second row Mike Nicholas. The remainder of the Wire's points, other than a couple of drop goals by captain/coach Alex Murphy, came from the boot of Whitehead, who was successful with all but his conversion attempt of Nicholas' late effort, leaving him only one short of the record of eight set in a Challenge Cup Final the previous year by another fullback, Featherstone Rovers' Cyril Kellett. He had done enough with his goalkicking, and his general play, however, to earn the accolade as the Lance Todd Trophy Man of the Match, offering the kind of accuracy that made him the fifth highest goal scorer, and the sixth highest points' scorer, for Warrington.

During his time at Wilderspool, Derek Whitehead earned six Lancashire caps, scoring a try and five goals, and three Great Britain caps. He made his international debut in the 16-8 defeat by France at Toulouse in February 1971, scoring a goal through converting a try by Leeds winger Alan Smith. In the return the following month at St Helens he contributed a try and three goals to a 24-2 success in which Smith again crossed; other touchdowns went to Hull KR stand-off Roger Millward, with a brace, St Helens centre Billy Benyon and Featherstone Rovers second row Jimmy Thompson.

Whitehead retained the no 1 shirt for the First Test of the incoming New Zealand tour of 1971. The Kiwis, however, won the game, at Salford, 18-13; Whitehead landed a couple of goals, with home tries going to Benyon, Salford centre Chris Hesketh and Wigan second row Bill Ashurst.

Castleford fullback Derek Edwards got the nod for the Second Test – at Castleford – which Great Britain lost 17-14, despite tries by Hull winger Clive Sullivan, Leigh winger Joe Walsh, Millward and Salford prop Mike Coulman; Salford's David Watkins scored the only goal.

Edwards was again preferred for the final Test, at Leeds, which Great Britain won 12-3. At the turn of the year, however, Salford's Paul Charlton was selected at the rear, and remained the first choice until the mid-seventies.

Whitehead focused on his club commitments, confirming his loyalty and value by turning out in various positions towards the end of his career. His last game was in the closing stages of the 1978-79 season, as a substitute at Rochdale, helping out a Warrington outfit that, after having first been approached with perhaps some dismay and trepidation, had become dear to his heart.

That feeling was reciprocated. He was made a member of the coaching staff and, in 1979-80, was awarded a richly deserved benefit. He remained on the coaching team until 1985, and was inducted into Warrington's Hall of Fame, together with Jim Tranter and Ray Price, in 2008.

12

Alex Murphy

ALEX MURPHY may have been a shade past his prime as a player when he joined Warrington in May 1971; but the Wire arguably enjoyed the best years that Murphy had to offer as a player/coach.

When Warrington prised Alex Murphy from Leigh's clutches in the immediate aftermath of the latter's great victory over Leeds in the 1971 Challenge Cup Final, the Wire were at one of the lowest ebbs in the club's history. The side had finished 22nd in the 30-team table that season, Warrington's worst-ever position and two spots lower than the previous nadir of 20th in 1923-24. The tale of woe included a 50-0 hammering at Wilderspool by Salford, who had been an unthinkable 29-0 ahead at the interval and who closed with 12 tries.

The Wire, in fact, were in some danger of heading into freefall. After having enjoyed some success in each decade throughout the twentieth century, the 1960s had been comparatively barren after the Championship Final defeat at the hands of Leeds in 1960-61. Warrington had lifted the Lancashire Cup in 1965-66, and had been runners-up in the 1967-68 season, during which the Wire had topped the Lancashire League. That wasn't an insignificant record, but it was one which paled by comparison with the successes of the 1950s. And despite the presence of such as scrum-half Parry Gordon and fullback Derek Whitehead in the ranks, there was little sign of any return to the glories of old.

It was against that background that Chairman Ossie Davies, who had joined the club only months earlier and who, ultimately, should be credited with Warrington's subsequent successes, decided to push the boat out for the services of the veteran Alex Murphy, who had proven beyond doubt his qualities as a player/coach by guiding Leigh to Wembley glory over the Loiners. Murphy, it is often overlooked, had also achieved success at league level, the men from Hilton Park having finished fourth in the table to Leeds' third to suggest that their victory wasn't quite the shock that it is often considered to have been.

Their faith – and sheer audacity, Murphy being enticed from Hilton Park even as Leigh were celebrating their Challenge Cup success – was vindicated by subsequent events.

Alex Murphy set about rebuilding the Warrington side in an image which embodied that of many sporting sides of the 1970s, many of which appeared to take their stylistic lead from the Spaghetti Western films which were popular at the time. Moustachioed, hard-faced to the point of being surly (and occasionally beyond), and aggressive, teams such as the Australian cricket side, Leeds United's soccer team and, it has to be said, Warrington, played to the limits of the rules of their respective sports – and, often, beyond – in their pursuit of victory. It was an approach, underpinned by no little skill throughout each team, that often paid off, and Warrington supporters, starved as they had been of something to celebrate on a regular basis since the retirement of Brian Bevan in 1962, certainly had few if any complaints.

During Alex Murphy's seven years at Wilderspool the Wire picked up six major trophies, including lifting the Challenge Cup in 1973-74, to retrieve their standing as one of the major forces in the game. Murphy didn't achieve the success on his own, of course; he brought in players whom he knew could be relied upon to prosper in a supportive role. A key figure was his hooker at Leigh, the ebullient Kevin Ashcroft, who followed Alex Murphy to Warrington 12 months or so after the pair had shared in Wembley glory.

Over the next couple of seasons, with the support of Ossie Davies – who raised funds by selling off the popular side stand area, erecting in its place a leisure complex which housed a concert hall, saunas and squash courts – Murphy set about building a strong pack which included the likes of prop Dave Chisnall, Brian Brady - who was rated by many opponents as the best around - and second row Mike Nicholas, a blonde-haired firebrand who was persuaded to come north from Aberavon Rugby Union club in 1972.

Murphy wasn't neglectful of his backs. Goalkicking fullback Derek Whitehead, a former Oldham player who had also graced Swinton, and the loyal and incisive scrum-half Parry Gordon were already at Wilderspool, imbuing the existing squad with quality. The new coach, meanwhile, acquired such as centre Derek Noonan from St Helens RUFC and, out wide and a couple of years later, Welsh rugby union winger John Bevan, who had played for the British Lions in 1971. And, of course, the maestro himself remained on the park, at stand-off, as the orchestrator-supreme of a fine side.

Success wasn't entirely immediate, which perhaps suited a coach who understood that candy built on floss can all too swiftly dissipate. However, the team enjoyed an incredible Challenge Cup run which ended in a 10-6 semi-final replay defeat to St Helens in front of 32,180 spectators at Wigan. The team finished fifteenth in Murphy's first season in charge, as perhaps an essential part of a rational rebuilding process; 12 months later, the Wire were top of the pile in the last season of the 30-team league structure, the Rugby Football League switching to two divisions for the 1973-74 campaign after several previous attempts, all of which had been aborted. Not that Alex Murphy was necessarily too bothered about league football, other than as a means of sustaining form for knock-out fare. Prior to the launch of Super League in the mid-nineties, league honours were generally regarded as secondary to success in the Challenge Cup, and Murphy certainly viewed Wembley as Rugby League's major stage.

The Wire missed out at the semi-final stage (and at Wilderspool at that) to eventual title-winners Dewsbury, who had future Sky TV pundit Mike Stephenson at hooker, in the 1972-73 championship play-offs. The side, though, went on to reach Wembley in each of the following two seasons. They were occasions on which Murphy brought the knowledge gained in three previous outings at the Twin Towers, each time as a winner, to bear – albeit with mixed results.

Alex Murphy's first experience of Wembley was in 1960-61, when he was a try-scorer at stand-off in the St Helens side that beat old rivals Wigan 12-6. He was back again five years later, again against Wigan but this time in the centre and, crucially, as captain in a match which added, if any extra lustre were needed, to his mystique.

Wigan went into the game without their hooker, the suspended Colin Clarke, which was a serious handicap in the era of contested scrums. It was also in an era prior to the reintroduction of the tap penalty, which had been abolished in 1960. The effect of that was that Wigan, who had drafted Tom Woosey in at number 9, were starved of possession. Their predicament was made worse by what many observers felt was St Helens' tactic, with Murphy and his scrum-half Tommy Bishop seen as the chief culprits, of straying offside as a means of regaining possession under the unlimited tackle rule. Wigan, compelled by the rules to kick to touch, inevitably lost the resulting scrums, which Saints hooker Bill Sayer took almost 4-1, and the Saints duly won a controversial game 21-2.

Several pundits suggested afterwards that Warrington whistler Harry Hunt should either have dismissed Murphy for persistent offside, or simply ignored his transgressions.

There was more controversy surrounding the legendary Murphy five years later, when he returned to Wembley as player/coach of Leigh, this time in the scrum-half position against hot favourites Leeds. On this occasion Murphy failed to last the full 80 minutes, but his exit was even more controversial than had been his involvement in the 1966 decider. No player had been sent off at Wembley until 1971, when Leeds centre Sid Hynes became the first man to be dismissed on the major stage. Hynes was deemed by referee Billy Thompson to have pole-axed Murphy in an off-the-ball incident midway through the second period, when Leigh were leading 17-2. Murphy was stretchered off, apparently concussed, and Hynes followed, dejected.

Murphy emerged afterwards, sitting the match out on the bench, after having received treatment from the Leigh and Wembley medical staff. Arguments have raged over the ensuing decades as to whether Alex Murphy was 'shamming', in an effort to secure Hynes' dismissal; the two men subsequently became good friends, but the definitive story has perhaps yet to be told.

These, then, were the qualities of gamesmanship – quite apart from his sublime skill as a player and his talents as a motivator – that Alex Murphy brought to the table when Warrington qualified to meet Featherstone Rovers in the 1973-74 Challenge Cup Final.

Featherstone travelled to Wembley as the holders, having beaten Bradford Northern 33-14 12 months earlier. They were to return to the West Riding pit village without the silverware as Warrington retrieved the Challenge Cup after a 20-year gap. The game turned out to be one of the most ill-tempered finals in the history of the competition, with some – including Featherstone coach Peter Fox – pointing the finger of blame at Murphy, who had been involved in a strong challenge on Rovers' centre David Hartley in only the third minute.

Fox also had words of criticism for the match official, Oldham's Sam Shepherd, reflecting, 'The referee was totally irresponsible. The first incident of the match, Murphy's stiff arm tackle on Hartley, caused all the trouble afterwards. We were suffering through penalties and that upset the lads.'

Murphy, meanwhile, established a proud record of being the only man to captain three different teams to Challenge Cup success. That

R. J. E. WARREN (President). 2.—MR. T. PEMBERTON (Treasurer). 3.—MR. H. ASHTON (Secretary). 4.—D. ISHERWOOD —A. NAYLOR. 6.—A. E. BOARDMAN. 7.—E. BROOKS. 8.—J. H. TILLEY. 9.—J. FISH (Capt.) 10.—S. LEES. 1.—J. BELTON. 12.—T. HOCKENHULL. 13.—I. TAYLOR. 14.—G. THOMAS. 15.—F. G. SHUGARS. 16.—G. HEATH.

JE Warren: A proud President is pictured at the centre of a montage of Warrington players of 1906-07

Alf Boardman, honest
and upright

In proud consideration
– Alf Boardman

Jack Fish displays the Rugby League Challenge Cup, won by
Warrington for the first time in 1904-05

Ernie Brookes

Ernie Brookes embraces
the Challenge Cup
in the immediate
aftermath of victory

Billy Cunliffe, a member of the
1920 Northern Union touring party
to Australia and New Zealand

Bill Shankland, captured to fine effect by a
cartoonist in the 1930s

OGDEN'S CIGARETTES

W. SHANKLAND (WARRINGTON)

Cigarette card images of leading players
such as Bill Shankland were popular for
much of Rugby League's history

Gerry Helme displays his passing skills in a training session

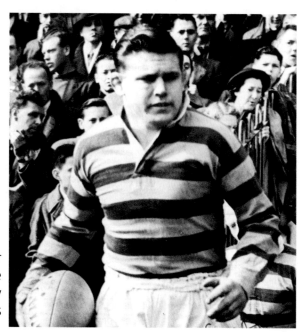

Inspirational skipper Harry Bath led the Wire out on many occasions

Brian Bevan sets off on a rare raid in the defence-dominated drawn 1954 Challenge Cup Final against Halifax. Gerry Helme watches events with interest as, in the background, does chief guest, the Earl of Derby, in the Royal Box

Parry Gordon – one
of Warrington's finest
servants

Alex Murphy and Derek Whitehead
flank Dave Chisnall as Warrington
line up at the 1974 Challenge Cup
Final against Featherstone Rovers

At the veteran stage, but still possessing fine technique, Alex
Murphy pumps the ball downfield

John Bevan in typical attacking mood

Welsh winger John Bevan, eyes
focussed on the tryline, rounds
Salford speedster Keith Fielding.
The Red Devils' David Watkins
looks on in vain

Kevin Ashcroft, accompanied by winger Mike Philbin, takes care of the plinth after the Wire's Challenge Cup win in 1974

Mike Gregory clutches the
Lancashire Cup, and Des
Drummond looks on benignly,
following Warrington's win
over Oldham in the 1989-90
Lancashire Cup Final
© RLPhotos.com

Not easy to take. Mike
Gregory reflects on the
defeat at the hands
of Wigan in the 1990
Challenge Cup Final
© RLPhotos.com

Des Drummond had few running
opportunities in the 1990
Challenge Cup Final. Here, with
fullback David Lyon in support,
he illustrates just what a threat
he presented to Wigan

Lee Briers looks to launch
his threequarter line

Normally the orchestrator, Lee Briers opts to take on the Huddersfield defence on this occasion

Jon Clarke nips over the tryline against Hull KR

Adrian Morley lifts the Challenge Cup in 2010 – the Wire's second successive triumph in the competition after a barren period spanning 36 years

The man who led Warrington Wolves to the heights – coach Tony Smith after the victory over his former club Leeds in the 2010 Challenge Cup Final

proud record of winning at Wembley was to end the following season when Warrington missed out to neighbours Widnes in another dour decider. Alex Murphy was, on this occasion, hampered by the fact that he was no longer able to directly influence events on the field of play, having retired as a player at the beginning of the campaign. The opposing coach, his old friend and team-mate, with St Helens and Great Britain, Vince Karalius – the loose forward known as the 'Wild Bull of the Pampas', who had given Murphy much-valued protection around the scrum – was to have the upper hand as Widnes prevailed 14-7.

Warrington's success story under Murphy's leadership, however, was not about to end. A couple of seasons later the Wire battled their way through to the Premiership Final – the culmination of a competition introduced, following the advent of two divisions, to replace the popular championship play-offs. Murphy's old team, St Helens, provided the opposition for the clash at Swinton. The Saints had appeared in each of the previous two Premiership Finals, losing 26-11 to Leeds at Wigan in 1974-75, but beating Salford 15-2 at Swinton 12 months later.

St Helens were to retain their grip on the trophy, thanks largely to fullback, Geoff Pimblett, who contributed a try and seven goals to his side's cause. The Saints, who scored six tries to four in the 32-20 win, also posted touchdowns by centres Billy Benyon and Eddie Cunningham, winger Roy Mathias, scrum-half Ken Gwilliam and second row Mel James. Scrum-half Parry Gordon, stand-off Alan Gwilliam, prop Dave Weavill and loose forward Barry Philbin also crossed the whitewash for the Wire before a disappointing gate at Swinton of 11,178, a drop of nearly seven thousand on the previous season's attendance.

Alex Murphy completed his term of tenure at Wilderspool with another piece of silverware to add to the cabinet – the Players' No. 6 Trophy, secured with a 9-4 victory over old rivals Widnes in the 1977-78 decider at St Helens. A crowd of 10,258 gathered at Knowsley Road, St Helens, for the final of a competition which emulated, in its format, the Challenge Cup. Left winger John Bevan scored the only try of the game, while right winger Steve Hesford landed three goals. Widnes, meanwhile, had to settle for a couple of goals by Welsh winger Paul Woods.

That victory brought the curtain down on Murphy's time at Warrington, the maestro moving on to Salford, He subsequently coached Wigan and St Helens, in addition to Lancashire, before having a spell at Huddersfield.

The Wire's successes, meanwhile, would continue, Billy Benyon taking over from Alex Murphy and steering the side to the John Player Trophy Finals of 1978-79, when Widnes won 16-4 at Knowsley Road, St Helens, and 1980-81, when Barrow were accounted for 12-5 at Central Park, Wigan. The foundations for that sustained period of prosperity had been set in motion in 1972-73 when Murphy's Warrington headed the table with 27 wins, two draws and only five defeats in their 34 outings. Although Wigan (30-15) and Rochdale Hornets (16-9) were beaten in the opening rounds of the Top 16 play-offs, the magnificent Dewsbury side of the era ended Warrington's campaign with a 12-7 semi-final verdict at Wilderspool.

The next season, highlighted by the win at Wembley over Featherstone Rovers, was perhaps Warrington's most successful since the campaign of exactly 20 years earlier, when all but the Lancashire Cup had been won in the 1953-54 campaign. In addition to prevailing in the Challenge Cup, Warrington lifted the Club Championship, the Players' No. 6 Trophy and the Captain Morgan Trophy.

The Club Championship, a complicated concept involving teams in the First and Second Divisions, with a preliminary round in the bottom tier helping achieve a 16-team play-off, was won with a 13-12 victory over St Helens at Wigan. Although the competition was not persevered with, being replaced immediately by the Premiership, the Wire had no complaints; nor did the majority of the 18,040 fans who turned up at Central Park for the final.

The Captain Morgan Trophy, meanwhile, had been introduced to fill what Rugby League bosses felt was a void in the fixture programme, and perhaps as a means of boosting the county cups, and lasted for only one season. The seven survivors of the first round of the Lancashire Cup, together with the 'best loser', were joined by the eight winners of the first round of the Yorkshire Cup; a notion that was meant to eliminate weaker teams but which failed in that aim when Dewsbury, Hull KR and St Helens all lost their opening county cup games. The first round of the Captain Morgan Trophy was zoned on a county basis, with the second round draw being made in an open format. Warrington made it through to the final with victories at Wigan (12-4), against Castleford (15-7) at Wilderspool, and at Leeds (20-13) in the semi-final. Fullback and man of the match Derek Whitehead, with two goals, helped the Wire to a 4-0 victory over Featherstone Rovers in the decider at Salford, before a crowd of only 5,259. Murphy, who was injured, missed out on the game. He was also an absentee in that season's Players' No. 6 Trophy final when Warrington beat competition surprise packets Rochdale Hornets 27-16 at Wigan. Whitehead again led the way with a try and six goals, with centre Derek Noonan bagging a brace, and winger John Bevan and substitute Mike Nicholas also crossing.

The following season Warrington, in addition to being Challenge Cup runners-up, reached the BBC2 Floodlit Trophy Final under Murphy, losing to Salford in a replay at Wilderspool after having drawn 0-0 at the Willows; home advantage in the replay, however, failed to help the Wire, who slipped to a 10-5 defeat, posting a try by Bevan and a goal by Whitehead but conceding touchdowns by speedy wingers Keith Fielding and Maurice Richards, plus two goals by centre David Watkins, the former Wales rugby union captain and stand-off who had been a big-money capture by the Red Devils' chairman Brian Snape.

Watkins would, throughout the 1970s, find himself frequently on the receiving end of Murphy's tongue, the League-reared maestro perhaps railing at the tendency of the media to occasionally attach more importance, and offer more status, to rugby union imports than to the talents brought through Rugby League's own nursery systems.

The men came head to head during the period that Murphy was Head Coach of England, with Watkins acting as player/coach of Wales; roles from which both derived great pride. Murphy, indeed, was noted for the gratification he derived from playing for his country, earning 27 Great Britain caps between 1958 and 1971, plus two caps for England. In addition, he made 14 appearances for Lancashire during the same period.

His first opportunity to force his way into the Great Britain side came in March 1958 when, at the age of 18, he was invited to play in the first of two trial matches ahead of that summer's Lions tour to Australia and New Zealand, Murphy securing inclusion in the 26-man squad after impressing against Oldham's Frank Pitchford, who also made the final party when first choice Jeff Stevenson, of Leeds, withdrew because of business commitments.

By the time he played his first Test match, the St Helens protégé was only just 19 yet, during the tour, he played 20 games, scoring 21 tries and kicking three goals. He also established a reputation as a superb young footballer with 'attitude'; a quality that remained with him throughout his career. Not that his international debut could be described as successful, Keith Holman getting the better of him in the First Test at Sydney, which Australia won 25-8 before a 68,777 crowd.

That kind of reverse can be a defining moment for a player, either halting a promising career in its infancy or prompting the man in question to rise to the challenge. The latter option applied to Alex Murphy, who was one of several inspirational figures in the famous Second Test, at Brisbane. On that occasion, however, he had to cede pride of place – not an eventuality that would occur very often thereafter – to another man. That man was his captain, club colleague Alan Prescott, who fell awkwardly in the fourth minute and broke his arm. The prop, amazingly and heroically, carried on, all too acutely aware in the era before substitutes that his withdrawal would condemn the depleted Lions to an almost certain defeat, and with it the loss of the Series. Prescott offered nuisance value, bravely passing and tackling with one arm dangling uselessly by his side. And his colleagues, including Alex Murphy, also rose magnificently to the occasion, particularly when Wigan stand-off Dave Bolton had no alternative other than to go off with a broken collar bone. With loose forward Vince Karalius suffering from a back injury, but filling in superbly for Bolton, the Lions had, surely, no right to do anything but succumb. Instead, they registered a 25-18 victory, one of the greatest in Great Britain's history, to level the Series.

Murphy was at the hub of the success, the manner of which even prompted home supporters in the 32,965 crowd to cheer the Lions on. The young halfback scored a try of his own and was heavily involved in three of the other four touchdowns, with Workington Town's Ike Southward bagging a brace and Jim Challinor (Warrington) and Mick Sullivan (Wigan) also crossing. Another Warrington man, meanwhile, fullback Eric Fraser, kicked five goals. Australia were left adrift despite Newtown fullback Gordon Clifford, in his last Test series, kicking three goals to accompany tries by Norths centre Brian Carlson, Wests winger Peter Dimond, Holman and prop Bill Marsh, of Balmain.

Britain, suitably inspired, went on to win the Ashes with a 40-17 victory in the Third Test at Sydney. Murphy again scored a try, while Sullivan got a hat-trick. Southward also raced over, and other tries went to Oldham centre Alan Davies, St Helens prop Abe Terry and Hull second row Johnny Whiteley, with Fraser landing eight goals. Clifford kicked four goals for the Kangaroos, for whom Holman, Wagga stand-off Greg Hawick and St George forward Norm Provan crossed.

It would be tempting to reflect that life with Great Britain, for Alex Murphy, never again quite reached those spectacular heights. And it wasn't without controversy, notably when he refused to tour Australia in 1966, having been selected at centre rather than in his preferred halfback slot. It later emerged that another reason for his decision was dissatisfaction at being overlooked for the tour captaincy, which went to Hull KR back row man Harry Poole; Poole, in the event, failed to play in a Test match.

In opting not to travel, Alex Murphy spurned the chance to equal the record of completing three Great Britain tours, having been a pivotal figure in the 2-1 Ashes success Down Under in 1962. Murphy dominated matters in the 31-12 opening win, before 70,174, at Sydney, and scored a try in the 17-10 Ashes-clinching success at Brisbane, where 34,766 were present.

The battered Aussie public turned up in reduced numbers for the last Test, at the Sydney Cricket Ground, where a try by the mercurial scrum-half appeared to have sealed a 3-0 whitewash until a controversial touchdown by Kangaroos winger Ken Irvine, converted by the same Norths player from the touchline, helped the hosts to an 18-17 win against a Lions side that had had Derek 'Rocky' Turner, of Wakefield Trinity, and Mick Sullivan (St Helens) sent off, together with Australia's Dud Beattie.

That was Alex Murphy's nineteenth international appearance; he was, thanks in part to his decision not to travel in 1966, to gain only eight more caps before his final outing, against New Zealand at Castleford, on 16 October 1971, shortly after he had joined Warrington from Leigh, in a 17-14 defeat which enabled the Kiwis to win the series.

The paltry crowd of 4,108 – an improvement on the derisory 3,764 who had shown up at Salford for the First Test, and both improved on only marginally by the 5,479 who gathered for the Third Test at Leeds – could scarcely have thought that they were seeing Murphy in a Great Britain shirt for the last time. It was not a fitting end to an illustrious international career; albeit a career that was to continue to hit the heights at club level.

His achievements were recognised by the Rugby Football League, which included him in the initial Hall of Fame, in 1988, alongside eight other great players. He was awarded the OBE in 1999.

13

John Bevan

WHEN John Bevan arrived at Wilderspool in 1973 from Cardiff rugby union club, he faced two hurdles.

The first was that which all converts from rugby union encountered – the difficulty of making a mark in a sport that was at once similar, but very different, to the one in which he had been brought up. He had no great problems with that. As a winger, he had fewer issues to attend to. His main job, after all, was to make the most of any try-scoring opportunities that came his way, a duty that he undoubtedly fulfilled.

The second matter was, however, more problematic, and not one that he could do too much about, or even wanted to: his surname. John Bevan was joining a club that had, from 1945 until 1962, boasted in its ranks the man generally rated as the finest winger of all time, in the shape (an unlikely one, it has to be said) of the great Australian Brian Bevan.

Comparisons were going to be inevitable, particularly as the Bevan's both operated on the wing. So, unfairly but inevitably, John Bevan was up against it from the start. To his immense credit, however, he made such an impression that, while not seriously challenging (or even seeking to) Brian Bevan's position on the highest pedestal of all at Wilderspool, John Bevan made his own lasting impression in the history of Warrington RLFC, remaining at the club for 13 years to become, with his namesake, one of the Wire's finest servants. Along the way he totalled 201 tries in 332 appearances, to help the club to sustained success in a productive era for Warrington.

It was John Bevan's good fortune, in being compared to Brian Bevan, that his style was totally different to that of his illustrious predecessor. If Brian lacked one thing in his armoury, it was sheer blockbusting power. That was an attribute that John possessed in abundance, and supporters of the era continue to relish memories of his enthusiastic and robust approach, in which his preferred option of taking the direct route to the line often brought due reward. In addition, he got off to the best of starts at Wilderspool, a factor that was perhaps crucial, by registering a try on his debut, against Castleford. If John Bevan had, for whatever reason, failed to score in his first two or three games, it's reasonable to speculate that the mood on the terraces and in the stands could perhaps have been so very different. Instead, he immediately worked his way into the hearts of the Warrington faithful with a trademark touchdown in the 22-5 success.

He later recalled of that pivotal game:

> I knew about Brian, of course, and I was aware that it could easily have gone against me if I hadn't started my career at Wilderspool well. The spectators were great, though, and gave me an immediate and warm welcome which became long-lasting. Scoring on my debut was, without question, a huge relief. It's a match which I'll always remember vividly, for several reasons. It was a tough encounter, and I recall that Alex Murphy got sent off. One of the Castleford players tried to break my ribs, if I remember rightly, but the result was right and I went ok. And there was a good crowd there.

Another way in which John Bevan differed from Brian Bevan was in temperament. The wizened wonder was famously taciturn and introspective, while his Welsh successor was much more outgoing and, in time, began to develop a rapport with supporters to such a degree that he would get involved in conversations with regulars on the terraces. He said:

> Sometimes it can get lonely on the wing, so I did develop a habit of chatting to the people in the crowd when I could. After a while I got to know a few faces, and the fans were always up for a laugh and a joke. I used to enjoy that side of things.

The Wire's faithful fans certainly enjoyed having John Bevan, one of several notable captures from the Valleys, on board during the successful period of the 1970s.

Persuaded to join Warrington by the legendary Alex Murphy, Bevan later admitted that he may have been a tad spoiled by his early experiences with the Wire. He knew little about the north west of England, and not much more about Rugby League. In fact he spoke, on his retirement, perhaps tongue in cheek, of having expected to play at Wembley every year following his early experiences with

Warrington. Within a year he was striding out onto the lush turf of Wembley Stadium, ready and willing to face the might of Challenge Cup holders Featherstone Rovers, who had lifted the prize piece of silverware with a record-breaking success 12 months earlier over Bradford Northern. Other Welshmen in the Warrington side that day included second row Mike Nicholas, a tough and uncompromising blond bombshell of a packman, blessed with pace and power, who had been snapped up by Murphy from Aberavon RUFC, and substitute Bobby Wanbon, born in Swansea but transferred from St Helens.

The game was an abrasive affair, its ugly spirit captured by a photograph of Wire substitute Billy Pickup landing a punch on the chin of Rovers hooker Keith Bridges. But the record books confirm that Warrington had emerged as winners, beating Featherstone by an utterly convincing 24-9 margin after having trailed 9-8 at the interval. That closing scoreline hadn't looked too likely during the half-time interval. In a defence-dominated affair, Warrington had led 8-4 as the hooter beckoned, fullback Derek Whitehead having landed four penalty goals in response to a couple by his Rovers counterpart Harold Box. But the Wire were rocked and Featherstone were given a massive boost when, with Murphy off the field because of a rib injury, scrum-half Steve Nash took a quick tap and second row Jimmy Thompson powered into the Warrington line before sending his captain, stand-off John Newlove, over the whitewash. Box's conversion put the Yorkshiremen ahead for the first time since the 10th minute – and, with scrum-half Parry Gordon being forced to withdraw during the break through injury, the situation was serious.

Alex Murphy's world-class match-winning temperament and motivational abilities – not to mention sheer courage – came to the fore, the captain receiving five pain-killing injections and returning to the fray. Within three minutes he had turned the contest back towards Warrington, freeing centre Derek Noonan who punched a vital hole in the Featherstone cover and, finding Kevin Ashcroft on his shoulder, sent the hooker over for a crucial try. Whitehead added the extras, and Warrington never looked back. Two further penalties by their fullback, who was voted as the Lance Todd Trophy-winning man of the match by the assembled members of the Rugby League Writers' Association, eased the Wire eight points clear, and a drop goal by Murphy on the hour stretched that advantage to 10 points. Another Murphy 'drop', in the era when such goals were worth two points, in the 72nd minute put the issue beyond doubt, and there really was no way back for Featherstone when hard-running second row Mike Nicholas crashed past a posse of defenders four minutes from time. Whitehead was unable to convert, thus missing out by a whisker on equalling the record of eight goals at Wembley set 12 months earlier by Featherstone's Cyril Kellett.

Twelve months later Warrington returned to Wembley to take on Widnes, their closest and most deadly rivals. The Chemics, while generally a tough nut to crack, had tended not to be among the honours in their long history. Challenge Cup successes in 1930, 1937 and 1964 being the sum total of their endeavours to date. That was about to change as Widnes became known as the Cup Kings of Rugby League, with Warrington their first victims on the major stage.

Vince Karalius, who had captained the Chemics to victory over Hull KR in the 1964 decider, was now coach, and not a man to contemplate the prospect of defeat lightly, if at all. That attribute could, equally, be accorded to Alex Murphy. The two men knew all about each others' strengths – and weaknesses, if any – having played together in the St Helens side that won the competition in 1961 (beating Wigan) after having taken part in the magnificent Championship Cup Final victory over Hunslet at Odsal in 1958-59.

The honours, on this occasion, were to go to Karalius, Murphy sampling the agony of defeat at Wembley for the first time. Not, however, as a player. The great halfback's 100 per cent record on the pitch was to remain intact, Murphy having retired; but he was to experience the frustration of life in the dugout, with the opportunity of directly influencing events now denied to him. The game was something of a mirror image of the previous season's affair. Warrington opened the scoring in the fifth minute, John Bevan pouncing after a kick by hooker Kevin Ashcroft had bounced off a number of defenders. Whitehead added the extras, but Widnes were to have the better of the rest of the contest, thanks in part to supreme levels of fitness instilled by Karalius, a man who had been in the habit of running 10 miles to and from training in his days as a player. The Chemics clawed their way back into the equation with a couple of penalties by fullback Ray Dutton, who was to collect the Lance Todd Trophy for his input, and went close when stand-off Eric Hughes was bundled into a corner flag. Warrington, though, were patently missing the on-field guidance of Murphy and fell behind seven minutes before the interval, Chemics centre Mal Aspey making a break and Hughes feeding giant prop Jim Mills – who benefited from the tactic of being played out wide – the latter's power and pace proving to be too much for the Wire's defence. Dutton added the extras and, on the stroke of half-time, a penalty to stretch his side's lead to six points, meaning that Warrington would have to score twice, in the era of the three-point try, to retrieve the advantage. That rarely looked likely as Widnes took a stranglehold, despite a Whitehead penalty three minutes after the resumption. A drop goal by Dutton – the first at Wembley since the reduction in the value of that mode of scoring from two points to one – seven minutes later, was followed by a penalty in the fifty-third minute by the fullback, who was also prominent in defence to thoroughly deserve his man-of-the-match accolade in the 14-7 win. John Bevan and his team-mates could only watch on, with 85,098 fans, as Widnes captain Dougie Laughton collected the Challenge Cup from HRH Princess Alexandra.

While that was hardly the best way in which to end a season, the overall success of the campaign for Warrington was not in doubt. The Wire, while not being able to sustain the heady four-trophy success of the previous campaign, had again featured on the major stage and, in addition, had reached the final of the popular BBC2 Floodlit Trophy. Bevan, after being involved in the scoreless draw against Salford at the Willows in the final, was a tryscorer in the replay at Wilderspool; but it wasn't enough to prevent a 10-5 defeat at the hands of the Red Devils.

The Challenge Cup Final and the Floodlit affair were, of course, among the many happy memories John Bevan was able to reflect on from his time at Warrington when he retired in the mid-80s. Another long-running theme from which he was able to derive great satisfaction was the re-emergence of the Wales Rugby League side, after a gap of five years, in 1975. Bevan, who made 17 appearances for his country after having played 10 times for Wales at Rugby Union, and once for the British Lions, was in at the centre of the action from its early, exhilarating revival.

There was nothing more exciting than the first match of the new era played by Wales, against France, on Sunday 16 February 1975; a game in which Bevan and Wire second row Mike Nicholas both featured. The scenes outside the St Helens Ground, Swansea, were nothing short of astonishing. Wales, whose last outing had been against England at Headingley in February 1970, when England won 26-7 before a 9,393 crowd, were caught on the hop by the level of interest. France, after all, were arguably not the most attractive of visitors at that stage, described as 'emerging from a limbo of mediocrity' by Paul Rylance of the Daily Telegraph in his subsequent report.

The Tricolors had lost the opening game of the new Triangular tournament at home to England a month earlier, slipping to an 11-9 reverse in front of between 8,000 and 12,000 spectators in Perpignan. While there may have been eyebrows raised at the uncertainty regarding the crowd in France there were certainly doubts over how many folk watched the Wales v France clash in Swansea. Organisers, it became clear, had failed to quite anticipate the passions aroused by the prospect of seeing former Wales rugby union heroes back on home turf, in the 13-a-side code. But what was a gamble in taking Wales' home game to an area which could have reacted with real hostility to the idea of an international game of Rugby League – hated by so many folk in the Valleys, if quietly and grudgingly respected in equal measure – paid off handsomely, helped in part by the decision to appoint David Watkins, the former Salford and Swinton stand-off or threequarter, as player/coach to the Wales side. Interest in the Triangular event was increased by the fact that England's coach was Alex Murphy, who rarely wasted time in rushing to belittle the perceived talents of the diminutive former Wales Rugby Union legend.

Perhaps partly because of the increased temperature surrounding the competition, and also possibly through interest in watching their former stars back on their old territory, even if playing an 'alien' game, the folk of south Wales turned up in huge numbers for the match. Not enough turnstiles had been opened to cope with the rush, creating real worries that a major incident was in danger of occurring. Against that backdrop, the gates were thrown open 15 minutes before the scheduled kick off, allowing an estimated 3,000 Welshmen to enter for free.

There has never been a definitive declaration of the attendance that day, but the general view is that 20,000 or so had already paid at the gate, taking the number of folk present to around 23,000. Those Welshmen and Welshwomen celebrated the return of Rugby League as only people from the Valleys can; by giving full vent to their emotions in a way that stirred their team to a superb 21-8 win. Only the players could reveal how important the crowd's support was to the Wales side, but the fact that they recovered from 3-2 down at the interval to win in comfort perhaps tells its own tale.

Wales had been limited to a penalty goal by St Helens loose forward Kel Coslett in the first half, but it was a totally different story after the break. Bevan himself raced over for two tries – celebrating, to the joy of the fans, in his own inimitable style, with arms raised aloft – while St Helens' Roy Mathias crossed on the opposite wing. Wales' remaining touchdown went to the fearsome prop Jim Mills, while Coslett totalled four goals and Watkins chipped in with a drop goal. France closed with a try by stand-off Michel Molinier, of St Gaudens, with prop Nestor Serrano, also of St Gaudens, landing a couple of goals and Avignon scrum-half Jean-Marie Imbert kicking a drop-goal.

Bevan and his colleagues therefore travelled to Salford nine days later aiming to account for England and lift the Jean Galia Trophy, so named in honour of the godfather of French Rugby League.

England prevailed 12-8, thanks to a 10-3 interval advantage, holding on for a victory which involved tries by Warrington centre Derek Noonan and Leeds winger John Atkinson, with Wigan hooker John Gray, who would eventually move on to Australian Rugby League, kicking three goals. Wales posted a try, a goal and a drop goal by Watkins in response, and Coslett also kicked a goal.

John Bevan went on to feature in Wales' assault on the 1975 Rugby League World Championship. The competition stretched from early March, when Wales played France at Toulouse, to early November, when France made the return trip, for a game played at Salford. Wales enjoyed a reasonable record in the event, closing with three victories and five defeats from their eight games, beating England in Brisbane (during the Australian leg of the competition) 12-7 before accounting for New Zealand 25-24 at Swansea on 2 November (when only 2,645 showed up in a remarkable turnaround from the delight of eight months earlier) and France 23-2 at Salford four days later.

Bevan missed out on the first four games, the 14-7 defeat by France in Toulouse, followed by the three games on the Australian 'leg' of the tournament, when Wales followed up the success over England in Brisbane with reverses at the hands of Australia (30-13 at Sydney, before 25,386) and New Zealand (13-8 at Auckland).

Back in the team for the European section of the tournament, he played in Wales' final four games, starting with a 22-16 defeat by England at Warrington and an 18-6 reverse at the hands of Australia at Swansea, when 11,112 showed up, followed by the one-point verdict over New Zealand at Swansea, in which he scored a crucial try, and the closing win over France, in which he again crossed the whitewash.

He was moved in from the wing to the centre, not scoring in either of the 1977 European Championship games against England and France, in which England were beaten 6-2 at Leeds and France prevailed 13-2 in Toulouse.

Missing out on the following year's series, he was back in the fold that October, selected on the wing for the game against Australia at Swansea, won 8-3 by the Kangaroos before 4,250 people.

He was in the centre the following year, when Wales lost 15-8 to France at Narbonne and 15-7 to England at Widnes, and scored from that position in January 1980 when Wales lost 21-7 to France, again at Widnes, in the following year's competition, before being switched to the second row for the game, the next month, against England at Hull KR, which was lost 26-9.

That kind of commitment was recognised by the Welsh management when he was appointed captain in 1981, Wales slipping to defeats; 23-5 by France at Narbonne, and 17-4 by England at Hull KR.

John Bevan's Wales career closed with his appearance, as captain, in the side that faced the Australian 'Invincibles' of 1982, Wales suffering the fate of most other host sides on that trip in losing heavily, in their case 37-7 before 5,617 supporters at Cardiff. The winger, meanwhile, made six appearances for Great Britain, earning selection for the 1974 tour to Australia and making his full international debut on 15 June in the First Test at Brisbane.

Great Britain lost the game, which was watched by 30,280 folk, 12-6 and Bevan missed out for the Second Test, which the Lions won 16-11 before 48,006 residents of Sydney and its environs. Bevan was back in the side for the deciding Third Test, at Sydney, when 55,505 folk watched Australia retain the Ashes with a hard-fought 22-18 win.

The winger played in the First and Third Tests of the New Zealand leg of the tour. He scored a try in the opener, which resulted in a 13-8 defeat at Auckland before a 10,466 crowd, and he crossed twice in the Third Test – the decider after Great Britain had beaten the Kiwis 17-8 in the 'middle' game. Those two touchdowns helped the Lions to a 20-0 victory, before 11,574 at Auckland, which sealed the Series.

John Bevan didn't play for Great Britain again, however, until the 1978 Ashes Series. The Warrington winger scored a try in the First Test, at Wigan, but it wasn't enough to prevent a 15-9 defeat. Missing out on the Second Test – the notable win at Odsal – he was recalled for the all-important Third Test at a packed Headingley, Leeds. He again contributed a try to the cause, as did Hull KR stand-off Roger Millward; but the Kangaroos, in easing to a 23-6 victory, served notice that they were about to enter a period of dominance.

Bevan continued to serve Warrington well, helping guide the Wire to triumph in the John Player Trophy in 1980-81.

Warrington were faced with something of a banana skin when they went out at Central Park, Wigan to face a 12,820 crowd (a record, at that time, for the competition) and Barrow who, with the likes of former Rugby Union centre Ian Ball, one-time Leeds stand-off Mel Mason, and fearsome hooker Eddie Szymala – not to mention a certain Dave Chisnall – in their ranks, were riding the crest of a wave.

The Cumbrians, who spent much of the season battling against relegation from Division One, were the surprise packets of the competition and arrived at Wigan in confident mood, giving Warrington a real fright before the Wire edged the issue 12-5. Bevan was a key figure in the victory, claiming both his side's tries in a game in which second row Tommy Martyn picked up the man of the match award. Fullback Steve Hesford was also influential, contributing two goals and a couple of drop goals, while Barrow could hold their heads up high after posting a Mason try and a Ball goal.

A little over five years later Bevan, one of the most wholehearted of Warrington's many enthusiastic captures from Welsh Rugby Union, retired in his mid-thirties, bringing the curtain down on a rousing career with a trademark outing in the 8-4 win over Oldham on 2 February 1986, shoulder and arm injuries compelling him to call it a day. He reflected:

A few clubs were after me when I was still in Rugby Union, and I was extremely lucky in opting for Warrington, because it turned out to be a tremendous place. Having such fine players around me gave me the confidence I needed to enjoy my game and, even when things weren't always going right they and the supporters, who were wonderful, always stuck by me.

I have to admit that we were quite a tough team in the 1970s, particularly, and I was glad to be playing alongside some of those blokes rather than opposite them. I don't think I'd have lasted 13 seasons otherwise!

14

Kevin Ashcroft

KEVIN ASHCROFT, a larger than life character, can be seen in various ways. The hooker has been the subject of several iconic photographs of major events in Rugby League, notably of post-match celebration, when he appeared to draw the attention of cameramen as if he were a magnet. That unbridled joy at success, whether expected or merely hoped for, was perhaps one of the reasons that Alex Murphy acquired his services: firstly at Leigh, were the pair tasted the glory of the win over Leeds at Wembley in 1970-71, and again at Warrington, where Ashcroft enjoyed similar, if more sustained, success.

While Ashcroft could be viewed, perhaps, as a faithful lieutenant to Murphy's generalship, he was certainly an accomplished leader in his own right, as he proved on retirement, when he took the reins successfully at Leigh, Salford and Warrington.

A hooker of vision and skill, his hopes as an enthusiastic youngster of being snapped up by his hometown team Leigh came to nothing, at least initially, but word of his promise had spread further afield, and he fetched up across the Pennines, at Dewsbury, where he was enticed by the Welsh coach Gwyn Davies. Crown Flatt failed to galvanise the youngster, who switched to Rochdale Hornets, where he began to make a real impact. His first appearance on the major stage was in the Lancashire Cup Final of 1965-66, when Hornets forced their way through to the Red Rose decider and a meeting with, ironically, Warrington.

The majority of neutrals in the crowd were undoubtedly rooting for a Rochdale outfit that had not appeared in a major final since 1921-22, when the Challenge Cup had been won with a 10-9 victory over Hull at Leeds. There was to be no such luck this time for Hornets, who lost 16-5 to the Wire. Ashcroft, however, had made folk sit up and take notice with a series of fine displays at the Athletic Grounds and beyond, including one Alex Murphy.

Murphy, on switching to Leigh from St Helens in 1966, made it his business to get Ashcroft on board as a singularly enthusiastic centrepiece of his pack. Ashcroft revealed, in John Huxley's *The Rugby League Challenge Cup*:

> More signings came after me, and once the men became touched by our increasing team spirit the ball just started rolling along.
>
> We were not a particularly great footballing team but we were fully committed and played for each other.
>
> When the 1971 Challenge Cup came around I couldn't have predicted what was going to happen but each time we overcame a team I started to believe that we were in with a chance of going all the way to Wembley.

Leigh didn't have it easy en route to the Twin Towers, accounting for Bradford Northern, Widnes and Hull before setting up a semi-final with Huddersfield.

14,875 showed up at Central Park, Wigan, for the game, which Leigh won 10-4 to mark a first appearance in the Challenge Cup Final since 1920-21 and, of course, a first visit to Wembley.

Leeds, who had beaten Castleford 19-8 in the other semi-final, at Odsal Stadium, Bradford before a 24,464 crowd, were viewed as hot favourites – despite having finished third in the league that season to Leigh's fourth, and despite lacking international stand-off Mick Shoebottom, who had sustained what would be a career-ending injury a couple of weeks earlier in a game against Salford. The Loiners were also without scheming loose forward Ray Batten and powerhouse winger Alan Smith.

In those circumstances, a Leigh win was not perhaps such a major surprise, although their hopes were hit when 21-year-old packman David Chisnall was ruled out through suspension.

The Lancastrians were certain, under Murphy, to make the most of any opportunities that came their way and had a goal-kicker, in Welshman Stuart Ferguson, the former Swansea RU winger, who would certainly make the Loiners pay for any transgressions. They also had the backing of a local spiritualist, Mrs Helen Smith, who revealed to a doubtful reception, 'Over the last fortnight I have received pictures of Alex Murphy holding the Cup no less than three times, and I keep getting the figures of 4 and 2'.

Those figures represented Leigh's total, on the day, of 24. More importantly, Leeds only scored seven points in a game in which the Loiners were kept at bay until the closing seconds, when stand-off

Tony Wainwright claimed an obstruction try. That score came far too late to rescue Leeds, who, by that stage, were 24-2 down and had lost Syd Hynes, who had been sent off after an incident which led to Murphy being stretchered off. Arguments have raged ever since as to whether Murphy was shamming, and whether the Leeds centre deserved to be the first man to be dismissed in a Challenge Cup Final at Wembley.

The agenda was set as early as the fifth minute, when prop Jim Fiddler landed a drop goal in line with Murphy's maxim of 'never come away without anything'. Ferguson added a penalty six minutes later and, with the Leigh pack getting on top as loose forward Peter Smethurst led by example, the game went further away from Leeds when centre Stan Dorrington raced over off a Murphy ball. The conversion, by Ferguson, was quickly followed by a Murphy drop goal, slammed over from 30 yards out, and a heady half ended with Ferguson kicking his third goal for a 13-0 lead.

Fullback John Holmes opened Leeds' account with a penalty eight minutes after the restart – a score that was quickly wiped out by another drop goal by Murphy. That effort, in the fifty-sixth minute, was followed in the next 12 minutes by a Ferguson penalty and, after Hynes' dismissal, a drop goal by fullback David Eckersley. Eckersley, who had moved up to stand-off when Murphy went off, closed his side's account with a bustling touchdown, Ferguson adding the extras, before Holmes improved Wainwright's last-gasp try.

Murphy collected the Lance Todd Trophy for his performance, while Hynes said, 'I tackled Murphy and I thought that was that. He just fell back and was laughing. I could not believe I had been given my marching orders.'

Ashcroft, meanwhile, revealed that the game had effectively been won the day before. A member of Great Britain's World Cup squad from the previous year, he had been surprised when none of the Leeds players who had been his team-mates in that side wanted to talk when the sides were strolling around Wembley on the Friday afternoon. He said:

They just couldn't bring themselves to speak to us, and you could see the tension written all over their faces. We went back to our hotel and the relaxed air went with us. Of course we were nervous, but we weren't frightened. We'd seen enough, especially when Leeds turned up at Wembley for their walkabout in jeans and leather jackets. We were in our official suits, and we looked and felt like a million dollars. By contrast, they hardly looked like a professional sports team. For some reason, the press had written us off. Alex didn't need to motivate us; he just showed us the press cuttings. We would have beaten anybody in the world that day. Everything we tried came off.

He added,

People always point to Sid Hynes' dismissal as being a key moment in that game, but we had the match won before he walked.

When Alex Murphy moved on to Warrington, almost before the champagne corks had finished popping, it was natural that several of his acolytes would follow him from Hilton Park to Wilderspool. Prop Dave Chisnall, the man whose moment of madness, leading to his suspension, had caused him to miss out on one of the most glorious of Challenge Cup Finals, was one of them. Kevin Ashcroft was another, although the lad from Leigh encountered pause for thought before making the move. Eventually, Ashcroft concluded that the chance of further domestic honours would be higher at Warrington than at Leigh; and subsequent events proved him to be correct. Not, though, without having played one last season for his beloved Leigh. The side lost its grip on the Challenge Cup, but not without a battle.

The tough Cumbrian outfit Workington Town were seen off 19-4 in the first round, at Hilton Park, but Swinton edged a tight second round clash, again at Hilton Park, 4-3. Leigh, meanwhile, slipped from the heights of fourth in the league in the Wembley season to sixteenth. The side would rise slightly, to thirteenth, in the following campaign, serving some kind of notice that Kevin Ashcroft hadn't left them in the lurch when he agreed to follow Alex Murphy to Wilderspool.

Warrington paid Leigh a transfer fee of £7,000 – a decent enough figure for a player reaching the veteran stage – and Ashcroft quickly became vice-captain to Murphy. His impact was immediate. The Wire, who had finished fifteenth in the league in Alex Murphy's first season of 1971-72, shot through the ranks in 1972-73. Warrington headed the pile at the close of the campaign, winning 27 and drawing two of their 34 games to close with 56 points, two ahead of second-placed Featherstone Rovers.

Kevin Ashcroft made his debut for the Wire in the first league game of the season, the home fixture with Hull on Sunday 20 August 1972. Warrington won the game 31-20 and, after slipping 15-11 at St Helens a couple of days later, got back to winning ways with a 17-14 victory at Swinton and a 13-4 success at home, over Widnes, on Monday 28 August; an opening spell of four games in eight days for the enthusiastic part-timers of the age.

The side then lost 18-16 at home to St Helens – perennial bete noirs – in the first round of the Lancashire Cup, before accounting for Blackpool Borough at Borough Park (42-8) and Wigan at Wilderspool (26-7).

Defeat at Huddersfield in the first round of the Players' No 6 Trophy (which subsequently became the Regal Trophy) was perhaps no bad thing for a team with league glory now firmly in its sights,

Revenge was secured six days later, also at Fartown, in the league and, before October was out, the 'double' had been posted over Barrow, with Rochdale Hornets and Workington Town seen off between-times.

That month closed with a draw against Widnes in the BBC2 Floodlit Trophy, the Chemics winning the replay 14-11 in another result that was, perhaps, advantageous to Warrington.

Meanwhile, the league procession continued unabated for the Wire, who had beaten York at home, and edged Whitehaven away 12-11, before that mid-November reverse at Widnes.

1972 closed with victories over Salford, Huddersfield, Whitehaven (58-9, in a remarkable change in fortunes for the Cumbrians), and Hull, with only Leigh putting a dent in the momentum with a 6-6 draw at Wilderspool on Boxing Day.

Oldham were seen off 20-10 at home on New Year's Eve, and 1973 opened with league victories over Huyton and Swinton before Halifax were pipped 7-4 at Thrum Hall in the first round of the Challenge Cup, thanks to a try by Welshman Clive Jones and a couple of goals by Derek Whitehead; Halifax were limited to two penalties by David Willicombe.

Retribution was gained against St Helens for the two early-season reverses with a 13-11 success in the league in early February, and that victory was followed by a 20-8 traducing of Widnes, at Wilderspool, in the second round of the Challenge Cup. Ashcroft and Dennis Curling scored the Wire's tries, before a 16,000 crowd, and Derek Whitehead landed five goals. Dennis Brown and Eric Hughes replied for Widnes, and Mal Aspey kicked a conversion.

The heady heights of that win were followed, seven days later, by perhaps the upset of the season, a 17-5 home reverse at the hands of Rochdale Hornets in the league; although Hornets would finish eleventh in the ratings, and thus qualify for the newly-launched First Division in 1973-74.

A rare second defeat on the trot followed that setback, Warrington losing to Featherstone Rovers at Wilderspool in the quarter-finals of the Challenge Cup. Rovers, who went on to beat Bradford Northern in the final at Wembley, progressed to the semi-finals with tries by Mike Smith and Mel Mason, supported by five goals by Cyril Kellett and one by Steve Nash. The Wire had to concede, despite thrilling their fans in the 15,600 crowd with tries by Derek Noonan and Brian Brady (a man rated by many opponents, incidentally, as perhaps the best prop around, despite his lack of representative honours), and four Whitehead goals.

While the Challenge Cup was undoubtedly a key target for Murphy's men, the saving grace was that attention could be focussed entirely on league football. Warrington embarked on a run of seven games without defeat, broken only by a 16-16 draw at Workington, in which Huyton, Oldham, Dewsbury (at Wilderspool), Salford, York and Wigan were accounted for.

The sequence was brought to a halt at Crown Flatt where Dewsbury gained revenge for the 23-19 defeat at Warrington with an 18-14 win in mid-April.

Blackpool Borough were put to the sword, 51-20, only two days later, but the Wire's league season closed with defeat at Widnes and Leigh, in the space of three days.

Warrington and Kevin Ashcroft, however, had already done enough to secure the League Leader's Shield. And with that came guaranteed home advantage in the Top 16 Play-offs.

Wigan presented few problems in the first round, Warrington winning 30-15 with the help of two tries each by Bobby Wanbon and Curling, with veteran Tommy Conroy and Noonan also crossing and Whitehead landing five goals. Ashcroft also landed a drop goal for good measure in a match in which Stuart Wright bagged a brace for Wigan and Bill Francis touched down, with Bill Ashurst (2) and James Nulty kicking the goals.

Rochdale Hornets weren't able to repeat their league win in the next round, conceding tries by Frank Reynolds and Dave Chisnall, together with four Whitehead goals and one for Wilf Briggs, in a

16-9 defeat. Albert Hillman – a Warrington lad – replied for Hornets, with Bill Holliday kicking two goals and Peter Gartland one.

Warrington's season ended seven days later when Dewsbury arrived at Wilderspool for the Championship semi-final. A crowd of 9,810 watched Dewsbury, captained by Great Britain hooker Mick Stephenson and coached by former Featherstone loose forward Tommy Smales – and including the likes of a young Jeff Grayshon, Nigel Stephenson, Allan Agar and the Bates brothers, Alan and John, in their ranks – win 12-7. Fullback Adrian Rushton and Nigel Stephenson got the Yorkshire outfit's tries, and Nigel Stephenson, Agar and prop Trevor Lowe landed the goals. Warrington, meanwhile, had to settle for a Noonan try and two Whitehead goals in a season that, nevertheless, had been highly successful.

Dewsbury went on to win the championship with a stunning 22-13 win over Leeds at Odsal in one of the most memorable of championship finals. Kevin Ashcroft, meanwhile, could reflect on a tremendous debut campaign in which he made 41 appearances – bettered only by Dave Chisnall, who had 42 outings – scoring an impressive 13 tries to come fourth in the club's list, behind Wilf Briggs (23), Curling (16) and Brian Gregory (15), and kicking six goals.

Warrington, for their part, had established the platform for what was to be one of the Wire's finest seasons. The side went into the 1973-74 campaign with one trophy on the sideboard, and closed it with four.

Several pundits have volunteered that, in describing that season, it's simpler and easier to detail what Warrington DIDN'T win. The silverware that eluded the Wire included the Championship – won by Salford in the first season of the 'Two Division' era, with Warrington closing at fifth, on 33 points, 14 points adrift of the Red Devils' total of 47. Warrington also missed out on the Lancashire Cup, which was won by a Wigan outfit that accounted for Salford 19-9 in the decider – although the Wire did have some involvement, Wilderspool hosting the final.

The BBC2 Floodlit Trophy, meanwhile, went most memorably to Bramley, who magically saw off all-comers, including St Helens in the semi-final and Widnes in the decider (played at Naughton Park during the day, because of continuing industrial action on a national basis).

The Wire, though, collected everything else: the Challenge Cup, the Club Championship (introduced to emulate the drama of the

Championship Play-offs, and to be replaced after a single year by the Premiership Play-offs), the Players' No. 6 Trophy, and the Captain Morgan Trophy. Kevin Ashcroft was, in his inimitably ebullient style, a key figure in each success.

Warrington were up against it at half-time in the Challenge Cup Final against Featherstone Rovers, finding themselves 9-8 down and having lost scrum-half Parry Gordon and stand-off Alex Murphy through injury. It was Ashcroft who got the show back on the road – with a little help from his mentor, Murphy, who opted to return to the fray with the help of pain-killing injections. With only three minutes of the second half gone, Murphy put centre Derek Noonan through a gap, and Ashcroft was on hand to dive over for a vital try which, with fullback Derek Whitehead's conversion, put a different perspective on a contest that Warrington went on to win 24-9.

He packed down in the 27-16 Players' No. 6 Trophy Final win over his old cub Rochdale Hornets, and was in the side that lifted the Club Championship by beating St Helens 13-12 at Wigan, before over 18,000 supporters. Mike Philbin, Brian Brady and Derek Noonan crossed for Warrington, with Derek Whitehead adding a couple of goals. Kel Coslett converted both of Frank Wilson's tries for the Saints, and landed a penalty in a game of missed drop goals, with Murphy and Ashcroft being wide with a total of nine attempts, and Coslett having a 40-yard effort miss the target at the death.

Ashcroft, meanwhile, was at his bustling best in the Captain Morgan Trophy Final win over Featherstone Rovers, in which two goals by Derek Whitehead were the only scores.

The next season was to be his last as a player, with his grand finale a second successive appearance in the Challenge Cup Final. Warrington lost the game, against old rivals Widnes, 14-7, despite having led throughout the opening quarter.

Kevin Ashcroft's career had closed in defeat, with a mid-season reverse at the hands of Salford, after a replay, in the BBC2 Floodlit Trophy, also in the last-season mix. Ashcroft, however, will be recalled, as a player, as a winner who won with an endearing smile on his face. And a winner of some class, as evidenced by his six Great Britain caps. The hooker earned his first five while with Leigh, and not at a time when the Hilton Park outfit, although strong enough, was exactly carrying everything along before it.

Leigh finished seventh in 1967-68, but Ashcroft had impressed enough to get the call-up by Great Britain for the 1968 World Cup, held in Australia and New Zealand. He appeared in the opening match, against Australia at the Sydney Cricket Ground, a game that was lost 25-10 before a 62,256 crowd. The Kangaroos only registered three tries to the Lions' two, with scrum-half Billy Smith, second row Ron Coote and loose forward Johnny Raper crossing in response to touchdowns by Wakefield Trinity winger Ian Brooke and Hull winger Clive Sullivan, but Australia fullback Eric Simms made the most of a heavy penalty count in his side's favour to land eight goals, while Great Britain and Leeds fullback Bev Risman, the captain, had to settle for two successes from limited opportunities.

Ashcroft didn't play in the last two games, in which France won 7-2 in Auckland, and New Zealand prevailed 38-14 in Sydney. He was, however, back in the line up when Great Britain met France at St Helens the following November, scoring a try in a 34-10 victory in which Barrow winger Bill Burgess claimed a hat-trick, Hull centre Dick Gemmell – a future tour manager – bagged a brace, with winger Alan Burwell (Hull KR) and Halifax second row Colin Dixon also sweeping in; Wakefield Trinity centre Neil Fox kicked five goals.

Ashcroft was a member of the side that lost 13-9 at Toulouse in the return, Fox landing three goals and Dixon again crossing, but missed out on the Ashes-winning tour of Australia in 1970. He was, however, selected for that autumn's World Cup, in England.

Bradford Northern's Tony Fisher got the nod for Britain's opening game, in which Australia were beaten 11-4 at Headingley, Leeds through a try and a goal by Leeds centre Syd Hynes, with Widnes fullback Ray Dutton kicking three goals; Simms and centre Bobby Fulton landed a penalty apiece for the Kangaroos before 15,084 folk.

Ashcroft donned the number 9 shirt for the 6-0 win over France at Castleford, where 8,958 souls watched Dutton kick three goals. He retained the berth for the tilt with New Zealand at Swinton, watched by 5,609, in which Great Britain completed a 100 per cent record with a 27-17 verdict involving tries by Hynes, Salford centre Chris Hesketh, Leeds winger John Atkinson, St Helens' cockney prop Cliff Watson and Wigan loose forward Doug Laughton, Dutton adding six goals. Captain Fletcher Christian – a descendent of the hero of 'Mutiny on the Bounty' – second row Garry Smith and loose forward Tony Kriletich replied for the Kiwis and fullback Don Ladner fired four goals.

Having won all their games – and with Australia, France and New Zealand having won just a single match apiece – Great Britain lost in the final, the Kangaroos grinding out a 12-7 win before 18,776 on a windy afternoon at Headingley, Leeds. Leeds winger John Atkinson claimed Britain's only try, with Dutton and Hynes each kicking a goal. Australia prevailed through tries by winger Lionel Williamson, and centre John Cootes, Simms adding three goals.

Kevin Ashcroft, who missed out to Fisher for that game, slipped out of the international scene, until 1974, when – as a Warrington player – he was called up for the tour of Australia and New Zealand.

Featherstone Rovers' Keith Bridges was selected for the First Test, in Australia, with John Gray, of Wigan, being picked for the last two Tests in that country, and for the three in New Zealand. Ashcroft, though, was selected as a substitute for the First Test in New Zealand, which the Lions lost 13-8 in Auckland, despite tries by Warrington's John Bevan and Featherstone Rovers scrum-half Steve Nash, one of which Oldham prop Terry Clawson converted.

Coming on for Featherstone's Jim Thompson, it was Kevin Ashcroft's last appearance for his country. Seven months later, he would bring the curtain down on his domestic career, again in a high profile match, in the Challenge Cup Final defeat by Widnes. His career record with Warrington comprised 123 games, plus one as a substitute, in which he scored 20 tries and 23 drop goals – including the first single-pointer for the Wire, following the reduction in value from two points – for a total of 101 points.

In June 1975 he returned to Leigh as player/coach, making 34 appearances in 1975-76 and scoring three tries and three drop goals. He guided the team to promotion from Division Two, finishing fourth behind Barrow, Rochdale Hornets and Workington Town, and edging Hull FC on points' difference.

He also steered Leigh to the quarter-finals of the Challenge Cup. He was a try-scorer in the 37-8 first round win over amateur side Pointer Panthers, of Castleford, who were in the competition as Yorkshire Cup winners and who posted four goals by Ian Murray before a crowd of 2,170.

Doncaster were seen off in the second round, 29-6, and Leigh had a great opportunity to reach the semi-finals when they were drawn at Keighley, who were battling unsuccessfully against relegation from Division One, in the quarter-finals.

A 7,000 crowd at Lawkholme Lane saw Keighley win 13-7 after the sides had been locked at 2-2 at the interval; Keighley subsequently went very close to booking a place at Wembley, losing 5-4 to St

Helens in the semi-final at Huddersfield before 9,829 folk, hitting back from a 5-0 interval deficit with a penalty and two drop goals by charismatic fullback Brian Jefferson. Prior to the reduction in the value of the drop goal, Keighley would have won the game 6-5.

Kevin Ashcroft remained at the helm at Hilton Park until 1977, setting the platform for the side's promotion from Division Two, as champions, in 1977-78. Along the way, he guided the team to the 1976-77 BBC2 Floodlit Trophy Final, in which Leigh faced Castleford at Hilton Park before a 5,402 crowd. Castleford, traditionally the top dogs of the Floodlit Trophy, having won the competition in its first three years in the mid-sixties, were too strong on the night, winning 12-4 through tries by winger James Walsh and stand-off Bruce Burton, with second row Sammy Lloyd kicking three goals. Leigh posted a try by centre Joe Walsh in response; and, typically in a final, Ashcroft landed a drop goal.

Ashcroft, after a three-year sabbatical, moved on to Salford, coaching the side between November 1980 and March 1982. The Red Devils were relegated, as the third-from-bottom side, from the top flight in 1980-81, and finished fifth in Division Two the following season. Kevin Ashcroft left in March, before the end of the campaign, to return to Wilderspool as Head Coach, winning the Lancashire Cup the following October. He left Warrington in the summer of 1984 for another stint at Salford, steering the Willows outfit to promotion this time. He remained in charge at Salford until October 1989.

The highlight of his second spell at the Willows was an appearance in the Lancashire Cup Final in 1988-89, earned with a 15-2 home win over Warrington at the penultimate stage in which the Wire were limited to a Robert Turner penalty, Salford progressing through tries by Keith Bentley and Tex Evans, with Adrian Hadley landing three goals and Bentley chipping in with a drop goal.

The Red Devils met a Wigan outfit arguably reaching its peak in the decider. If one side was able to upset the Pie Eaters during the period of Wigan's dominance, however, it was Salford who, under Ashcroft, tested the Central Park outfit more than most; Ashcroft's team almost staged an upset, losing only 22-17 before a 19,154 crowd at St Helens.

Wigan owed their victory to a three-try blitz in a five-minute spell towards the close, with Salford hitting back from 22-9 to rattle Wigan with late tries by Bentley and Steve Herbert, both courtesy of New Zealand prop Peter Brown, whose wayward goalkicking – with only two successes from seven attempts – cost Salford dear. The Red Devils also missed suspended Australian fullback Steve Gibson, while the loss of captain Peter Williams with concussion was a further blow. Evans scored Salford's opening try, and Mick Worrall kicked a drop goal, while Wigan won through two tries and three goals by Kiwi centre Kevin Iro and touchdowns for fellow New Zealanders Adrian Shelford and Dean Bell. The defeat, however, was honourable, the team mirroring Kevin Ashcroft's unquenchable spirit.

15

Mike Gregory

BLOND locks flowing – as much as they could, given the trademark strapping around his head – features etched with determination, and with every ounce of his athletic body committed to the task in hand, his focus totally on the demands of the moment, Mike Gregory was the epitome of the ideal Rugby League player. The image of the Warrington loose forward steaming away from the Kangaroos defence in Great Britain's victory in the Third Test of the 1988 tour of Australia – the Lions' first win in 16 games against the old enemy – is among the most iconic of that decade, while it was almost equally impossible for Gregory to appear anything other than Adonis-like, however he was captured in camera.

Mike Gregory served Warrington with distinction for nearly 12 years, from his debut against Huyton in September 1982, through to his final game, against Leeds, in February 1994. During that time he earned the enduring affection and admiration of Wire fans who, as Gregory related in his book *Biting Back* were – and remain – unfailingly appreciative of players of his ilk who were ready, always, to give everything to the Warrington cause.

Perhaps the most remarkable aspect of Mike Gregory's playing career, however (and perhaps of a life most cruelly cut short) is, apart from his propensity to suffer injuries, the fact that he played for Warrington at all. A Wigan lad born with an ironic nod to his future position in the game at 13 Mitchell Street, Pemberton (his grandparents' home) Gregory had no thought as he came through the ranks of playing for anyone other than his hometown club. Wigan, though, declined to show any interest in a major young talent operating right under their noses until it was too late, Warrington having beaten off Salford and St Helens for his services largely through the huge impression made on the prodigal youngster by former player and club stalwart Jackie Melling; and by the fact that the Wire were, at the time, operating without a recognised loose forward, Welsh winger John Bevan filling in at the base of the pack.

Mike Gregory saw, in that scenario, a potentially quick route to the first-team, and he was to have no regrets after putting pen to paper at Wilderspool on 8 June 1982, even when Wigan got in touch days afterwards after hearing the news. The Wire were, in snaring Gregory, acquiring a player who had added, at the age of 15 or so, a mean streak – a readiness to play 'dirty' even, if required – through an incident in a training session with his school team, St John Fisher, which appeared to transform his personality, on the field of play at least.

Prior to that injury, incurred when the team's captain, Mike Hancock, upended him in a perfectly fair tackle, fracturing his collarbone in two places, Gregory had been a hard-working, back row forward, blessed with some pace and plenty of commitment but lacking, on his own admission, a 'nasty' side. That changed on his return – for no readily explicable reason, as Gregory recounted in his autobiography *Biting Back*. Shortly afterwards, playing for the Wigan Under 15s Town team against Oldham, Gregory was sent off for the first time in his Rugby League career after an altercation involving an opponent sparked a mass brawl.

The injury at training may have had something to do with his change of attitude and, possibly, with the abiding and painful memory of having missed out on an appearance in the Schoolboy curtain–raiser to the 1975 Challenge Cup Final between Widnes and, ironically, Warrington at Wembley (now named the Steven Mullaney Memorial Match, in memory of the player who was killed in a motor accident only months after having shone in the 1986 game). That was an all-too early experience, for Mike Gregory, of the anguish that can face all sportsmen who are denied their place in the limelight through injury.

The youngster had been looking forward with huge anticipation to turning out for Wigan Schools against Widnes Schools in the first of what has become a memorable aspect of the Wembley occasion, only to break a toe in the weeks before the match. He recounted in *Biting Back*:

> I was devastated, as it's every boy's dream to play at Wembley. I've always had injuries at the worst times, but this was a particularly bitter pill to swallow. I wasn't allowed to walk out with the team, but I was allowed to sit on our substitutes' bench. We lost the game 8-0 and came back home the same day on the coach with the Widnes lads.

That episode could perhaps have been behind Gregory's thinking when he chose to play in the 1989 Challenge Cup semi-final at Maine Road, Manchester, hiding a debilitating hand injury which had been self-inflicted in extraordinary circumstances less than 24 hours earlier. Gregory, for some reason, had found himself in Blackpool with friends the previous day, fetching up at the Pleasure Beach where he was unable to resist the temptation to have a go on one of the punchbag diversions which are spread around the site. He mistimed his punch and realised immediately that he had damaged his hand; with one of the most important games of his career beckoning the next day.

A couple of injections and an expanse of strapping enabled Mike Gregory to play in the game, but with restricted movement; worse, the cause of the injury wasn't divulged to coach Brian Johnson until a few days after the game, which ended in a defeat caused largely by an astonishing drop goal measured at 61 yards by Wigan fullback Joe Lydon – an old friend of Mike Gregory's, who 18 years later would be a pall-bearer at Gregory's funeral.

The score, registered when the game was very much in the balance, was worth much more than its face value of a single point and Wigan went on to book a place at Wembley with a 13-6 victory in which Lydon, the clear man of the match, also scored a try and two goals to help his side to the second of what was to be an eight-year sojourn at Wembley.

Warrington, who had not appeared at the Twin Towers since the 1974-75 defeat at the hands of neighbours Widnes, were left to hope for another day, while Mike Gregory vowed to never again put himself at risk so carelessly prior to a game. He could, however, at least console himself with the knowledge that his parents had been told, when he was just four years old, that he would be unable to ever play contact sports, following a fall from a slide while visiting family in London, his treatment for a broken jaw continuing to the age of 14.

The wait for an appearance at Wembley wasn't to last for too long, however. The Wire, and Mike Gregory, reached the Challenge Cup Final 12 months later. Warrington, who finished eighth in the league, battled their way through to the Empire Stadium to earn a tilt with Wigan in the decider.

Warrington, who had already won the Lancashire Cup that season – granting Gregory his first major trophy as captain, the loose forward having been made skipper in February 1988 – were unable to overcome a Wigan side that, as the only fulltime club in the country at the time, was becoming all-powerful and which also boasted many of the finest players of the era.

Wigan had reached Wembley by edging Hull KR 6-4 in the first round, winger David Marshall scoring the only try of a hard-fought game at Craven Park, before beating Maurice Bamford's Dewsbury 30-6 in a second round tie in which the Yorkshiremen, of Division Two, had been only 2-0 adrift shortly after half-time.

The Pie Eaters accounted for Wakefield Trinity 26-14, helped by an injury to Trinity's talismanic Australian Test loose forward Ray Price, who was carried off in the 37th minute with a back injury at a time when Wigan were only 12-10 ahead.

Wigan's luck, even if it was the reward for hard work and a never-say-die attitude, continued in the semi-final at Old Trafford, in which they and neighbours St Helens appeared to be heading for a 14-14 draw before captain and loose forward Ellery Hanley, with a little over a minute remaining, blasted his way past four defenders before sending second row Andy Goodway over the whitewash, Lydon adding the extras.

Warrington, meanwhile, had set their assault on the Challenge Cup in motion with a 20-12 first round success at Wilderspool over Featherstone Rovers, the side they had toppled in the abrasive 1973-74 final. The Wire had looked poised for a comfortable win when they went in at the break 17-0 ahead, only for Rovers to hit back forcibly in the second period. Gregory's try was crucial to Warrington's progress, while his workrate was also pivotal in the 12-10 quarter-final verdict at Odsal, where Bradford Northern scored two tries to one, Paul 'Rocky' Turner's four goals, including his conversion of Bob Jackson's touchdown, proving to be seminal.

The Wire had struggled to eliminate lowly Trafford Borough in the second round, having to overcome a 7-6 interval deficit before posting a 20-11 success, while Division Two outfit Oldham, the surprise packets of the competition, almost pulled off a major upset in the semi-finals, holding Warrington to a 10-6 scoreline at Wigan. Gregory and his team-mates owed a nod of gratitude to substitute Mark Thomas, who helped create tries in the second period for Martin Crompton and Mark Forster in a game in which Warrington were denied the services of scrum-half Paul Bishop through a freak accident in his home that morning, when he put his hand through a glass door.

Oldham, meanwhile, were left fuming when referee John Holdsworth ruled out what would have been an equalising try in the last minute, winger Paul Lord being deemed to be offside before pouncing on scrum-half Mike Ford's smart kick.

Warrington headed to Wembley aware that Wigan had won each of the two previous Challenge Cup Finals in comfortable fashion, having accounted for Halifax 32-12 in 1987-88, and St Helens 27-0 in 1988-89. The portents, therefore, suggested that Warrington could be in for similar treatment, and the 36-14 scoreline would suggest that. The Wire, however, offered stronger resistance than the result indicated – even if Wigan fell only a couple of points short of the record set by Wakefield Trinity in the 38-5 routing of injury-hit Hull in 1960 – before going down to a Wigan outfit that set a new record with three successive wins in Challenge Cup Finals. Neither side, nor the 77,729 fans present at the game, knew that Wigan would go on to record five more wins at Wembley, before Bradford Bulls and St Helens broke the spell by contesting the 1996 decider.

Ultimately, Warrington paid the penalty for an uncertain opening before Wembley's first all-seated crowd, Wigan scrum-half Andy Gregory (a former Wire favourite) making the most of that hesitancy by dominating proceedings to become the first player to win the Lance Todd Trophy twice at Wembley, thereby rubbing a little more salt into the wounds of a Wire outfit whose illustrious folk hero Gerry Helme had also secured the coveted award on a couple of occasions, although Helme's second nomination was for his display in the 1953-54 replay against Halifax at Odsal Stadium, Bradford.

Wigan's eleventh win in the Challenge Cup final set a new benchmark, as they extended the record for appearances in the most glittering of occasions to 20, and the most at Wembley to 16, which included a record 10 victories. It was, meanwhile, Andy Gregory's fifth winners' medal, including the two he had pocketed whilst at Widnes.

Warrington appeared, in the early stages, to be almost willing to stand back and admire Wigan's attempt to record these achievements; achievements perhaps earned by a willingness to battle through the pain barrier, epitomised by stand-off Shaun Edwards, who sustained a facial injury in the tenth minute but who refused to depart the fray until the closing stages, when he learned that he had suffered a double fracture of the eye socket and a depressed cheekbone; injuries which ruled him out of that summer's Great Britain tour to Papua New Guinea and New Zealand.

Wire scrum-half Paul Bishop was another central figure. The mercurial Bishop was wide with a couple of relatively simple penalty attempts, before landing a goal in the twenty-fifth minute after Wigan had gone eight points clear with a penalty by Lydon, who then improved a touchdown for second row Denis Betts, who steamed in for an opportunist score after a clearing kick by Bishop had been charged down.

Another Wigan try, this time by winger Mark Preston after another Warrington kick had gone wrong, helped Wigan stretch their advantage to 12 points as the interval approached, a Lydon penalty in the thirty-seventh minute putting the Pie Eaters firmly in control.

Mike Gregory, producing his best display of the season and setting a real captain's example in brushing aside the pain of an Achilles tendon problem that had plagued him throughout the campaign, immediately hauled his side back into the frame, sweeping in for a try after Bishop, who added the extras to reduce the interval deficit to 16-8, had broken the Wigan defence.

Any hopes Warrington may have harboured of forcing their way back into serious contention were dashed, however, when Wigan registered two quick tries after only thirteen minutes of the second period. Kiwi centre Kevin Iro grabbed the first, and Preston the second. Mike Gregory did his best to prevent that score, chasing back when Hanley broke clear and continuing to track back when his opposite number passed on to Edwards. Gregory caught the Wigan halfback, only for Edwards to feed the supporting Preston.

A touchdown for Hanley took Wigan clear as the game entered the closing quarter, and the Pie Eaters closed with a touchdown by Iro, who was unfortunate not to finish with a hat-trick (he would have been the first player to have done so at Wembley) after having another effort ruled out; the giant centre had scored two tries at Wembley for the third successive year, his total of six touchdowns being twice a many as any other player had scored at the famous ground. Between-times, Warrington at least had the satisfaction of registering a try by fullback David Lyon, who latched on to a superb break from the base of the scrum by Mike Gregory to race in from 40 metres, with centre Paul Darbyshire converting.

That defeat left the Wire with the Lancashire Cup unaccompanied on the Wilderspool sideboard. Warrington had swept to the final – their fourth Red Rose decider of the 1980s – with a series of emphatic victories, overcoming in quick succession Swinton, at home, 16-6,

Salford (away) 27-4, and Widnes, at Wilderspool, 28-6.

Warrington had earned the right to meet Oldham, of Division Two, in the final at St Helens, and perhaps the prospect of a runaway win for the Wire led to folk staying away, the crowd of 9,990 being way down on the 19,202 who had turned up to watch Warrington lose to Wigan at the same venue in 1985-86, and the 20,237 who paid to see the same two sides in the 1987-88 decider.

The Roughyeds had last won the Lancashire Cup in 1958-59 (beating St Helens 12-2 at Swinton before 38,790 fans in the third of three successive triumphs, 39,544 turning up at Wigan for the 10-3 verdict over St Helens in 1956-57 two years earlier, and 42,497 at Swinton, in the middle of the three games, to watch Oldham topple Wigan 13-8).

Warrington – who had seen off St Helens 5-4 at Wigan, in front of 39,237, in the year after Oldham's period of success – were inspired by Gregory, who was in the running for the Great Britain captaincy ahead of the home series against New Zealand following an injury to incumbent Ellery Hanley.

Feeding off Gregory's powerful raids, the Wire blasted to an early 12-point lead, stand-off Robert Turner converting tries by right centre Joe Ropati and left winger Mark Forster. Oldham, though, belied their status in the lower section to bounce back with touchdowns for left centre Richard Irving and right winger Steve Robinson, fullback Duncan Platt converting the first before retiring through injury, and right centre Gary Hyde the second.

Warrington, who had been limited to another Turner goal in response, were under the cosh until the intervention of Australian second row Bob Jackson. The former Fulham mainstay, enjoying a second spell at Wilderspool, halted Oldham's momentum with a stunning charge to the line from 30 metres.

A try from left winger Paul Lord, who had been unfortunate to have had a previous effort ruled out by Castleford referee Ray Tennant, meant that Warrington were unable to breathe easily, but a second score by Jackson eight minutes from time, courtesy of a well-timed pass by right-winger Des Drummond, and with Turner adding his fourth goal of an entertaining clash, put paid to Oldham's hopes.

The Lancashire Cup had given Mike Gregory his first taste of silverware, seven years earlier and while still in his first season. It couldn't have been any better for Gregory than when, in his inaugural 1982-83 campaign as a professional, he shared in the 16-0 success over St Helens, operating at loose forward in a final played at Wigan before a 6,462 crowd. His input was important from the first round stage, when he made his debut for Warrington in the home tie with Huyton. No one in the 2,042 crowd at Wilderspool that day could have predicted that they were witnessing the first game for the Wire of a man who would become one of the club's finest servants, but few could have left the ground unaware that they had witnessed a prodigious talent. That evidence came early in the game, the ball popping out of a scrum close to Huyton's line and Gregory opting to go on his own, successfully, down the blind side to open Warrington's account for the day and his own account for what was to prove to be a glittering career. Winger Phil Ford helped himself to a hat-trick in the 43-5 win, while second row Bob Eccles bagged a brace. Other tries went to centres Ronnie Duane and John Bevan and prop Tony Cooke, while fullback Steve Hesford chipped in with five goals and Duane three.

Gregory's next try for the club was also in the Lancashire Cup; but altogether more important, his score helping the Wire to a 16-14 victory over Oldham in a game played only four days after the Roughyeds had accounted for the Wire 22-12 at Watersheddings. Derek Finnigan grabbed Warrington's other try, and Hesford totalled five goals.

The exciting Fulham side of the early 1980s provided the opposition at the penultimate stage. The London outfit, invited to take part in the Lancashire Cup as a guest entry in similar fashion to the inclusion of Cumbrian sides Whitehaven and Workington Town, had reached the last four through a 20-8 home win over Swinton and a stunning 15-4 success at Wigan in which player/coach Reggie Bowden, Tony Gourley and John Crossley scored tries, with future Warrington player Steve Diamond landing three goals. Fulham returned to Wigan for the semi-final – and a meeting with Warrington, who were unable to stage the game at home because of the lack of working floodlights at the time at Wilderspool.

Warrington limited Fulham, this time, to tries by hooker John Dalgreen and winger Hussein M'Bsrki, with Diamond kicking a goal. The Wire duly booked their berth in the final with tries by Eccles, winger Mike Kelly and scrum-half and skipper Ken Kelly, with Hesford kicking four goals.

Gregory, therefore, was in his first final, and conscious after the euphoric win that his coaches, while a junior player at Wigan St

Patrick's, Tony Scahill and Jackie Melling, had offered him totally sound advice in recommending that he join Warrington, partly on the basis that he would quickly be offered a spot in the first team and possibly because both had played for the Wire.

The youngster's contribution to the cause that day at Wigan was largely defensive; and effective, given that a St Helens outfit boasting the talents of such as scrum-half Neil Holding, loose forward Harry Pinner and centres Roy Haggerty and Chris Arkwright was kept at bay in that 16-0 win.

Gregory duly paid tribute to such men as Melling, Scahill and Ray Unsworth, also at Wigan St Patrick's in his autobiography, stating:

> I was fortunate that Jackie and Ray were the coaches of the Under 17s side, and I was proud when they made me captain, because there were phenomenal players in that team.
> Talent was just oozing out of the side and it was the first time that we were really coached. We were learning about modern set-plays and game plans, who to run at, what moves we were putting on. For an amateur set-up, it was very professional.

Gregory also revealed that he realised he had much to learn when tackling Holding hard, expecting the scrum-half to stay crumpled on the ground. Holding, instead, got up as if nothing had happened and nonchalantly played the ball; possibly in a classic example of never letting the opposition know they have hurt you. Mike Gregory was also of that mindset, a factor which may have limited his career which, taking into account the Great Britain tours of Australia in 1988 and New Zealand in 1990, and Warrington's pioneering game against Wigan in Milwaukee in 1989, all prefaced by a stint with Aussie outfit Cronulla in 1987, went without respite for four years, putting extra strain on his body.

His playing career with Warrington didn't quite end where it had started, with a match against Huyton, but in a sense an era came to a close when Gregory played against Huyton's successors, Runcorn Highfield, in the first round of the Regal Trophy in the 1990-91 season; a competition Warrington went on to win. The game was a routine 33-7 success, and a tackle made on Gregory was equally routine, and innocuous. There was nothing routine, however, about the consequences. Gregory said:

It was a nothing tackle, in fact I think I did the damage before the tackle was made. I remember planting my right foot and I twisted my body to give the ball out to my right. As I twisted I felt an explosion in my right knee and then, after I had offloaded the ball, I got tackled. As I went down, the pain was excruciating.

Gregory, on his own admission, was never the same player again. All seemed well when, in a pre-season Locker Cup game against Wigan, he shot onto a well-timed pass by scrum-half Kevin Ellis and sped over the whitewash, leaving his old friend and rival Joe Lydon trailing in his wake. He was announced as man of the match, but was unable to get out of bed the following day, having been months out of the game.

His last match for Warrington was in the first round of the Challenge Cup, at Leeds, on February 1994; a match that ended in a 38-4 defeat.

Mike Gregory's career with the Wire, however, involved far more successes than disappointments, even allowing for defeat by Wigan in the 1985-86 Lancashire Cup Final, followed by a setback against Wigan in the Red Rose event's 1987-88 decider. Notably, Warrington featured in the Premiership Final in successive seasons, in 1985-86 and 1986-87.

Those finals, of a competition which had been introduced by the Rugby Football League with the aim of preserving the principle of the popular end-of-season play-offs – previously Top Four, and subsequently Top 16, and both as a means of settling the championship – following the introduction of two divisions in 1973-74, straddled the switch between single-game events, at various venues, and the popular 'double-header' event at Manchester United's Old Trafford ground.

The last of the 'nomadic' events took place at Elland road, the home of Hunslet, who rented the stadium from Leeds United soccer team. A crowd of 13,683 turned up for the Wire's 1985-86 meeting with a Halifax outfit which was in the middle of a heady spell under Australian coach Chris Anderson, having already secured the Division One championship. Twelve months later, the men from Thrum Hall would add the Challenge Cup to their trophy cabinet, with a dramatic victory over St Helens at Wembley.

Warrington, meanwhile, were coached by Tony Barrow, who had taken over the previous March from Reggie Bowden and who had appointed the notoriously committed Australian Test prop Les Boyd as his assistant. The Wire, who finished fourth in the table, were in superb form that day, particularly Boyd, who grabbed two tries in a real blockbusting display to pick up the Harry Sunderland Trophy as the man of the match.

Brian Johnson, who came on as a substitute, raced over direct from a drop-out in the emphatic 38-10 victory – a record for the Premiership Final, both in terms of the points' tally and the winning margin – earned on the back of an awesome pack which had a front row of Bob Jackson and Boyd, with Kiwi Kevin Tamati at hooker, with Gregory packing down behind the second row duo of Gary Sanderson and Mark Roberts, Billy McGinty later coming off the bench. Halfbacks Andy Gregory and Paul Bishop had the quality and enterprise to make the most of the strong platform established by one of the most robust packs around, and a threequarter line comprising Mark Forster, Paul Cullen, Ronnie Duane and Brian Carbert, with the enigmatic Welshman Phil Ford popping in to the line, was not to be sneezed at, and had proved its worth by battling through to the final with a 10-8 home win over Widnes, followed by a 23-12 semi-final victory at Wigan.

That success, which also involved a try and five goals by Bishop and touchdowns by Forster, Tamati and Jackson (with Halifax limited to a Chris Anderson touchdown and three goals by fullback Colin Whitfield), eased the anguish of the previous autumn's 34-8 defeat at the hands of Wigan in the Lancashire Cup Final, Warrington disappointing their fans in the 19,202 crowd at St Helens, with only a Brian Johnson try and a couple of goals by Carbert to show for an effort in which Gregory played in the second row, the enigmatic Alan Rathbone wearing the number 13 shirt.

It was Wigan who were to deny the Wire in the 1986-87 Premiership Final, taking the trophy off the Wilderspool outfit with an 8-0 victory before an Old Trafford crowd of 38,765 which fully vindicated the decision of Rugby Football League officials David Oxley and David Howes to introduce the concept of a 'double-headed' Premiership Final, also including the Division Two decider. The attendance, almost three times the previous year's, was close to 10,000 more than the previous highest of 29,448 that had turned up to watch Hull KR beat Hull 11-7 at Headingley, Leeds, in 1980-81.

Gregory and his colleagues watched Swinton – a team he would, ironically, subsequently coach – beat Division Two champions Hunslet 27-10 in the preliminary match.

There was to be no joy when the Wire took to the field themselves. Joe Lydon, so often Warrington's bête noire, was again the tormentor in chief in a game in which Gregory was on the substitute's bench, coming on in the second half for second row Tony Humphries. By that stage Warrington, who were hampered by the absence through injury of hooker Mark Roskell and stand-off Keith Holden, together with skipper Les Boyd, were 6-0 down, Lydon having beaten Des Drummond and the rest of the Wire defence to a telling kick by scrum-half Andy Gregory, who was a pivotal figure against his former club. Mark Roberts, standing in at number 9 for Roskell, lost the scrums 12-6, although Warrington could have made up for that through a 19-8 penalty count in their favour. A disallowed 'try' for second row Gary Sanderson early in the second period, hotly contested by the Wire camp, was the closest that Warrington came to opening their account, and a penalty by Lydon – who was the Harry Sunderland man of the match – sealed a momentous win for Wigan.

Warrington were also runners-up in the John Player Trophy that season, in what was a real 'bridesmaid' campaign. Wigan were, again, the stumbling block, halting Warrington's progress after a stuttering route to the decider at Bolton Wanderers in which the Wire had almost lost at home to Division Two title-chasers Hunslet in the first round, having hooker Kevin Tamati sent off and trailing 10-6 at half-time to tries by Jed Coates and Jimmy Irvine, plus an Alan Platt goal, before scraping an 11-10 win with the help of three goals and a drop goal by Bishop.

Halifax, who dropped fullback Colin Whitfield and scrum-half Gary Stephens for being late for training, were beaten 44-10 in the second round, and the Wire, ahead 14-8 at half-time in the quarter-final at St Helens, subsequently found themselves behind before snatching a 22-20 verdict with a late touchdown for former St Helens winger Kevin Meadows.

Warrington, however, hit top form to ease to a 35-4 semi-final win over Widnes in which fullback Brian Johnson and centre Paul Cullen bagged a brace apiece; that ascendancy, however, wasn't to be repeated in the final itself, despite the pre-match perception that the Wire were favourites to prevail.

Coach Tony Barrow had steered his side to a winning run of 14 games, including the 'double' over Wigan, against whom Warrington had been unbeaten in their previous four meetings. Only nine days before the final the Wire had ground out a 6-4 verdict over the Pie

Eaters at Central Park, earned with a Cullen try and a Bishop goal and, as such, were strongly fancied to add to their sequence. That rating was, perhaps, the spur that the full-timers of Wigan needed. Burnden Park, which boasted undersoil heating, and which was hosting a major Rugby League game for the first time, witnessed a closely-fought first half in front of 21,144 spectators (the third-highest crowd in the competition's history) before the Pie Eaters pulled away in the second period for an 18-4 success.

Without Bishop, who had been suspended following his dismissal, together with the Chemics' Paul Hulme, in the semi-final, the Wire were already hampered, but were nevertheless on level terms at the interval at 4-4. Great Britain winger Henderson Gill had opened Wigan's account, but Mike Gregory was a central figure in the response, breaking clear off a pass by hooker Kevin Tamati before feeding supporting scrum-half Steve Peters. Peters' pass to Mark Forster was collected superbly by the winger, who had to reach low before diving over in the corner.

Tamati, however, was unable to resume in the second period, having suffered a hamstring injury, while captain and prop Les Boyd had a rare off-day. Second row man Mark Roberts, switched to hooker in Tamati's absence, performed superbly for his side, winning the scrums in the last 40 minutes 5-1, but Wigan were to dominate affairs in the loose. Gill grabbed his second score, popping up in midfield to throw an outrageous dummy which bamboozled the Wire defence. With the game still in the balance on the hour, a chip by Warrington fullback Brian Johnson which could, if slightly better flighted, have led to a try, was intercepted by Wigan loose forward Andy Goodway, who sprinted clear over 65 metres for the game's seminal score. Gill's conversion put the Cherry & Whites 10 points clear, and there was no way back for Warrington when New Zealand centre Dean Bell swept over in the closing seconds.

Mike Gregory's playing career at Warrington, therefore, closed with three winners' medals – for the 1982-83 and 1989-90 Lancashire Cup, and the 1985-86 Premiership. He had collected five runners-up medals, for the Lancashire Cup in 1985-86 and 1987-88, the John Player Trophy and Premiership in 1986-87, and, of course, the Challenge Cup in 1989-90. Meanwhile, Warrington had never finished lower than eleventh (on three occasions, in his first season of 1982-83, in 1984-85, and in 1988-89). The Wire's highest rating in that spell was third, in 1983-84 and 1986-87.

Gregory's contribution to that highly-satisfactory record was immense, and was recognised by his record of 19 Great Britain caps, plus one as substitute. He made his international debut in 1987, in Great Britain's 52-4 win over France at Headingley, Leeds (a game that, apart from being the regular annual fixture between the two countries, was also a World Cup game), and closed it in 1990, as a substitute against Australia in the 14-0 defeat at Elland Road in the series-deciding Third Test, a match which doubled as a World Cup match.

Along the way, he achieved arguably the highlight of his career, when he was captain of the Great Britain side that toured Papua New Guinea and New Zealand in 1990. His career started well, with him scoring two tries in the success over France on that balmy day in January, and he retained the loose forward role in the return, in Carcassonne, in which Great Britain prevailed 20-10.

After missing out on the home World Cup game against Papua New Guinea, and the two matches against France in 1988, Gregory was selected for that year's tour of Papua New Guinea and Australia. He scored a try in the 42-22 win over PNG, helping earn Great Britain a couple of points in their World Cup bid. He retained his berth in the second row for the First Test against Australia, impressing in a 17-6 defeat at Sydney in which a disallowed try for scrum-half Andy Gregory, following a run-round with prop Kevin Ward, proved to be costly.

The Kangaroos retained the Ashes with a 34-14 verdict in the Second Test at Brisbane – a game in which Gregory played at loose forward, with Wigan's Ellery Hanley switched from loose forward to centre – and the Lions prepared for the Third Test at the mercy of the Australian press, which was arguably at its most vindictive in rubbishing the tourists.

Great Britain certainly went into the game with little hope. With hookers Kevin Beardmore (Castleford) and Paul Groves (St Helens) both injured, coach Malcolm Reilly had little option other than to draft Widnes back row man Paul Hulme into the vital role. Injuries in the backs meant that Bradford Northern's Phil Ford – a former team-mate of Gregory's at Warrington – was switched to fullback, and a makeshift side led to only 15,994 turning up at the Sydney Cricket Ground on 9 July 1988 for what was, to the majority of observers, a foregone conclusion. No one, however, had imparted that information to the Great Britain side who, apart from playing for pride, were also aware that World Cup points were at stake.

In one of the most sensational Test matches ever played – one which ranks, in the opinion of many observers, alongside the 'Rorke's Drift' win over Australia in 1914 and the 'Alan Prescott' Second Test success in Brisbane in 1958 – Great Britain shot into a 10-point interval lead with tries by Widnes winger Martin Offiah and Phil Ford.

Wally Lewis crashed over for the Kangaroos shortly after the resumption, but the Lions had the bit between their teeth and hit back when Wigan winger Henderson Gill sped onto a kick by Andy Gregory.

Australia appeared to be set to rescue the situation when prop Sam Backo powered over after 62 minutes to reduce the deficit to only four points.

The Lions restored their cushion with Gill's second try, courtesy of a superb break by St Helens centre Paul Loughlin, whose three goals were vital to the win. Then came the moment which, when the name 'Mike Gregory' is mentioned, will conjure up an image in the minds of most Rugby League fans. As Gregory relates in *Biting Back*:

> It started when Andy Gregory drove the ball up from dummy half and evaded four Aussies with his nuggety strength. He ducked under a few swinging arms, drew fullback Garry Jack, and gave me the ball.
>
> I was still on our 25-yard line, but I knew I had the fitness and strength, and I just went for it.
>
> Wally Lewis and Wayne Pearce were chasing me down, but I had the step on them, and I knew Martin Offiah was supporting me.

Gregory, seeing that Lewis had given up the chase, realised that he could also hold off Pearce and said to himself 'If I'm going to run all this way, I might as well score'. And that he did, drawing on all his energies to race the last few yards for one of the most glorious of Great Britain's many tries. He admitted 'I lay on the ground realising what I and the team had just done. I was physically and emotionally knackered, and I couldn't even get up. But Ellery Hanley had come over with the rest of my team-mates and said, "Get up, don't show them you're tired."' Gregory did just that and Australia, despite having the capacity to score the three tries that could have overturned the deficit, were beaten.

The Lions inexplicably lost 12-10 to New Zealand in the game that decided which of the two countries would meet Australia in the

World Cup Final; a game in which Andy Gregory was again denied a try after a run-round with Kevin Ward.

Mike Gregory, however, had done enough on the tour to be recognised as, alongside Aussie Paul Sironen, one of the best two second row forwards in the world, and scored the first try against Australia when he was selected for the Rest of the World team, under Wigan coach Graham Lowe, that lost 22-10 to Australia.

Gregory had, without doubt, cemented his place in the Great Britain team and was in the side, at second row, that did the 'double' over France in early 1989, winning 26-10 in Wigan and 30-8 in Avignon.

He was appointed skipper of his country, taking over from the injured Ellery Hanley, for the New Zealand tour of England later that year, and led Great Britain to a 2-1 victory in a memorable series in which New Zealand won a classic First Test at Old Trafford 24-16 (the responsibilities of captaincy, on his own admission, affecting his performance) before Great Britain prevailed 26-6 at Elland Road in the Second Test in another magnificent backs-to-the-wall display after Wigan fullback Steve Hampson had been sent off in the early stages for an attempted head-butt on Kiwi scrum-half Gary Freeman, with second row Andy Goodway pulling off two outstanding tries.

Great Britain won the Third Test, at Wigan, 10-6, thanks to a huge defensive performance after New Zealand had hit back from 10-0 down. And there was no prouder man on the planet that day than Mike Gregory, when he went to lift the trophy on the ground on which he had himself watched his illustrious predecessors, with his family looking on.

Gregory played in both games against France at the turn of the year, Hanley resuming the captaincy for the 8-4 win in Perpignan, and Wigan scrum-half Shaun Edwards skippering the side in the return, when the Tricolors pulled off a shock 25-18 win at Headingley. Neither Hanley or Edwards, however, were fit for the 1990 tour of Papua New Guinea and New Zealand – and Gregory, who had battled through the season with an Achilles tendon problem, was only too delighted to accept the captaincy of a very young squad which also included the inexperienced but high-profile convert from rugby union, Jonathan Davies.

With physio Dave Fevre treating his Achilles injury three times a day, Gregory was able to circumnavigate the tour, including the First Test against Papua New Guinea at Goroka. The Lions, despite the oppressive heat and humidity, were 6-0 ahead when a riot broke out, prompting the police to fire tear gas into the crowd. The vapours blew back into the faces of the British players, causing complete debilitation and leading to New Zealand referee Denis Hale suspending play for a period.

On the resumption, the home side hit back to lead 14-8 at the break, with some overly aggressive play helping their cause. Gregory said, 'I told the referee we needed a bit of protection, but he told me he just wanted to get off the pitch in one piece.' The Lions subsequently slipped to a 20-18 defeat despite a try and three goals by Widnes' Davies and touchdowns for Hull winger Paul Eastwood and Wigan scrum-half Bobbie Goulding.

It was a different story in the Second Test, at Port Moresby, however. The game, which was also a World Cup match, was won 40-8. Great Britain had been 34-2 ahead when Gregory came off because his Achilles injury was playing up a little.

The Lions broke an 11-year duck in New Zealand by winning the First Test at Palmerston North 11-10, hanging on magnificently in a game in which a drop goal by Leeds' Garry Schofield was the seminal score. And the series was clinched with a 16-14 victory in the Second Test, at Auckland, secured with a late try by Widnes winger Martin Offiah after Bradford Northern prop Kelvin Skerrett had sparked a raid continued by Schofield and Sheffield Eagles centre Daryl Powell. Gregory had defied the pain of his Achilles injury to play throughout that match, in which Wigan scrum-half Bobbie Goulding – who had narrowly escaped being sent home for being involved in a melee in a bar – excelled.

Great Britain were only denied a whitewash, under Mike Gregory's stewardship, through a rare mistake by Offiah, who dropped the ball in the act of touching down in the closing stages of the Third Test at Christchurch, the Kiwis benefiting to win 21-18. Gregory reflected, 'We'd started as no-hopers, but went home heroes'.

A finger injury sustained in the Third Test, which Gregory neglected to monitor properly, going on holiday before having it properly attended to, kept him out of the first two Tests when Australia toured England the following autumn. Great Britain had beaten the Kangaroos at Wembley, and lost controversially at Old Trafford, before he was fit for the Third Test, at Elland Road. The game ended in defeat for the Lions, bringing the curtain down on an international career in which Mike Gregory had scaled the heights.

Gregory had, following the end of his playing career at Warrington, the option of joining one of two clubs – Keighley Cougars and Salford. The offer from Keighley was hugely tempting. The Cougars were, at the time, setting a standard in terms of razzmatazz and pre-match (and during – and post-match) entertainment that would set the early template for Super League; an adventure from which they were questionably excluded. Keighley, however, is not the easiest place to get to from Wigan (or, some would say, anywhere else, possibly even Keighley) and Gregory opted for Salford, whose chairman John Wilkinson had made such a big impression on him 12 years earlier, in 1982. A two-year contract was agreed, and Mike Gregory had every intention of making a big impression at the Willows.

In the event, his body wasn't up to the task, and he featured in only 18 games for the Red Devils, admitting that he only played well (by his standards anyway) in one of them, ironically against Keighley. That episode, entered into by Mike Gregory in all honesty but, in the cold light of day, more in hope than expectation, was one of the few regrets of his illustrious playing career. It was, however, during that spell that he spent time as an assistant coach, under Clive Griffiths, with Wales in the 1995 World Cup, after playing his last game of Rugby League, in Salford's home win over Hull FC on 1 October 1995. The following year, a chance meeting with Shaun McRae led to Gregory being appointed as the Aussie's assistant at St Helens.

Within a month of joining St Helens, Gregory had been close to the action as Saints recovered from 26-12 down against Bradford Bulls in the 1996 Challenge Cup Final to win 40-32. And, by the end of the campaign, he had been part of a double-winning outfit, the men from Knowsley Road also securing the Super League title, clinching the silverware at the expense of Wigan with a 66-14 verdict over Warrington in the decisive final league fixture.

Twelve months later, St Helens retained the Challenge Cup with a 32-22 success over luckless Bradford. But, at the end of the 1998 season, the contracts of Gregory, McRae and Chief Executive David Howes were not renewed; on Gregory's analysis, the trio had developed too strong a bond with the players for the board's liking.

After missing out on the vacant job at Widnes, he was approached by Swinton, and spent a couple of seasons with the Manchester outfit, impressing with his attention to detail but eventually conceding that a coach at that level can benefit from deeper knowledge of the amateur game than he had. The fact that he was informed of the club's decision that he should step down on returning from New

Zealand and Australia, where he had had charge of the England Academy side, perhaps illustrates how his expertise related to the sport's elite. He focussed on the England Academy side, earning plaudits when the team overcame the mighty Australian Schoolboys 28-20 in 2002.

It got even better when England won the Second Test, and Mike Gregory then joined the Great Britain Under 21s on their tour to South Africa, working under John Kear who, impressed, recommended him to Stuart Raper when he returned to Wigan. He became skills coach at Central Park and took charge of the Under 21s, keeping in touch with the international scene by coaching the England Sevens side in 2003. Following the departures of Kear and Raper (the former to Hull at the end of the 2002 season, the latter when he parted company with Wigan the following year) he became caretaker coach of Wigan Warriors, his hometown club, before being offered the Head Coach position on the eve of the 2003 Super League Grand Final, which Wigan lost 25-12.

Gregory guided Wigan to the 2004 Challenge Cup Final – the game ending in a 32-16 reverse at the hands of St Helens before 73,734 fans at Cardiff – before the man who had once thrilled crowds with his all-action, committed and courageous style of play, hit the biggest of his challenges when, slowly, a debilitating illness became all too apparent.

Putting lethargy, headaches and a certain twitchiness in his biceps down to a mixture of factors, ranging from the pressures of the Head Coach job to the reaction of his body to no longer playing, and disruption to his sleeping habits caused by the illness of one of his sons, Mike Gregory unfortunately failed to seek medical attention until the effects of a tick bite incurred on the trip to Australia for the Sevens in 2003 had became too deep-seated. Sadly Wigan turned out, after having made encouraging noises initially, to be less than supportive; a real blow for Gregory and his family, who were faced with high medical bills for treatment in America.

A long and unseemly legal wrangle ensued over the implications of disability law. At a time when Gregory and his family needed support, both financial and emotional, they found that they had to spend time battling against obstacles put in their way. In *Biting Back* he criticises Chairman Dave Whelan and Maurice Lindsay for what he felt was their unhelpful approach, but insists, 'It's not the club I have fallen out with, but only two men. I want the club to do well, and win silverware. I love the club and being a Wiganer, I've no wish to see them at the foot of the table.'

By contrast, in thanking the many people who got behind him to help raise funds for his treatment, he says of Warrington, 'My former club Warrington have been exemplary in looking after one of their own. They have hosted two dinners for me, one on our tenth wedding anniversary, so that was really special.'

Despite the help over treatment, Mike Gregory's condition deteriorated. He passed away on 19 November 2007, at the age of 43, leaving his wife Erica and sons Sam and Ben. Joe Lydon read a tribute to his old friend and on-field opponent at the funeral service.

16

Des Drummond

AN abiding memory of the author's of Des Drummond is of the opening game of the 1987-88 season when Hunslet, promoted as Division Two champions, launched the new season in the top flight with a visit to Wilderspool. The south Leeds outfit who, remarkably, have never won at Warrington, were certainly up against it that day, the Wire having closed the previous season in third position in Division One.

The home side had in their ranks the Great Britain winger, Drummond having signed from Leigh the previous February, netting eight tries in his 17 appearances in the closing stages of that campaign. It wasn't, however, for his scoring exploits against Hunslet on that day in late August that he will be remembered. It will be for one of the most astonishing tackles many of the spectators will have been privileged to see.

Hunslet stand-off Jed Coates looked a certain scorer, at a stage when the game was still in the balance, when he was put through only a few yards from Warrington's line, seemingly with nothing else to do other than saunter over the whitewash and place the ball down. Drummond, however, was having none of that, despite being on the opposite flank. Flying, as if by magic, out of nowhere, he crashed into Coates in the manner of a super hero, upending the hapless halfback just as he was about to ground the ball, and denying Hunslet the most certain of touchdowns. It was a stunning moment, and one which encapsulated several of Des Drummond's many qualities: his speed, his agility, his timing, his intelligence, his commitment to the cause and, above all, a spirit which simply refused to give anything up as a lost cause.

Warrington went on to win 54-4; although there was not necessarily that much between the teams, Hunslet prevailing 20-16 at Elland Road in the return. It may have been, however, that Drummond's amazing stop on Coates not only knocked the stuffing out of the visiting stand-off; it may also have been the contribution that put paid to any thoughts Hunslet may have harboured of announcing their return to the top flight with a victory.

Such an episode marked Drummond out above many other wingers, the majority of whom – including the matchless Brian Bevan – focussed their minds mainly, if not solely, on getting among the tries and, with justification, left the defensive chores to others.

He was, however, equally effective with ball in hand, and served due evidence in that same season, with one of the tries of the campaign, registered against high-flying St Helens, again at Wilderspool, in which he left several players sprawling after breaking clear from deep in his own territory, registering the touchdown with a stunning mixture of power and acceleration.

Such touchdowns were, in fact, a fairly regular feature of his time at Warrington, with another memorable score being notched in 1988-89, at Hull KR, in which he again crashed his way through the first line of the defence before showcasing his blistering pace.

Des Drummond, in fact, showed a relish for the physical side of the sport that was remarkable for a man who had come to Rugby League late, and by chance.

A British amateur judo champion, Drummond, who had been born in Jamaica in 1958, had no notion of playing rugby when he went to watch his brother, Alva, turn out for Leigh 'A'. Leigh – lucky for themselves, Des Drummond, Great Britain and the game in general, not to mention Warrington – were a man short, and Alva's kid brother was persuaded to make up the numbers. He did more than that. His contribution was so impressive that within seven days an offer had been made and accepted, setting in motion a career that was to last from 1976 until 1993, when he brought the curtain down with a spell at Workington Town.

Missing out on the BBC2 Floodlit final of 1976-77, Drummond was a driving force in the promotion season of 1977-78, when Leigh finished top of the pile with 21 wins from 26 games; an identical record to that enjoyed by both Barrow and Rochdale Hornets, who had inferior points' differences. Leigh didn't allow the impetus of the campaign to dissipate. The side, under coach Tom Grainey, consolidated at eleventh in 1978-79, and moved up to sixth in 1979-80.

The return of Alex Murphy as coach in November 1980 perhaps helped Leigh step up to another level, despite slipping to ninth in his first season back at Hilton Park. The following season, in 1981-

82, Leigh pulled off the impossible for a small-town club and lifted the Championship with a dramatic victory at Whitehaven on the last day of the season, when the champions-elect needed only to draw to come top of the pile. There was rising anxiety among their 4,000 fans in the crowd when Whitehaven, who had been marooned at the foot of the table, led 4-1 at half-time through a try by Malcolm McClure and a drop goal by Arnold 'Boxer' Walker. It was a different story in the second period, however. A try by Des Drummond sparked the revival, with other tries going to David Dunn and Mick Hogan, with John Woods kicking a goal and Steve Donlan and Roy Howarth landing a drop goal apiece.

Leigh were the champions of the Rugby League, for the first time since the 1905-06 campaign, and in the likes of stand-off John Woods and winger Drummond they had players who were the equals of anyone in the world. Drummond had also attracted the attention of the international selectors, and duly made his debut for Great Britain in the 1980 home series against New Zealand, under motivational coach Johnny Whiteley.

He made his first appearance in the Second Test at Odsal, Bradford, taking the place of Barrow's Chris Camilleri, who had scored a try in the 14-14 drawn First Test at Wigan, before just 7,031 folk. Hull KR centre Mike Smith had claimed the other touchdown while Smith's club colleague, fullback George Fairbairn, landed four goals. New Zealand, meanwhile, had registered touchdowns by second row Tony Coll, a former captain of the Kiwis, and stand-off Fred Ah Kuoi – who would join Hull – with scrum-half Gordon Smith matching Fairbairn's four goals.

An improved crowd of 10,946 turned up at Odsal Stadium, Bradford, for the Second Test. There was disappointment for Drummond in a 12-8 defeat in a game in which the Kiwis prevented Great Britain from crossing the whitewash, the hosts' points coming from four penalties by Fairbairn. New Zealand took a grip on the Series through tries by fullback Michael O'Donnell and winger Dane O'Hara, with Smith adding three goals.

Drummond was not held to be at fault, however, for the unsettling reverse, and was retained for the crucial Third Test at Headingley, Leeds, played before 8,210 supporters. The Series was drawn through a 10-2 success, earned largely through the Leigh winger, who scored both of Great Britain's tries, with Widnes fullback Mick Burke adding a couple of goals. New Zealand could only muster a Gordon Smith penalty in response.

He also grabbed two tries in the 37-0 win over France at Hull over a year later in December 1981. Woods, who himself would subsequently join Warrington, was also called up, contributing a try and seven goals, while Drummond's co-winger, the Wigan wonder Henderson Gill, was the star of the show with a hat-trick. Hull Kingston Rovers stand-off Steve Hartley also touched down, and Fairbairn landed a conversion in a game witnessed by a 13,173 crowd (the best for a home clash with France since 14,196 had amassed at Odsal, Bradford, in March 1968 for a 19-8 Great Britain win) at the Boulevard.

Woods, however, was the only British player to score, in the return at Marseilles five days before Christmas, kicking a penalty in the 19-2 defeat before 6,500.

Drummond kept his place in Great Britain's side for the next international: the keenly awaited First Test, at Boothferry Park, Hull, the home of Hull City AFC, against the 1982 Australian tourists. It was an encounter that not only shook the British players – it shook the British game to its very core as the Kangaroos raced to a 40-4 victory which indicated that, only a decade after conceding the World Cup to the Lions, they were now operating not so much on a different playing field as in a different galaxy.

A healthy crowd of 26,771 had turned up for the game, many attracted by exciting displays in the opening stages of the tour by the likes of Kangaroos centre Mal Meninga and halfbacks Peter Sterling and Brett Kenny, the latter's outstanding form keeping Wally Lewis, the tour vice-captain and the first choice when the party left Australia, out of the starting Test line-up throughout the trip.

Great Britain were, notionally at least, still in the contest at the break, when the Kangaroos were only 10-4 ahead; but the writing, in reality, was on the wall in a game in which the perceived wisdom that Australian players were physically stronger, but British players were more skilful, was dealt a shattering blow.

The Lions flattered to deceive in the early stages, taking the lead after only two minutes with a penalty by 19-years-old Hull second row Lee Crooks, one of the few British players to emerge from the humbling experience with his reputation enhanced. Meninga, however, restored parity just four minutes later with his only penalty goal of the game and, midway through the first half, the giant centre scored a try that signalled, beyond question, Australia's superiority, crashing through from 35 metres, handing off Leeds centre Les Dyl on the way with an awesome fend, and heading to the try-line for a score that set an agenda that remains in place 30 years on.

Australia's captain, Max Krilich – a much-criticised selection by the Sydney press prior to departure – was a hugely influential figure, to a degree not perhaps always fully recognised by historians, regularly making important yards from the dummy-half slot in a manner that has come to be seen as central to that position.

Five minutes later Les Boyd, moved into the blind-side prop role from his usual second row slot in Sydney club football, crashed over, Meninga adding the extras. Crooks replied with his second penalty, giving Great Britain some hope as they trooped in at the interval with only a six-point deficit to make up. But the reality was that the Lions had a mountain to climb.

That became all too apparent within three minutes of the resumption, when powerhouse winger Eric Grothe crashed over in unstoppable fashion, Meninga adding the extras. Great Britain then crumbled, in a devastating 10-minute period around the hour mark in which the tourists registered four tries.

Loose forward Ray Price, a favourite of home fans if only for his riveting habit of standing, at penalty attempts, ready with arms outstretched in anticipation of the ball rebounding directly towards him, got the next try to perhaps reduce his popularity a shade.

Right winger Kerry Boustead was next to streak in, with Kenny following suit before 21-year-old second row Wayne Pearce, who had been shunted from loose forward to accommodate Price, capped a fine display in which he had had a hand in three tries with a long-range score in which he left the Lions' cover defence trailing with embarrassing ease.

Australia rounded off a seminal victory with a touchdown in the last minute by veteran second row Rod Reddy, Meninga adding his eighth goal to set a new record for an Ashes Test in England. One diversion for depressed British fans from beyond the city of Hull as they wound their way along the M62, other than the praise of Kangaroos coach Frank Stanton for having stayed until the end in appreciation of the Green & Golds' display, was that the sin-bin had been used for the first time in Great Britain; Krilich and his opposite number, Leeds' David Ward, copping yellow cards for technical offences in the scrums and both serving five minutes on the sidelines.

By general consensus few British players emerged with any real credit. One who did was Des Drummond, and the reason for the plaudits were telling; he had impressed with his unfailingly committed defence on an afternoon on which his running chances were somewhere between nil and non-existent.

By happy – or unhappy – chance, Des Drummond found himself facing Australia four days later when the Kangaroos turned up at Hilton Park to take on reigning champions Leigh. The script hadn't been changed significantly from the previous Saturday, Australia going in at half-time 11-4 ahead, and closing as 44-4 victors; a success which turned out to be their highest winning margin of the trip. Woods emulated Crooks by kicking a couple of goals in the opening period. The Kangaroos, meanwhile, registered hat-tricks by second row Paul McCabe, left-winger John Ribot and right-winger Chris Anderson. McCabe's back-row partner John Muggleton crossed twice, Wally Lewis chipped in with a try and a goal, and Meninga landed three goals.

Peter Fox's Bradford Northern showed – almost – how it could be done in Australia's next game, the wily Fox picking John Green ahead of international Keith Mumby at fullback, with the latter switched to the centre, specifically because of Green's superior kicking game. Fox's tactics centred on Green regularly kicking deep, often early in the tackle count, with the aim of keeping the Kangaroos pinned in their own territory. The strategy worked. With 72 minutes gone, Northern were only 7-6 down, Mumby having kicked three goals in response to a try by McCabe and a conversion and a penalty by the great centre Steve Rogers.

Australia, though, emphasised their class with a couple of late touchdowns, by fullback Greg Brentnall and giant centre Gene Miles, for a 13-6 victory before a 10,506 crowd that had learned that the Kangaroos were perhaps not quite as invincible as had been presumed. Green, meanwhile, impressed with some superb try-saving tackles, in addition to his kicking in the loose.

Great Britain made 10 changes for the Second Test, at Wigan. Bradford Northern's Keith Mumby was brought in at fullback for Hull KR's George Fairbairn, and Drummond was the only threequarter to retain his place. Mike Smith, of Hull KR, was his centre partner instead of Widnes' Eric Hughes while on the other flank Les Dyl (Leeds) and Steve Evans (Hull) were replaced by Wigan duo David Stephenson and Henderson Gill.

A new halfback pairing of John Holmes (Leeds) and Warrington's Ken Kelly took over from Salford's Steve Nash – who had been captain at Boothferry Park – and Leigh's John Woods while, up front, Fulham hooker John Dalgreen stepped in for Leeds' David Ward, and a back three of Warrington's Bob Eccles, Hull KR's Chris Burton and David Heron, of Leeds, took the slots of Les Gorley (Widnes) and Lee Crooks and Steve Norton of Hull. Woods was on the bench, together with Bradford Northern's Alan Rathbone. Apart from Drummond, the only players retained in the starting 13 were Bradford Northern prop Jeff Grayshon, who was appointed captain, and Hull prop Trevor Skerrett.

Despite the wholesale changes Great Britain fared little better, if at all, at Central Park, as it began to dawn on the authorities and everyone else, including a previously critical media, that the differences between the Kangaroos and the Lions were far deeper rooted than mere matters of selection. A crowd of 23,216, the majority of whom were fervently hoping for a Series-levelling home success, were to be disappointed, although not by the quality of the tourists' football; football, moreover, which remained of high quality despite the dismissal of prop Les Boyd – who would subsequently join Warrington – as half-time approached. When Boyd received his marching orders six minutes before the interval, incurring the wrath of French referee Julien Rascagneres for kicking Dalgreen, Australia were already 15-4 ahead.

Mumby, perhaps the great success of the British side, landed his third penalty, on his international debut, to reduce the deficit at lemons-time to only nine points and, in theory at least, the Lions had a realistic chance of keeping the Series alive. Those ambitions were rooted, unhappily for British hopes, in wishful thinking. Meninga, who had traded penalties with Mumby in the early stages of the contest, going on to convert tries by loose forward Price and Sterling, with his attempt to improve a Grothe score drifting wide, landed another penalty within a couple of minutes of the resumption to reignite Australia's bid for the Ashes.

Twelve minutes later came a moment which will live long in sporting folklore. Wally Lewis, only able to make the line-up as a substitute – a detail which says much about the calibre of the 1982 Kangaroos – produced a piece of sublime magic with a wonderfully long floated pass from in front of the posts to Meninga, who was free and unmarked on the flank.

Meninga strolled over for a try that was breathtaking in its simplicity, in its precision, and in its sheer audacity; a score which heralded, as much as any possible cameo could, the subsequent supremacy of Australian sides over their British counterparts.

Lewis, who had come on at half-time for the injured Grothe, wasn't the only Kangaroo to display skills of the highest calibre. Prop Craig Young, who had sparked the move that led to Meninga's First Test opener, offered a lesson in the kind of close-quarter handling skills that had once been the preserve of English front-row forwards, while coach Stanton perhaps said it all when he announced that he would be selecting his best possible side for the Third Test.

Australia, who inspired home fans to offer a standing ovation in response to a sublime 10-man passing move, closed their victory with a late try by centre Steve Rogers, with Meninga scoring 15 points from a try and six goals.

Great Britain again rang the changes for the Third Test, at Headingley, Leeds. Mumby, who had made three try-saving tackles on his debut, was replaced by Fairbairn, while Hull's David Topliss was confirmed as stand-off and captain (Topliss having to fly back from a pre-booked holiday in an embarrassing episode for the British game, the stand-off slot being left blank until his confirmation), with Widnes' Andy Gregory at scrum-half. Mike O'Neill (Widnes), Bradford Northern's Brian Noble and Paul Rose, of Hull, formed a new front row, and workhorse Peter Smith of Featherstone Rovers was drafted into the second row, alongside Crooks. Hull's Mick Crane packed down at loose forward, and Woods was on the bench, alongside Warrington's Neil Courtney.

Until 10 minutes from time, Great Britain were firmly in contention. A crowd of 17,318 had witnessed a brawl on the stroke of half-time, which suggested that the Lions were at least not disposed to concede the Ashes without a fight, or to allow Boyd to crash-tackle the diminutive Topliss without retribution. Boyd and Crane were sent back to the sin-bin by M Rascagneres when they came out for the second period while, five minutes later, Rose and Aussie fullback Greg Brentnall were also given 10 minutes in the cooler.

The first home try of the Series, by Hull winger Steve Evans 15 minutes from time, hauled Great Britain to only 14-8 adrift, after Crooks had already scored two penalties and a drop goal, and despite the dismissal of Crooks 13 minutes into the second period for punching an Australian player in the aftermath of a try by Kangaroos captain Krilich.

A more astute kicking game had helped stretch the Australian defence, as did Crane's unorthodox approach at loose forward. The young Gregory also shone at scrum-half, while Noble was busy in the loose and won the scrums 5-2. The tourists, though, closed their tour on a high note with touchdowns by winger Kerry Boustead, Steve Rogers, Pearce and Kenny. Meninga finished with seven goals in a 32-8 success which barely reflected the match as a whole, while there was some further satisfaction for Great Britain from the fact that their tryline had not been breached until the 50th minute, when Kangaroo winger John Ribot crossed.

The 1982 Kangaroos had created a record as the first touring side, from any country, to win all its matches in Britain, and the first to prevail in all three Tests. Their total of 99 points in the Series set a new benchmark, for either country, in Ashes history, and when Australia went on to win both internationals in France on the second leg of their tour, they had extended their sequence of victories to a new high of 15. Meninga, with 21 goals and 48 points in the three Tests, had broken two more records, while the 97 tries scored in their 15 matches was the most registered for 30 years, despite the fact that the Invincibles had played fewer games.

Only one man had featured in all three Tests for Great Britain. That man was Des Drummond, who had been given few running chances but who was perhaps one of the few players to match the tourists man for man. He remained a perennial fixture in the Great Britain team for much of the 1980s, making 24 appearances in total and scoring eight tries.

He appeared in both the 1983 games against France – who lost their Tests against Australia 15-4 at Avignon, and 23-9 at Narbonne – and although he didn't get on the scoresheet, he played a full part in a 20-5 success at Carcassonne and in a 17-5 victory in the return, at the Boulevard, Hull.

He was retained for the next international fixture, at Avignon in January 1984, when the Lions won 12-0 before, in his absence, grinding out a 10-0 victory in the return, at Headingley, Leeds.

Des Drummond was subsequently selected for the 1984 Great Britain tour to Australia and New Zealand and played in all seven Tests; the trip however, if viewed solely in terms of Test results rather than results as a whole, would have become the least successful in history but for a win over Papua New Guinea, in an innovative fixture, in the closing match of the tour.

The problems started before the party set off, captain Trevor Skerrett, of Hull, having to pull out through a shoulder injury;

although his replacement as skipper, Bradford hooker Brian Noble, made a huge impression in the role, despite testing circumstances, duly signalling his abilities as a leader. Hard-bitten Hull KR packman Len Casey had to withdraw after being banned for six months, and St Helens' Chris Arkwright was ruled out through injury.

Warrington centre Ronnie Duane suffered the rare disappointment of being a tourist but of having minimal experience of it, when he was injured in the opening game – a 40-13 win over Northern Territory at Darwin – and had to return home, Widnes winger John Basnett flying out as a replacement.

The Lions opened the tour impressively, adding to the win over Northern Territory with five more victories before the First Test.

The bubble burst at the Sydney Cricket Ground. Australia won 25-8, limiting the Lions to a try by young Hull centre Garry Schofield and a couple of goals by Widnes fullback Mick Burke. Stand-off Wally Lewis scored a try and a drop goal for the Kangaroos, with winger Kerry Boustead, scrum-half Mark Murray and loose forward Ray Price also crossing the whitewash and winger Ross Conlon landing four goals before a 30,190 crowd.

Great Britain prevailed in their next three fixtures before losing their first and only game in the Australian section of the tour outside Tests, Toowoomba edging an 18-16 clash before 4,051 fans.

Lang Park, Brisbane, housed 26,534 spectators for the Second Test, most of whom went home happy that Australia had retained the Ashes with an 18-6 win. Drummond's centre, Schofield, was again the Lions' sole try-scorer, Burke kicking a goal, but it wasn't enough against a Kangaroos outfit that posted a try and three goals by centre Mal Meninga, with Grothe and Pearce adding touchdowns.

Britain again enjoyed playing success between Tests, beating Northern Rivers 24-12 at Tweed Heads and Northern Division 32-18 at Tamworth. The Lions, though, went down 20-7 in the Third Test at Sydney before 18,756 folk. Drummond, with few opportunities, was again unable to get over the try-line, with Bradford Northern's Ellery Hanley touching down from the other wing and Burke adding a goal, while St Helens scrum-half Neil Holding kicked a drop goal. Fullback Garry Jack, Grothe and Greg Conescu claimed the hosts' tries and Meninga landed four goals.

The Lions lost four of the eight fixtures in New Zealand – the last match of the leg, against Auckland, who won 18-16, and each of the three Tests, in which future Warrington hooker Kevin Tamati appeared for the home side.

Tries by James Leuluai and Fred Ah Kuoi, with Olsen Filipaina adding each goal, served the Kiwis in a 12-0 First Test win at Auckland, before 10,238. Hanley and Widnes stand-off Tony Myler got the touchdowns for Great Britain in the Second Test, at Christchurch, and Burke landed two goals. Sadly for the Lions, all New Zealand's threequarters raced over with household names such as Dane O'Hara (2), Dean Bell, Leuluai and Ah Kuoi getting the tries and Filipaina adding four goals in a 28-12 home success.

The Kiwis made it three out of three at Auckland, winning 32-16. Mumby, who was selected at centre by coach Frank Myler in each of the seven internationals, claimed one touchdown, while Drummond's centre Hanley also crossed. Burke closed the account with four goals, while New Zealand posted a brace apiece by substitute halfback Clayton Friend and Leuluai, with O'Hara also getting over the whitewash and Filipaina landing six goals.

The inaugural Test against Papua New Guinea at least helped the Lions close the trip reflecting on a victory. There were 7,510 people at Mount Hagen for the historic occasion. Drummond led the way in a 38-20 win with two tries, while Burke chipped in with a try and five goals. Mumby, Keith Rayne, David Hobbs and Hanley also crossed.

Papua New Guinea registered touchdowns by centre Noifa, winger Tolik, prop Jekis, and loose forward Arebo Taumaku. Centre Bal Numapo landed a couple of goals.

The tables were turned on New Zealand a little over a year later, on the 1985 tour of England, with Drummond featuring in all three Tests after having not played in either of the games against France the previous winter.

It didn't quite look that way after the Lions lost the First Test, at Leeds, before 12,591 people, 24-22; Britain missed out despite a try and two goals by Widnes winger Joe Lydon, touchdowns for Hanley and Wigan second row Andy Goodway, and three goals by Burke.

Drummond didn't score in that game, or in the next – for a very good reason. His centre, Schofield, added to his burgeoning reputation with four tries in a 25-8 win, with Lydon kicking four goals and St Helens loose forward Harry Pinner, the captain, firing a drop goal. New Zealand could only muster, before a 15,506 crowd at Central Park, Wigan, a try by winger Dean Bell try and a couple of goals by stand-off Olsen Filipaina.

The closing Test, at Elland Road, Leeds, attracted a crowd of

22,209 for a match which would settle the Series. The game will be remembered for the late equalising penalty by Hull substitute Lee Crooks, who had already kicked two goals to play a major role in a 6-6 draw. New Zealand had led in an abrasive contest which also doubled as a World Cup game through a try by second row Mark Graham and a goal by prop Dane Sorensen.

Great Britain's next game, against France at Avignon the following February, was drawn 10-10 – Hanley scoring a try and Crooks landing three goals – and Drummond was a try-scorer in the return, at Wigan, which was won 24-10. His centre, Schofield, chipped in with a try and two goals, and Castleford centre Tony Marchant also nipped over. Halifax second row Neil James added a try, and Crooks posted two goals.

Drummond missed out on the 1986 home series against Australia and on the two games in early 1987 against France, but returned to the international arena, as a Warrington player, that October for the Test, and World Cup match, against Papua New Guinea at Central Park, Wigan, watched by 9,121 folk. Although not among the scorers, the threat he posed out wide helped pave the way for a brace for Wigan stand-off Shaun Edwards, with other touchdowns going to centre Lydon (who had moved to Wigan), scrum-half Andy Gregory (who had also switched to Central Park), Bradford Northern's Welsh winger Phil Ford, powerhouse Leeds second row Paul Medley and Hanley; Wigan centre David Stephenson kicked seven goals.

The curtain came down on Des Drummond's Great Britain career at the turn of the year, on 24 January 1988, when he was a try-scorer (bagging his eighth for his country) in the 28-14 win over France at Avignon. His centre, Schofield, bagged a brace, Hanley – the captain – steamed in from the stand-off position, and Widnes winger Martin Offiah scored on his international debut. St Helens centre Paul Loughlin kicked three goals and substitute David Creasser, of Leeds, converted one try.

The winger would, in fact, have been on the plane with Great Britain for the 1988 tour to Australia and New Zealand, but for an incident in the 1987-88 Premiership semi-final at Widnes which left him sidelined from the trip.

An abrasive Premiership semi-final at Naughton Park, against old rivals Widnes, ended in a 20-10 defeat after the Wire had led by 10 points at one stage. Worse, Drummond, after the game had spilled over into a brawl, became involved with a spectator in an incident which led to police intervention.

Des Drummond was eventually deemed to have acted in self-defence. In the meantime, however, the Rugby Football League had opted to withdraw him from the tour.

Drummond subsequently focussed on his career at Wilderspool, where he gave exceptional service over five years, scoring 69 tries in 182 appearances, before moving to Workington in the twilight of a glittering career.

His qualities as a leader were recognised when he was handed the captaincy for the Regal Trophy Final 1990-91 against Bradford Northern.

Warrington won the game 12-2, but the abilities of Drummond and Welshman Allan Bateman on the flanks were wasted as the ball was rarely moved wide by either side in a dour affair watched by the lowest Regal Trophy crowd for seven years of 11,154.

Drummond, though, was no doubt more than happy to lift the trophy after substitute Mark Thomas had scored the only try of the game, in the very last minute. Fullback David Lyon, who defied an eye injury which had ruled him out of contention earlier in the week, was in superb form and kicked the four goals that had got the Wire in control; David Hobbs landed Bradford's penalty.

That was the second of two trophies Drummond won with Warrington. The previous season he was in the side that beat Oldham 24-16 to lift the Lancashire Cup at St Helens. Forward Bob Jackson got two tries and centre Joe Ropati and winger Mark Forster one each with four goals from the boot of stand-off Rocky Turner. He also featured in the side that reached the Lancashire Cup Final in the 1987-88 campaign, missing out 28-16 to a Wigan side that registered two tries by loose forward Ellery Hanley, touchdowns by winger Henderson Gill and substitute Graeme West, and five goals by centre Joe Lydon, with co-centre David Stephenson also kicking a goal. Winger Forster crossed twice for the Wire, loose forward Mike Gregory touched down, and Woods landed two goals.

Wigan were also the side that denied Warrington in the 1987 Premiership Final at Old Trafford – Drummond's valiant effort just failing to stop Lydon scoring the only try of the match in Wigan's 8-0 success – and again at Wembley in 1990, a match in which Drummond had few opportunities in the 36-14 loss.

That was a pity, not least for the wider TV audience, many of whom would have known Des Drummond very well from his exploits on the popular *Superstars* programme, in which he served evidence that he possessed levels of fitness and athleticism to match the best.

Following in the illustrious footsteps of another Rugby League winger, Salford's Keith Fielding, Drummond did his sport proud, catching the imagination by ignoring the rope when circumventing a high hurdle – merely leaping to the top and vaulting to the other side. He also set new standards in the sprints, serving his own and Rugby League's reputation well in the process; something he also did in the lower-profile setting of a beach at Lake Michigan when the players of Warrington and Wigan were relaxing together after their exhibition game in Milwaukee in 1989.

In his book *Biting Back* Mike Gregory recalled:

Desi Drummond and Rocky Turner were throwing a rugby ball about, just messing about, and two big Yanks came over and said 'would you guys like a game of two-on-two?' I thought, 'Oh no' but Desi thought and said, 'Yeah, why not?'

They were two typical beach bums – you could hear the lads on the touchline as the Yank with the ball looked towards Desi saying, 'Don't run to him.' Pound for pound Desi was the biggest hitter ever. He ran straight at Desi, who wasn't even blinking. He straightened his back and his head and put his right shoulder into the lad's sternum. There was blood, shit and snot everywhere, and the Yank couldn't move.

That was the shortest game of two-on-two that I ever came across. As he was on the floor, Desi kicked a bit of sand over his back and said, 'Pull me another beer.' What that young man will now realise is not to mess about with people who are smaller than you, but quite lethal. Desi was; he had this ability to snap in the tackle. I haven't seen anyone who can compare with his head tackling because Desi used to hit with his head first, not his shoulder.

Physically, he was an awesome specimen of a Rugby League player, and I'm just glad I played with him rather than against him.

17

Lee Briers

MERCURIAL, magical, irascible, infuriating – and incomparable. Those are all adjectives that could, and often have been, applied to the man who is perhaps Warrington's favourite son of the Super League era.

Lee Briers, one of the most gifted halfbacks of the first decade of the 21st century, has been the Wolves' pivotal guide throughout one of the most successful periods in the club's history; and, as such, he has been taken to the fans' hearts to a degree few others can emulate. His strengths include the ability to spot a half-gap and make the most of it, the vision to spot an opportunity out wide, and the capacity to fire out the required telling pass; all underpinned by the tactical nous to orchestrate his troops through the stages of each and every set.

Dramatically, he is as fine an exponent of the drop goal as the sport has ever seen, perhaps the equal of the legendary Albert Goldthorpe of the magnificent Hunslet 'All Four Cups' side of the Northern Union era. And, tellingly, Lee Briers is a master kicker in the loose, making magnificent use in particular of the 40/20 rule to drive opponents back mercilessly deep into their own territory.

The most remarkable factor, however, is that Lee Briers became a Warrington player at all. A St Helens lad born and bred, he signed for his hometown Super League team in 1997 but his time at Knowsley Road was brief, hectic, and successful – and closed dramatically.

Called into the side in place of injured scrum-half and captain Bobbie Goulding, Briers made his debut for Saints in the home fifth round Challenge Cup tie with Division One outfit Hull. His impact was immediate. The youngster contributed a try and five goals to the 54-8 victory played out in front of 10,251 appreciative fans, and his display in the quarter-finals confirmed that his performance against the Airlie Birds was no flash in the pan.

Keighley Cougars, on their home ground, offered stout resistance, but hard work and effort were not enough to prevent a 24-0 reverse in which Briers landed a couple of goals.

Briers sampled Super League fare, next, with the trip to the capital to take on a strong London Broncos outfit that was destined to finish second in the table. The Broncos, in fact, proved to be near-impregnable at the Stoop, dropping only three points in league games. Their one defeat, however, came in their opening match, St Helens returning north with a 28-24 win under their belts in which Lee Briers' four goals were vital.

Six days later, on 22 March 1997, Briers stepped out for the biggest match of his life to date – the Challenge Cup semi-final against Salford Reds – at the tender age of 18. The youngster was up to the task, turning in a man of the match display and landing six goals in the 50-20 stroll.

With Goulding still on the sidelines, Briers continued to have a major input into St Helens' progress, kicking three goals in the 22-10 Super League success at Wigan on Good Friday, with Dave Calderbank of the *Rugby Leaguer* enthusing 'scrum-half Lee Briers again proved a real box-of-tricks in the absence of Bobbie Goulding'. Three days later, Briers contributed four more goals to the 32-12 victory at home to Sheffield Eagles; neither he, nor anyone else at the time, knew it, but that was to be his last game for St Helens.

Goulding, back to fitness, returned for the trip to Paris St Germain on 5 April and Briers was left on the sidelines. That was understandable, given Goulding's standing, but eyebrows were raised when Briers wasn't on the list when the squad came to be measured up for their suits in the build-up to the Challenge Cup Final. And one or two of the Saints squad were taken aback, together with Briers, when he was not invited to Wembley.

Perhaps unsurprisingly, Briers was not long at Knowsley Road following that episode, transferring to Warrington Wolves. He had made six appearances for St Helens, scoring 52 points from a try and 24 goals. A fee of £65,000 was paid for his services, and he made his debut for the Wolves against, in a neat piece of symmetry, Paris St Germain – the opposition St Helens met when his run of appearances ended – on 27 April 1997. Equally appropriately, he marked his first appearance with a drop goal, also landing six two-pointers in a 37-34 success before a 4,576 crowd at Wilderspool.

That contribution – particularly the drop goal – heralded a career with Warrington that remains, in 2012, ongoing, and during which Lee Briers became recognised as one of the most talented and influential halfbacks of his generation, albeit missing out, inexplicably

– like another fine Warrington halfback in Parry Gordon – on a Great Britain cap.

During his career, Briers was overlooked for his country's number 6 shirt through the selectors preferring a one-time Warrington icon in Iestyn Harris, St Helens' Sean Long, and, from the turn of the century, the likes of Castleford's Danny Orr, Leeds Rhinos' Kevin Sinfield and Danny McGuire, and Leon Pryce, of Bradford Bulls and St Helens.

He opted, in 1998, to pin his colours to the Wales mast and made 23 appearances for the Dragons, shared almost equally between the two halfback positions. His Wales career opened with the 15-12 defeat at the hands of England on 19 July 1998, and closed with the 56-14 reverse against Australia on 13 November 2011, at Wrexham, in the Gillette Four Nations Series. Eleven other outings for Wales ended in defeat for Briers, with 10 closing in victory; a reasonable enough record for a country not perhaps seen, particularly in the modern era, as a major power.

Wales, with Briers at scrum-half, performed particularly well in the 2000 World Cup, held in England. The side won their first three games, beating South Africa 40-8, Cook Islands 38-6 and, more stoically, Lebanon 24-22, before slipping to a 58-18 hammering by New Zealand. Wales then got back to winning ways with a 22-8 success over Papua New Guinea – Briers adding a try to the touchdowns he had scored against Cook Islands and New Zealand – before meeting hot tournament favourites Australia at the McAlpine Stadium, Huddersfield, on Sunday 19 November. This was to be arguably Lee Briers' finest hour at international level; maybe, also, at any level.

Wales, who had suffered from the refusal of the Rugby Football League to offer a club franchise following the success of the 1995 World Cup, were obliged to draft in former stars John Devereux and Paul Moriarty, both of whom had returned to the Union ranks, to bolster their squad. Those problems, magnified by Australia's ability to select from a deep and rich seam of talent, appeared to be all too apparent when the Kangaroos went 8-0 up within 11 minutes through tries by scrum-half Brett Kimmorley and winger Wendall Sailor.

The Dragons, inspired by Briers, fullback Iestyn Harris and hooker Keiron Cunningham, simply refused to buckle. Harris, scrum-half Ian Watson and prop Anthony Farrell worked a well-crafted move for Watson to shoot over the whitewash and, in the 17th minute, a mistimed Harris pass wrong-footed the Australian defence, centre Kris

171

Tassell weaving his way over from 30 metres and Harris' conversions giving Wales a four-point advantage.

It got even better for the Dragons when Briers took a grip. The Warrington ace, operating at stand-off for Wales for the first time, had no right to score when Harris hoisted a high bomb, but Briers, no respecter of reputations, simply snatched the ball from Lockyer's fingertips to saunter over unopposed from 10 metres. Harris improved from in front of the posts to put Wales 10 points ahead after 22 minutes.

Briers, the ace exponent of the drop goal, kept the Kangaroos under the cosh with two one-pointers, in the 26th and 27th minutes respectively, to suggest that the 8,114 crowd could be treated to a huge upset, before Australian stand-off Brad Fittler forced his way over, centre Ryan Girdler landing his first goal.

Winger Anthony Sullivan came agonisingly close to responding in kind, with only a couple of minutes of the first half remaining, but was unable to pull off what could have been a killer of an interception try. Sailor, meanwhile, was denied a touchdown at the other end by a stunning tackle by second row Paul Highton.

Wales stretched their lead to 22-14 shortly after the restart with a Harris penalty, before the Kangaroos forced their way back into contention in the 54th minute when second row Brian Fletcher went over off a contested pass by Kimmorley. Lockyer, who had added the extras, got the Kangaroos back in front with a try – again courtesy of Kimmorley – only a couple of minutes later, and the lead was stretched when Fittler crashed over as the hour beckoned.

A penalty by Lockyer eased Australia eight points clear, and Wales' spirited display was ill-served by late touchdowns that gave the score a lop-sided look, Lockyer, Gower and Ben Kennedy powering over in the last 14 minutes and Lockyer adding a couple more goals. The abiding memory, despite that shattering finale, is of Wales' first half dominance, and Briers' glorious five-minute contribution in which, almost single-handedly, he stretched the Dragons' lead from four to 12 points in a display that epitomised his mercurial talents.

Wales, perhaps because of a lack of strength in depth, all too often saw promising positions ebb away at the business end of games. The following July, Briers and his team-mates established a 23-10 interval lead against England before eventually losing something of a thriller 42-33, and in November 2002 Wales completed an unfortunate three-match sequence by going down to New Zealand 50-22 after having only trailed 18-10 at the break. Lee Briers contributed a try, four goals and a drop goal in the England clash and five goals in the reverse against the Kiwis.

Briers formally retired from international football in 2007 following Wales' failure to qualify for the following year's World Cup. Happily, a career with Wales didn't, in the event, culminate with the 50-26 reverse at the hands of Lebanon on 9 November 2007 – a game in which the Dragons had led 16-10 at the interval and in which he offered a goal. A subsequent rethink led to the maestro turning out in the 2010 European Cup and Briers excelled, captaining Wales to the title with the help of a 60-22 win over Scotland and a 31-30 verdict over Ireland, when Briers kicked the vital drop goal.

Briers closed his international career in the 2011 Gillette Four Nations Tournament; a competition in which Wales, compelled to field a number of part-time players, lost each of their games, to England, New Zealand and Australia, by margins of 42-4, 36-0 and 56-14.

The 2009 and 2010 seasons, while quiet for Briers on the representative front, were conversely his most successful on the domestic scene. With only three trophies to play for in the Super League era – the Challenge Cup, the League Leaders trophy and the Championship – the opportunity to appear on the major stage for Briers and his colleagues was limited by comparison with that afforded to their predecessors. Warrington, during Briers' time at Wilderspool and, subsequently, the Halliwell Jones Stadium, were denied opportunities to achieve glory in competitions such as the Lancashire Cup, the Regal Trophy and the Premiership, all of which had been summarily ditched by the Rugby Football League, although the Grand Final play-offs effectively replaced the Premiership (with the winners being declared champions rather than Premiership winners). As a result, Briers had to wait a long time before appearing in a final for the Wolves: until 2009, in fact, after having experienced three defeats at the penultimate stage, each of them reasonably emphatic.

Warrington missed out twice to Bradford Bulls in successive seasons, losing the 2000 semi-final 44-20 in a game in which Henry Paul excelled. Along the way, Briers had been the man of the match in the 84-1 success over York in the fifth round.

Defeat was even harder to take 12 months later, Briers pulling off another man of the match display but still missing out on a final, with the Bulls prevailing 39-22. Briers was clearly the best player in the field, scoring three tries and three goals for the Wolves, with Warrington's other touchdown going to winger Rob Smyth. The anguish of that reverse, however, was put in its proper perspective, for Lee Briers and for the Warrington club, by tragic events during the following week.

On the same day – the Thursday – the Wolves' Kiwi back row man Tawera Nikau returned to his home to find that his wife Letitia had committed suicide. Meanwhile Lee Briers, his family and friends were in mourning for his older brother, Brian, who succumbed to cancer after a long and courageous battle. A minute's silence was held at the following Sunday's game against Castleford (one of Nikau's former clubs) at the Jungle. Nikau did not play; Briers opted to turn out in a game which ended in an 18-0 defeat.

Three years later, after home defeats by St Helens in the fifth round and Bradford in the fourth round, to the tune of 36-14 and 38-12, respectively, the Wolves hit rampant form on the 2004 Challenge Cup trail. Warrington were drawn away in each of their three ties before the semi-final stage, crushing Rochdale Hornets 80-0, winning 44-10 at Oldham and, in the quarter-finals, prevailing almost as emphatically, 42-10 at Whitehaven. The momentum was halted, though, against Wigan, who carved out a 30-18 win to book a berth at the Millennium Stadium, Cardiff, for the final with Leeds Rhinos.

Warrington slipped to narrow early round defeats in each of the 2005 and 2006 campaigns, losing, respectively, 26-22 at Leeds Rhinos in the fourth round and 40-36 at Hull Kingston Rovers in the fifth round.

St Helens won 25-14 in a quarter-final clash in 2007 – Warrington having gained quick revenge over Hull KR with a 38-10 romp a couple of rounds earlier – and the Saints posted their third Challenge Cup victory of the decade over Warrington in 2008 with a 40-34 success.

The waiting ended, however, both for Briers and his team-mates, in 2009, when Warrington, under coach Tony Smith, reached Wembley for the first time since 1990, when they had lost to Wigan. Smith, a coach of the highest abilities, had turned the team around from a side languishing in the lower reaches of Super League in March to one bidding for major honours. Their opponents, Huddersfield Giants, had not appeared in the final since 1962, while the clubs had met at Wembley in the 1932-33 Challenge Cup Final, Fartown succeeding 21-17.

Warrington eased to the quarter-finals with a 56-10 success over York City Knights in which Lee Briers scored a try, followed by a 56-8 result at Featherstone Rovers.

The semi-final was reached with a stunning 25-24 win, earned in extra time, at Hull KR. Briers, inevitably, was the man who took the Wolves through to the last four with his crucial drop goal. Another late Briers drop goal, added to an earlier try, rounded off a 39-26 semi-final win over Wigan at Widnes.

Perhaps predictably, the stand-off also fired a one-pointer, from the scrum-half position, in the Challenge Cup Final, his drop goal two minutes from time sealing a 25-16 victory over the Giants. His contribution wrapped up a performance in which Warrington Wolves hardly looked in danger of missing out against a Huddersfield outfit that rarely got going. Briers, despite – or possibly because of – his long wait for an appearance on a major stage, was not prepared to be minded to let the occasion get the better of him. He told *League Express*, in the aftermath of one of his greatest days:

> It was a bit eerie on Friday at the walkabout, but just being here on the day before the game with all the fans here, the drums, the hooters going made it all a totally different feeling. It's what dreams are made of.
>
> To be here as an eight-year-old kid watching, and then to be here as a player, is just fantastic. There'll be plenty of kids in that crowd looking to do the same. Trust me, if they do it they'll be really proud, because it's an immense feeling.
>
> I wasn't even going to go for a drop goal, but it's nice to get one.
>
> The occasion was everything I thought it would be. Even though the pitch is no bigger than any other pitch, your legs don't half wobble. It's a freakish feeling. You get cramp and feel a bit drained, but you get through it.

Briers was a serious contender for the Lance Todd Trophy, but conceded that he had no doubts as to the right of the Wolves hooker to collect the prize. He said,

> I think Mike Monaghan was badly done by in the semi-final, I think he deserved it then, and he deserved it today. I love the guy; he's an awesome player and an awesome friend.

He also revealed the impact Alex Murphy had had on him,

> I read a piece from Alex Murphy, who my dad says was the greatest player ever, and he says you should never come away without a point. I just thought that at that time it would be nice to get one over, and the game was done then.
>
> We were always in control, eight points in front with three minutes left, and I thought we're not playing Saints, who are the only side who come back at us from that position!
>
> And it was a perfect start. We carried the game-plan off to a 't'. It was fantastic.
>
> If they throw me out at Warrington that's the only way they're going to get me out. It's the be-all and end-all.

Lee Briers was reflecting on a game in which, together with Monaghan, he called the shots throughout, particularly with his kicking game. Warrington opened their account in the second minute, making the most of territory and possession gained when Kiwi second row Louis Anderson charged down a clearing kick by Giants (and future Wolves) fullback Brett Hodgson, getting away with a knock-on in the process. Monaghan sent fullback Richie Mathers over the whitewash in the next play, video referee Phil Bentham giving the thumbs-up to the effort, and centre Chris Bridge added the first of his four goals.

The Giants hit back through hooker Shaun Lunt, whose touchdown after supporting a break by Brett Hodgson sparked by loose forward David Faiumu was allowed by referee Steve Ganson after an effort by Lunt only a couple of minutes earlier had been ruled out by Bentham.

Brett Hodgson's conversion levelled matters but when Monaghan bustled over from dummy-half in the twelfth minute, the Wolves had established a lead they were destined not to lose.

Bridge stretched the advantage to 12 points with his conversion, two minutes later, of right winger Chris Hicks' score; a touchdown engineered by Briers, whose pinpoint crossfield kick found left winger Chris Riley in space to set the platform for a further raid in which Briers gave Bridge the opportunity to send Hicks outside opposing winger David Hodgson.

Warrington's Australian centre Matt King then had a 'try' disallowed for ball-stealing, with David Hodgson also unlucky to have a touchdown chalked off; in his case for a contentious obstruction ruling against Bridge, on Lunt, in the build-up.

Strong defence in which Briers and Hicks were especially outstanding kept the Giants at bay until three minutes before the break, when Brett Hodgson crossed out wide off winger Leroy Cudjoe's pass, his conversion attempt drifting past the posts to leave Huddersfield only eight points in arrears.

But, after a scoreless opening 20 minutes in the second half, Warrington registered the score that put them back in control. Vinnie Anderson – operating, unusually, at stand-off – was rewarded for his courage in returning to the fray with six stitches in a cut head, slicing between Huddersfield scrum-half Luke Robinson and centre Paul Whatuira, after another scoot from dummy-half by the irrepressible Monaghan.

Bridge's goal stretched the lead to 14 points, and the margin should have been increased in the 64th minute, only for Bridge to skew a penalty attempt wide from close to the posts.

The Giants threatened to rescue the situation when David Hodgson shot over, namesake Brett adding the extras, with four minutes remaining. But any lingering hopes Huddersfield may have harboured vanished with Briers' audacious drop goal, his 60th for the Wolves and one of his most memorable, to seal a 25-16 win.

Modest Smith said:

> These guys were going in a pretty good direction anyway. I've been able to come in and jump on the back of a lot of good things they were already doing and are about to do.

Twelve months later, Lee Briers collected another winner's medal at Wembley – and, for good measure, was named as the Lance Todd Trophy winner. Operating on this occasion at stand-off, with Monaghan at scrum-half, Briers was the central figure, despite not registering any score on his own account, in a 30-6 victory over a Leeds Rhinos outfit that was returning to Wembley after an 11-year wait, although the Rhinos had featured in several finals away from Wembley.

Briers was at his orchestrative best, and found ready support from his front row of Adrian Morley, Gareth Carvell, Paul Wood and David Solomona, with the rest of the side responding superbly to the platform. The match, marred a little for spectators by the Rugby Football League's decision to allow both teams to wear their regular colours – Warrington's primrose and blue clashing with Leeds' blue and yellow – started superbly for Briers, his lofted kick-off deceiving

Leeds hooker Danny Buderus into knocking on in the shadow of his own posts. Buderus' blushes were rescued by his team-mates, who bundled Wolves centre Ryan Atkins into touch when the ball was worked wide from the scrum.

Leeds fullback Brent Webb and prop Ryan Bailey went close at the other end, the latter being held up by fullback Richie Mathers and second row Louis Anderson.

Warrington's well-organised defence rode a Rhinos storm in which centre Keith Senior, Buderus and diminutive halfback Rob Burrow all went close.

Briers went on to punish Leeds for not making the most of their pressure, firing a high pinpoint kick to the corner which Atkins rose to in style, beating Rhinos centre Brett Delaney to the flight. That score, in the 14th minute, was followed four minutes later by a touchdown presaged by a Briers 40/20 – fired in the third tackle – followed by a crossfield passing move, and a return attack to the other flank, with Briers sending out a long pass to centre Matt King who turned the ball inside to winger Chris Hicks, the latter forcing his way past several defenders in a committed surge which denied both Senior and Bailey.

Second row Ben Westwood's conversion attempt rebounded off a post and the Wolves stayed 8-0 in front until five minutes before the break, when Atkins punctured the Rhinos' challenge with one of the more astonishing – and controversial – tries seen at Wembley; scored less than a minute after Briers had pulled off a try-saving tackle on flying Rhino Ryan Hall.

Winger Chris Riley, after collecting the ball from what seemed to be an offside position after fullback Richie Mathers had been unable to collect a kick by Leeds loose forward and captain Kevin Sinfield, raced clear before being caught by a fine cover tackle by Leeds fullback Brent Webb.

Atkins, in at dummy half, raced at offside defenders Ryan Hall and Ian Kirke, scorching away to cross beneath the posts; even if he left the act of touching down a little late as the dead-ball line approached. That score, converted by Westwood, left Leeds staring into the abyss, and Warrington came close to finishing them off shortly after the resumption when Briers sent Westwood through with a sweet short ball, the latter kicking on before feeding King, who was hauled down by Burrow.

Delaney was denied twice at the other end, on the second occasion by a strong joint stop by Mathers and Atkin.

Briers, again, lofted precision kicks to the corners, which Leeds only just survived, and continued in his role as tormentor-in-chief by linking with Monaghan to send Hicks steaming down the flank. Hicks was hauled down by the cover, and a Briers kick at the play-the-ball to the opposite flank was inches away from presenting King with a glorious score.

As the game entered the final quarter, Leeds found themselves unable to deny Briers yet again, his high kick to the corner enabling Hicks to rise above Hall for his second try of the afternoon. Westwood's goal gave Warrington a 20-point cushion which wasn't needed, although Leeds did hit back with a try by winger Lee Smith, off a pass by stand-off Danny McGuire, which was confirmed by the video referee and which Sinfield converted from the touchline.

Mathers hit back immediately against his old club, only to have his effort ruled out for obstruction, Westwood being deemed to have got in Kirke's way in the build-up.

Warrington, unfazed by that setback, crossed a couple of minutes later, Hicks netting his hat-trick from a move involving Louis Anderson, Mathers and Westwood but sparked, inevitably, by Briers, who learned after Hicks crossed that he had won the Lance Todd Trophy.

The Wolves completed a 30-6 win with Louis Anderson's try four minutes from time, Westwood adding his third goal from six attempts, and as the final whistle blew Briers gazed to the skies, as if thanking the gods for the most glorious of occasions.

A pertinent point was made by *League Express*' Martyn Sadler, in his analysis of the game in the following Monday's issue. Sadler said:

Watching Lee Briers' majestic performance took me back almost ten years, to Huddersfield on 19 November 2000, when Briers, then 22 years old, had a storming game for Wales against Australia in the World Cup semi-final. Early in the second half of that game, Briers had played a key role as Wales led the Aussies 22-14. At half-time the Australian captain Brad Fittler had apparently demanded to know why his side hadn't been warned about just what a dangerous player Briers was.

Eventually the Australians composed themselves, and ran out 46-22 winners, but anyone watching that game would have been convinced that Briers had a great future as a Great Britain star for the next decade.

In the intervening years, it is tempting to wonder how many times we would have beaten the Aussies if Briers had been selected for Great Britain or England. He is just the sort of player, always doing the unexpected, who the Australians have always struggled to handle. But for some reason he has always been ignored. It's almost as though the respective coaches of our national team have feared the very quality that Briers would have brought to the side. And of course there have been fears about the quality of his defence, although anyone who saw his possibly try-saving tackle on Ryan Hall in the 34th minute on Saturday would struggle to believe that he could be a defensive weakness.

The calls of Sadler and others for Briers to be included in the international set-up continued to be ignored, and there was to be no repeat of Wembley glory in 2011 for the halfback, with the Wolves slipping out 44-24 at eventual competition winners Wigan Warriors at the quarter-final stage. Along the way, though, Briers rewrote the record books, at club and league level, with his 44 points, with three tries and 16 goals, in the 112-0 victory over Swinton – the Championship One leaders – in the fifth round. The result beat Warrington's previous best win of 84-1 over York at Wilderspool in the Challenge Cup in 2000, while the 20 tries notched against the Manchester outfit equalled the number posted in the 78-6 verdict over St Helens on 12 April 1909. It was also Swinton's heaviest defeat, higher than the 78-0 hammering by Wigan on 29 September 1992. Briers beat his own 40-point record (set in the victory over York) and his 16 goals marked a new high for a Warrington player, leaving behind the previous best of 14 which he had shared with Harry Palin, who landed that number in a win over Liverpool City in 1950. Coincidentally, Briers also became Warrington's top points scorer, easing past the figure of 2,416 amassed by Steve Hesford. Joel Monaghan helped himself to four tries in the romp, which also included hat-tricks for Gareth Carvell and Chris Riley and a brace for Ben Westwood. Ryan Atkins, Simon Grix, Michael Monaghan, Chris Bridge and Rhys Williams closed the account.

Calls were made, following the rout, for future Challenge Cup competitions to be seeded, with only two teams joining the 14 Super League sides in the closing stages. Those were calls that Briers resisted. He said:

The RFL shouldn't make sweeping changes. The Challenge Cup, as it is, gives teams from the lower divisions the chance to appear on a major stage, and their players have the opportunity to play in front of much bigger crowds than the few hundred that is often the norm.

It's their Wembley, stepping out at Warrington, Leeds, Wigan or Hull and, for their players – many of whom have ambitions to play at a higher level – it's a chance to make a big impression on a Super League coach, even if the gulf is getting wider between the full-time pros of Super League and the part-timers of the Championship.

He added,

Summer rugby doesn't help the lower clubs either. The old muddy pitches of yesteryear added to their chances of pulling off an upset, but that's much more difficult on dry grounds. Shocks, though, can still happen. Hunslet Hawks beat Huddersfield Giants in 2003, and Barrow won at Castleford last year. David v Goliath clashes are integral to the Challenge Cup and, if Super League clubs are very confident of victory, they can always rest one or two players and blood a few youngsters. Gaz O'Brien made his debut in the fourth round, against Keighley, and that was a marvellous experience for him.

Reflecting on a sequence of 12 successive wins in the Challenge Cup since the fifth round defeat at St Helens in 2008 Briers said,

I wouldn't have imagined, when I signed in 1997, that one day I'd beat Steve Hesford's record. I'll certainly relish that when I retire. Records, though, are made to be broken.

Records may have been broken during the 2011 season, but so were hearts – Warrington hearts – at the end of an otherwise hugely successful campaign. The Wolves finished top of Super League, and were hot favourites to force their way through to the Grand Final at Old Trafford and win the championship for the first time since the 1954-55 season. However, in a remarkable echo of the 1972-73 campaign, when the Wire lost at home to Dewsbury at the semi-finals stage after having won the League Leaders' Trophy, the Wolves fell at the final hurdle to a Rhinos outfit that became the first side in the Super League era to make it to the Grand Final from outside the leading four.

The disappointment of the 26-24 home defeat at the hands of Leeds in the Qualifying semi-final was increased for three reasons: the Rhinos prevailed through a penalty by Kevin Sinfield with less than two minutes of normal time remaining; the Wolves had opted to host Leeds, rather than Wigan Warriors, at the penultimate stage, suffering from the poisoned chalice of the Clubcall 'right' for the League Leaders, introduced the previous year by the Rugby Football League to add extra interest to the play-offs; the Wolves had finished the regular league season with 44 points, with 22 of their 27 games being won; Leeds had finished in fifth place, winning 15, drawing one and losing 11 of their programme; and it was, of course, Leeds who had disposed of Warrington in the 1961 Championship Final.

Warrington had secured the coveted League Leaders Shield – which, in the light of subsequent events, acquired extra lustre from supporters throughout the game, with the *League Express*' Mailbag packed with letters bemoaning the fact that the side that was clearly the best of the Super League season had been so cruelly denied – with a stunning 34-12 victory at Hull FC in the final game of the campaign.

Atkins, one of the heroes at Wembley the previous season, was again a catalyst, claiming an astonishing try when he stole the ball from Hull second row Joe Westerman's grasp, after driving the back row man back several yards, before racing away over 40 metres; for good measure, the pursuing Sam Obst tweaked a hamstring in the chase and had to be withdrawn.

That victory set up a Qualifying Play-off tie at the Halliwell Jones Stadium against Huddersfield Giants, who crossed the Pennines with expectations high. Most neutrals expected a close contest. Instead, the Wolves ran riot, cruising to a 47-0 win in which a 25-point advantage had been established by the interval. Briers had landed a drop goal by that stage, while Warrington's other scorers by the close comprised Joel Monaghan and Chris Riley, with a brace apiece, and Chris Bridge, Matt King, Brett Hodgson, Ryan Atkins and Richard Myler, with Bridge kicking two goals and Briers having three successes in front of a 10,008 crowd.

A gate of 12,074 turned up at the same venue a fortnight later to witness one of the turn-ups of the season, with the Wolves, who had gone straight through to the Qualifying semi-finals as a result of their having, as League Leaders, won their opening game, not necessarily benefiting from the fortnight's break against a Leeds Rhinos side that arrived at Halliwell Jones battle-hardened from a 34-28 success at the very Huddersfield side that Warrington had already put to the sword.

Leeds had prevailed at the Galpharm Stadium after having seen an early 16-point lead reduced to 16-12 and, after having been 34-12 ahead with only 12 minutes left, finding themselves having to hang on grimly for victory when the Giants blasted back with three tries in five minutes; only for the Rhinos to survive an agonising spell from the 75th minute to the close.

The Rhinos, whose coach Brian McDermott had, unfairly, been singled out as being in danger of the sack during an indifferent sequence of results earlier in the season, with five games out of seven ending in defeat at the height of the summer, had hit a rich seam of form and arrived at Warrington with four successive wins, including the victory at Huddersfield, behind them. That buoyancy was illustrated in the sixth minute when Carl Ablett forced his way over, Sinfield's conversion giving the visitors a surprise lead.

Briers helped get Warrington going, hoisting a kick which Matt King palmed back, Chris Bridge popping up to send Joel Monaghan over the whitewash.

The departure of fullback Brett Hodgson on the half-hour with ankle ligament trouble threatened to hamper the Wolves' hopes in the Grand Final. In the event, that consideration turned out to be superfluous, although the Wolves took the lead on the Aussie's exit when replacement fullback Chris Riley went past Ablett after having been fed by Michael Monaghan.

The Rhinos' response was immediate, Ryan Hall pulling off an interception of what could otherwise have been a try-creating pass by Simon Grix, two Wolves men having been clear on the outside.

Warrington bounced back from that levelling score when Richie Myler fired out a long pass to King, who steamrollered through a posse of defenders.

In a seesaw finish Leeds hit back with a second try by Hall, who finished off a raid by Burrow and McGuire which Atkins almost thwarted, followed by a trademark score by Burrow after fullback Brett Webb had bust the first line of the Warrington defence.

Briers and his colleagues were not about to concede, however, and it was Briers who created the gap, with a smart inside ball, for Riley to sweep over.

Sinfield then fell short with a 50-metre penalty attempt – but when Myler was ruled offside in attempting to block a drop goal attempt by Sinfield, the Wolves' dream of a berth at Old Trafford was destined to end in tears.

It was a sad end to a tremendous season for Warrington and for Briers, who made 25 appearances, scoring 21 tries, 35 goals and four drop goals. Happily, Briers enjoyed a cameo appearance with Wales in the Four Nations Series which may well have cleansed him for the 2012 Super League campaign.

18

Jon Clarke

THE greatest hooker in Warrington's history. That was the accolade bestowed on John Clarke by the Wolves' highly appreciative supporters when, in acknowledgement of the Lowton lad's unfailingly high quality displays for Warrington, they voted him above a litany of fine number 9s who have graced the famous Primrose and Blue.

Considering that Warrington have, during their illustrious history, boasted such fine hookers as Tom Fell in the early 1900s, Dave Cotton in the 1930s and Kevin Ashcroft in the 1970s, the honour is one which has some meaning. Add to that list the likes of Ike Fishwick and Frank Wright in the glory years of the 1940s and 1950s, together with John Thursfield and Mark Roskell, who came second and third in the standings, and the resonance of the accolade becomes even more impressive.

While some allowance has to be made for a tendency in the modern age for such ballots, in any walk of life, to lack proper historical perspective, there can be little doubt that Jon Clarke would have made a real impact at any stage in Warrington's history. The rationale for many supporters for putting a cross beside Clarke's name would, unarguably, have been respect for his highly impressive work ethic, in both attack and defence. He was – and remains at the time this book was published – not only one of the best tacklers in his position; he was one of the most reliable defenders in the game.

Clarke was, in fact, rated as the most efficient tackler in Super League in 2004, with an astonishing 99 per cent success record, and, the following season, posted the fourth highest figures for tackles made in the entire competition. It was those kinds of statistics that persuaded Warrington to sign Clarke on a permanent basis after he had been brought in on loan, to help resolve an injury crisis, in 2001. Clarke had, in fact, only made one starting appearance for London Broncos during that season, with another eight off the bench, when he headed north in aid of the Wilderspool cause. He made his debut in a 30-24 home reverse at the hands of Wakefield Trinity Wildcats on 20 May 2001 and by early July had more than done enough to persuade the Wolves to make the arrangement permanent.

During his opening campaign at Wilderspool, Jon Clarke made 17 appearances for Warrington, plus one as substitute, scoring four tries. His first touchdown for the Wolves was registered in the 26-18 defeat at Salford on 10 June, and he crossed the whitewash again seven days later in the 30-16 home success over Castleford. Those tries no doubt went some way to convincing coach Darryl Van de Velde and the Warrington board that terms should be offered, and so did Clarke's workrate and superb defence. He put pen to paper on 9 July 2001, ironically only two days after the Wolves had been put to the sword by St Helens at Knowsley Road.

Van de Velde lamented, in the press conference following that thrashing – which came hard on the heels of two wins and a draw, and which could be attributed, at least in part, to the fact that scrum-half Allan Langar was clearly jetlagged after having flown back from the midweek State of Origin match in Australia, 'We were beaten in every facet and it was our most disappointing performance of the season. It will be a waste of time watching the video.'

Not, perhaps, an entire waste of time. Van de Velde's subsequent viewing, whilst painful, will have revealed that Jon Clarke was one of the few Wolves players to show full commitment throughout, and that evidence no doubt went a long way to a full-time contract being offered which would keep him at Wilderspool until the end of the following year. In the event, Clarke was to remain with Warrington Wolves for a decade, offering superb service and becoming a firm favourite with the fans; including, it has to be said, those of the female gender, his Latin good looks and flowing dark locks adding to his appeal.

Clarke became central to Warrington's assault on Super League, his value to the side being enhanced by an ability to operate to equal effect in the second row. That kind of sustained good form led to Clarke earning the call-up for Great Britain's home series against New Zealand in November 2007.

The Wolves hooker, who may have feared that he would, in common with other Warrington legends such as Parry Gordon and Lee Briers, miss out on the international scene, was one of five uncapped players selected by Great Britain coach Tony Smith (who would, ironically, join Warrington several years later). Smith, an Australian who was to apply for and secure UK citizenship, also gave the nod in his 25-

man squad to other new boys in the shape of Bradford Bulls' fullback Michael Platt and his club team-mate, prop Sam Burgess, together with Leeds Rhinos packman Jamie Jones-Buchanan and, in a surprise choice that grabbed all the headlines, St Helens' Samoan-born prop Maurie Fa'asavalu, who qualified under the Rugby Football League's residency rulings, having lived in Blighty since 2003.

Including Fa'asavalu, St Helens had seven players in the party, while Warrington's nominees, in addition to Clarke, comprised centre Martin Gleeson and prop Adrian Morley. Morley and Gleeson got the nod for the First Test, at the Galpharm Stadium, Huddersfield, with Clarke missing out. Great Britain, despite being 10-8 adrift at the interval and finding themselves on the wrong end of a 8-6 penalty count, won 20-14 before a 16,522 crowd. Fa'asavalu scored on his Great Britain debut, with Hull FC winger Gareth Raynor and Burgess also crossing and diminutive Leeds Rhinos half-back Rob Burrow adding four goals to help put the home country 20-10 ahead with time running out.

New Zealand, who had opened with tries by Bradford Bulls centre Shontayne Hape and Huddersfield Giants centre Paul Whatuira, one of which prop Lance Hohaia converted, were unable to add to their tally until the closing seconds, when Hape claimed his second touchdown from a smart ball by Sydney Roosters fullback Sam Perrett.

Despite Bradford Bulls hooker Terry Newton and St Helens number 9 James Roby having impressed, Smith found room for Clarke in his starting line-up for the Second Test, at the KC Stadium, the home of Hull FC, seven days later. Roby, on parental leave as a new father, was unavailable, and Newton was left out of the side.

Great Britain got off to the best of starts, thanks in part to Clarke, who fed his captain – the Leeds Rhinos prop Jamie Peacock – who charged over in an arcing run in which half a dozen defenders, including South Sydney prop Roy Asotasi and West Tigers hooker Dene Halatau, were left sprawling. That touchdown, after only a couple of minutes, laid the platform for a 44-0 victory.

Clarke was to the fore as Great Britain repelled the inevitable Kiwi response, with Wests Tigers winger Taniela Tuiaki and Penrith Panthers second row Frank Pritchard being kept at bay. And it was Clarke, again, who supplied the final pass for Britain's second try, feeding St Helens stand-off Leon Pryce, who evaded Hohaia and a couple more defenders to crash over.

Clarke continued to orchestrate Great Britain to fine effect, and the Kiwis went further behind when Raynor, to the delight of the Hull fans in the 20,324 crowd, squeezed in at the corner. Leeds Rhinos loose forward Kevin Sinfield, who had improved both of the opening scorers, was off the pitch at this stage, and Burrow was unable to add the extras from wide out, but Britain went in at the interval well-placed to secure their first Series win over New Zealand (or anyone else for that matter) for 14 years.

After withstanding a strong opening following the break in which Leeds Rhinos centre Keith Senior prevented his club-mate, Clinton Toopi, from crossing, Clarke went off for a spell to the acclaim of the crowd, with Burrow temporarily taking over at dummy-half and substitute Danny McGuire, of Leeds Rhinos, slotting in at scrum-half.

A high kick by Pryce caused Toopi and Hape problems they were unable to resolve, Senior getting to the ball first and palming it back for supporting St Helens fullback Paul Wellens to pounce, Burrow improving. That score was followed by perhaps the best try of the night, in which St Helens winger Ade Gardner finished off a fine move in which Wigan Warriors second row Sean O'Loughlin stole the ball off the hapless Toopi, who had done well to collect a McGuire kick, before sending Burrow away, the halfback in turn feeding Gleeson, who supplied the final pass after bewitching the New Zealand rearguard.

A rare New Zealand attack was foiled by Wellens' ball-and-man tackle on Tuiaka, Wellens adding to his laurels by sending Burrow over within a minute, making the most of a platform set by Morley and Raynor.

The last 10 minutes were highlighted by tries by Senior, after Perrett had been unable to control a Wellens kick, before Pryce pulled off a 70-metre interception try off a telegraphed pass by Hohaia. Sinfield wrapped the win up with his fifth goal from as many attempts, and Clarke and his Great Britain team-mates duly celebrated a rare Series success.

He said:

I had to pinch myself really. To be part of a victory of that margin on your debut is fantastic and I couldn't really have asked for anything more. And to be part of a first Series win for Great Britain in 14 years is a dream. It's Tony Smith's decision, of course, but I'd like to think that I have done enough to get in the side next week.

He added,

> It's quite a difficult thing to make your debut. If you're not careful the pressure can get to you. I think the key is to try to control your emotions, and play the normal game you play for your club each week.
>
> It was fast, tough and very physical, in fact it was everything I expected and more. I'm delighted that I've been able to test myself against some of the best players in the world.
>
> Winning the Series after only two games hasn't really taken any pressure off us, because we will be putting pressure on ourselves, next week, to make it 3-0. That's very important to us, in fact it was the target we set ourselves before the First Test.

Clarke also revealed that he had set himself a target of securing inclusion in the Great Britain squad for the 2008 World Cup, in Australia.

Great Britain went on to win the Third Test 28-22, before a 21,235 crowd at the JJB Stadium, Wigan. The game was, however, not quite as successful from a personal perspective for Jon Clarke as had been the Second Test. New Zealand, whose coach Gary Kemble had made five changes from the side that had been humbled at Hull, were 12 points in front after 11 minutes, through tries by St George-Illawarra Dragons winger Chase Stanley – after a sweeping move involving Halatau, Bulldogs stand-off Ben Roberts and Toopi – and Whatuira, who started and finished a raid also involving Roberts and Melbourne second row Jeremy Smith, who converted both scores from wide out. Clarke was replaced by St Helens' James Roby after 20 minutes and had to wait until 10 minutes from time before being able to return to the fray. At that stage, Great Britain had battled back in some style but were only 26-18 ahead, Stanley having claimed his second try just three minutes earlier, and Smith having kicked his third goal.

He was, however, instrumental in Great Britain thwarting a Kiwi rally from 14 points down. His defence was a key factor, and he was also involved in the incident that enabled Burrow to land the penalty, a couple of minutes from time, that gave Great Britain a 10-point advantage, the Kiwis being sanctioned for interference at the play-the-ball after the hooker had burrowed towards the line.

With only 14 seconds remaining New Zealand posted a try by Tuiaki, who finished off a sweeping move highlighted by a long pass by Roberts; but it was too little, too late, for the Kiwis to avoid defeat.

Great Britain had clawed their way back into contention with three tries in a stunning seven-minute period before the break, sparked by a barnstorming try by substitute forward James Graham, who clattered and twisted his way over the whitewash after having charged onto Roby's pass.

Almost from the restart, the tourists' lead had been slashed to a couple of points, O'Loughlin sending Senior crashing over with a well-timed delivery. And, as the crowd waited for the interval hooter, Burrow and Senior combined to devastating effect to give Salford City Reds winger David Hodgson the chance to squeeze in at the corner. Burrow, who had improved the first score, had been unable to convert either of the other two tries, but Britain were now 14-12 ahead and had the momentum against a Kiwis outfit that, from being in total control, had been hit by a whirlwind.

Within three minutes of the resumption, the lead had been extended to eight points, Burrow grabbing a trademark touchdown in which he collected off Graham and, rounding Wests Tigers hooker Dene Halatau, scampered over in a diagonally weaving effort. It got even better for Great Britain as the hour mark approached, a pin-point long-range kick direct from a scrum by O'Loughlin giving McGuire the chance to show his paces, leaving Kiwi defenders trailing before reading the bounce well and sprinting over the whitewash unopposed. Burrow added the extras and, with Clarke returning to the scene, there was to be no way back for New Zealand.

Jon Clarke, however, missed out on the World Cup jaunt to Australia, and suffered a setback in 2009 which proved to be the low point of his career. The roots to this stemmed from ankle problems – which may have been endemic from much earlier, and which may have been caused or exacerbated by his high workload – which came to light with a vengeance, particularly for a player who, at 31 years of age, was clearly at the veteran stage.

There were concerns, at one stage, that his days as a player were over, and a series of operations ruled him out of the 2009 Challenge Cup Final. He said:

> It started with a little bit of pain in my shin, but over a period of a month or two it just got worse and worse. Things came to a head in the game against Wakefield; the match before we were due to appear at Wembley. I had to come off with the injury, and afterwards I couldn't move my foot.

Clarke underwent a scan within a couple of days, and the results were devastating, x-rays revealing a stress fracture through his inside ankle bone. The medics said, simply, that his season – due to finish on a real high, with Warrington set to face Huddersfield Giants at Wembley and also riding high in second place in the Super League table – was over. And it was largely his fault, as he had played on the damaged ankle for too long, causing further damage.

He said:

> It was very upsetting. Here we were, with a chance of winning the Challenge Cup for the first time in 35 years, and making our first trip to Wembley since 1990, and I was going to miss out. To make matters worse, I'd enjoyed 10 years at Warrington, without having had a chance of winning a trophy, and my big day had been snatched away from me.

He added,

> I was in bits over it, although in some ways I was relieved that the reasons for my troubles had been established, as it had been getting to the stage where no one seemed to know.

Clarke underwent an operation and seemed on course, after a period of rehabilitation, for a rewarding 2010 campaign. He suffered pain, however, during pre-season training in November, and investigations revealed that the original crack in his bone had spread along the ankle. Clarke said:

> At that point, I wondered not only about whether I'd ever play again, but whether the injury would ever heal. At 31, recovery times are much longer than they are when you're a younger player.

The recovery process was, however, successful and Clarke, looking ahead to the new campaign under Tony Smith, said:

> We've got good coaches at Warrington, and a good squad. It'll be a competitive season, with such as St Helens and Wigan Warriors in the frame, as always. You can't dismiss Leeds, either. They are packed with experienced players, and they have big-match know-how. They know how to win.

Happily for Clarke, Leeds didn't know how to win at Wembley on

Saturday 28 August 2010. The Wolves registered a stunning 30-6 success, as the Challenge Cup Final dream came true, at long last, for the veteran hooker. But his dream of a Grand Final appearance, in what turned out to be his last season at Warrington, in 2011, was shattered when the Wolves, generally rated as the best side in Super League throughout the campaign, and awarded the *Rugby Leaguer & League Express*' Albert Goldthorpe Team of the Year Trophy in recognition of that status, lost at home to Leeds Rhinos in the Qualifying semi-final.

Jon Clarke at least had the consolation of closing his career with Warrington with a major medal to show for his efforts, the Wolves picking up the League Leaders' Shield after finishing, deservedly, top of the pile. He had made two starting appearances, and 16 off the bench, scoring one try, in his final season at the Halliwell Jones Stadium.

On 6 September 2011, a little over 10 years since his arrival at Wilderspool, the announcement had been made that Clarke would join Warrington's neighbours and old rivals Widnes Vikings – newly elevated to Super League – for the 2012 season. Widnes were acquiring a man who had carved out a deserved reputation as a fine player and, on and off the field, as the consummate professional. He said:

> The Vikings are an ambitious club and I'm an ambitious player. The goals I had as an 18 year-old making his way in the game are still the same to this day, and ultimately that is to perform to the best of my ability every single week both on and off the pitch. I've had ten fantastic years at Warrington but the time has now come for me to part company with the club and move onto the next chapter of my career. Before I do that, I'll be doing my utmost to make sure that I can go out on a high and finish my time there on the right note.

Jon Clarke had signed for his first professional club, Wigan Warriors, in the mid-90s, captaining the Great Britain Academy side after arriving at Central Park and making his debut in the 1997 season, during which he made six full appearances and three as substitute. He scored one try, in the 38-22 victory over Leeds in the quarter-finals of the Premiership Trophy, and was at hooker at the age of 18, packing down opposite a 20-year-old Keiron Cunningham, when Wigan accounted for St Helens in the decider at Old Trafford.

New Zealand stand-off Henry Paul claimed a sparkling hat-trick in the opening success over Leeds, with fullback Kris Radlinski and scrum-half Tony Smith adding touchdowns; young back row forward Andy Farrell landed seven goals. The Rhinos, meanwhile, had to settle for a brace for winger Francis Cummins, a touchdown by Keighley Cougars acquisition Phil Cantillon, a try by winger Leroy Rivett and two goals by halfback Iestyn Harris, with Graham Holroyd adding a conversion.

Wigan appeared to be coasting in the semi-final against a Sheffield Eagles outfit that, 12 months later, would stun the Warriors with a sensational victory in the Challenge Cup Final. The Warriors were served prior notice of what could happen at Wembley when the Eagles, who were 20-10 down at the break at Central Park but had much the better of the second period, posted tries by Johnny Lawless and Danny McAllister, plus a Mark Aston goal. Wigan, though, stayed secure with Farrell's fifth goal, having registered tries by Simon Haughton, Andrew Johnson and Jason Robinson in the opening period.

Coach Eric Hughes took his side to Manchester with his standing high after having been dismissed by St Helens the previous year. He was to add to his laurels by guiding Wigan to a glorious 33-20 success in which the Warriors were inspired by loose forward Farrell; who, at the age of 22, equalled the record of Widnes fullback Alan Tait by winning the Harry Sunderland Trophy twice as man of the match, having secured the coveted award the previous year, also for success over the Saints. Farrell, in addition to contributing a try and six goals to the cause, was also heavily involved in each of the Warriors' other four touchdowns.

Winger Andy Johnson set the agenda after only four minutes, stunning the 33,389 crowd with a coolly taken try off Farrell's precision kick to the corner.

A Farrell penalty goal was followed by St Helens' opener, second row Derek McVey forcing his way over the whitewash.

Farrell's second penalty put the Warriors 8-4 up, and he then put his dribbling skills to appropriate use at Manchester United's home, setting up a touchdown for Robinson.

The Saints hit back with a 40-metre touchdown by powerhouse centre Paul Newlove, reducing the interval deficit to 14-8, and young scrum-half Sean Long pegged Wigan back a shade more with a penalty on the resumption. The next 20 minutes, however, belonged to Wigan, who hit St Helens with a whirlwind.

Farrell kicked a penalty in the 44th minute, and three minutes later the mercurial Nigel Wright, plucked off the bench, kicked a drop goal.

That gust turned into a gale, Farrell and Haughton linking up to send Radlinski over.

The same three then worked a move finished off by Farrell and, in a rare episode, the trio were again involved in the third try of the sequence, Haughton stepping up on this occasion for the touchdown.

St Helens lent some respectability to the scoreline when substitute prop Paul Anderson and stand-off Karle Hammond crossed the whitewash in the closing stages – but Wigan were the better side, by some distance, on the day, and Clarke had his first major medal.

Wigan showed Hughes scant gratitude for an honour achieved against a backdrop of boardroom upheaval and financial worries, replacing him with Australian John Monie.

Clarke's progress stalled at Central Park the following year and he made only one starting appearance, with another eight off the bench, scoring one try. He missed out on the Challenge Cup Final, which ended in a 17-8 defeat at the hands of Sheffield Eagles, and on the inaugural Super League Grand Final, when 43,553 fans witnessed a 10-4 victory over Leeds Rhinos.

Twelve months later, Monie joined London Broncos, and Clarke followed, having made 28 appearances for Wigan, scoring five tries. In a season-and-a-half at London, he played 32 games, crossing twice, before heading for Warrington in a temporary move which was to last for 10 years, involving 263 games, 62 tries and 2 goals, and which was to leave a lasting legacy.

19

Adrian Morley

THE signing of Adrian Morley by Warrington in 2006 could be seen as the capture that transformed the Wolves from the nearly men of Super League to a side that seriously challenged for – and won – major honours.

Prior to Morley's arrival at the Halliwell Jones Stadium, Warrington had perennially been seen as a side that was difficult to beat and which could definitely make inroads in the Challenge Cup, or force its way into the Super League play-offs. That, however, was about as far as it went. The Wolves, who had rarely if ever been in danger of relegation since the launch of Super League in 1996, equally rarely made any real headway en route to Old Trafford, or on the road to Wembley. The side had got no further than the semi-finals stage in the Challenge Cup, and had not got as far as that in the Championship play-offs.

All that changed when Adrian Morley agreed terms midway through the 2006 campaign to move from Sydney Roosters to Warrington for 2007. The Great Britain prop proved to be the cornerstone of a pack that, while strong enough, had arguably lacked a man of his physical presence and sheer, unassuming commitment.

Morley, weighing in at 16st 7lb and standing 6ft 3in tall, had proved himself many times over since signing for Leeds in 1994, moving on to Sydney Roosters and, in a fleeting cameo, Bradford Bulls prior to switching to the Wolves. Most memorably, each of those clubs had acquired a player who was emphatically ready to 'mix it', in the time-honoured manner of the open-side prop. That much was plain when Morley was sent off by referee Steve Ganson after only 12 seconds of the opening Test of the 2003 Ashes series against Australia, for a high tackle on opposing prop Robbie Kearns.

The dismissal, the fastest in the history of international Rugby League, was highly controversial; not perhaps in terms of strict adherence to the rules, which by general consent were applied correctly by Mr Ganson. Many veterans of Ashes Tests, however, recalled that during almost a century of encounters between the two nations, the regular pattern had been for games to start with an almighty scrap, following which the match official would give both sides a stern talking-to. Both Australia and Great Britain then generally got on with the game. The key to Morley's dismissal in 2003 was that whereas, in the past, the team-mates of the floored Kangaroo would have flown in en masse to exact instant retribution, on this occasion, perhaps reflecting a more disciplined age, no Australian player took it upon himself to act in that way. As a result Morley was left to stand alone, waiting anxiously for Mr Ganson's decision; which was almost inevitable, particularly as, as an Englishman, he could so easily have found himself called to account by the Australian management had he opted for a more traditional approach.

While Morley was in hot water for his over-zealous act, and for the effect that it had on Great Britain, who went on to lose the Test by a narrow 22-18 margin, it had little effect on his career, most coaches and clubs recognising, at least privately, the value of an 'enforcer' in the pack. It was that kind of approach, within limits, that had persuaded Sydney Roosters coach Graham Murray to lure the lad he had nurtured at Leeds Rhinos to the other side of the world. The Roosters, however, took a dimmer view of an incident in a club game in the closing stages of the 2006 season, against Canterbury Bankstown Bulldogs, when he allegedly kneed Corey Hughes in the face as Hughes was playing the ball. The incident led to Morley being suspended, and to the Roosters releasing him from his contract, paving the way for a return to England for a player who, hailing from Salford, had been produced by the strong Eccles club, in the heart of Manchester; a club with whom he has retained close links throughout his career.

It was from Eccles that Morley signed for Leeds, making his debut in the 1994-95 season – the last before the launch of Super League – as a 17-year, having been signed by coach Dougie Laughton; a man who, while at Headingley, set in motion or transformed a number of careers, not least that of James Lowes, whom he bought from neighbours Hunslet as a scrum-half, but immediately switched to hooker. Morley made a full appearance and two as a substitute that season, scoring his first try in the 23-16 defeat, in the Stones Bitter Championship, at Halifax on 17 April 1995. His abilities, even at such a young age, were readily apparent and he quickly became a fixture in the first team; and a favourite with the fans.

Morley's form at Headingley was very quickly apparent to the Great Britain selectors, and he was duly selected for the 1996 tour of New Zealand, which was preceded by matches against Papua New Guinea and Fiji. The youngster, still only 19, didn't play in either of those games. He was, however, called up, as a substitute, for the First Test, against New Zealand, at Auckland on 18 October 1996. The game ended in a 17-12 defeat and Morley wasn't selected for the Second Test, at Palmerston North; a match which, again, went the way of the home side, who sealed the Series with an 18-15 victory. Morley was reinstated as a substitute for the Third Test, at Christchurch, another match that ended in defeat, this time 32-12. The powerful packman, however, had made a big impression, on the field and off it, and added to his laurels by scoring a try after coming off the bench.

Exactly 12 months to the day later, on 1 November 1997, Morley was again a Great Britain substitute, this time for the opening Test match at Wembley against the Australian Super League side (a team which wore a blue chevron, in addition to the two yellow chevrons, to distinguish it from the established article). Great Britain were beaten 38-14, but Morley had done enough to find himself elevated into the starting line-up for the Second Test, at Old Trafford, Manchester; a game in which he played a full part in a 20-12 success in which Wigan Warriors' Andy Farrell, switched to stand-off from loose forward, scored a try and six goals, with his club team-mate Jason Robinson also crossing, from the wing. The pattern of Australia winning the games that matter most continued in the Third Test, Morley retaining his place, at Hunslet's Elland Road Stadium, when the Kangaroos prevailed 37-20, limiting the host nation to a brace by Wigan substitute Simon Haughton, another Robinson try, and four Farrell goals.

The prop suffered a knee injury in a 22-10 defeat at the Boulevard, at the hands of Hull, in mid-June 1998 – Leeds, however, showing faith in their young front row forward, offered a contract extension which would keep him at Headingley until the end of 2000.

Morley was back in action by early August and was immediately back to top form – typified by a display in which he came off the bench, having sustained a head wound at the hands of Mick Cassidy in the previous week's win at Wigan Warriors – in a Super League clash with Sheffield Eagles at Headingley to help inspire a transformation from 12-2 adrift into a 36-22 victory. His coach, Graham Murray, enthused, 'We sure needed something when we went 12-2 down and Adrian gave it to us.'

Veteran scribe Richard Coomber reported for *Rugby Leaguer*:

> Morley, still wearing the black eye from 'that tackle' in the Wigan game, was colossal in defence and attack and his try was amazing as he somehow stretched out an arm, his giant hand gripping the top of the ball and touching down despite Willie Morganson's tackle.

That form helped steer Leeds to the 1998 Super League Grand Final at Old Trafford, Manchester; there was, however, to be no joy for the Rhinos, or for Morley, at the home of Manchester United. Wigan won 10-4 in the wet conditions after having been 6-4 ahead at the interval, thanks to a try by winger Jason Robinson which loose forward Andy Farrell improved. Leeds, who claimed an earlier touchdown by New Zealand centre Richie Blackmore, were left adrift before a 43,533 crowd by a couple of penalties by Farrell in the second period.

There was some solace for Morley, however, with his call-up by Great Britain coach Andy Goodway for the incoming tour by New Zealand. That solace, however, proved to be short-lived. Morley missed out on the First Test, in which New Zealand beat the Lions 22-16 at the McAlpine Stadium, Huddersfield, before 18,509 fans. Instead he was on the treatment table, trying to recover from an ankle injury sustained in the Grand Final in a tackle by, ironically, Great Britain captain Andy Farrell. The injury failed to respond to treatment. Morley missed out on the Second Test, in which Great Britain lost 36-16 at the Reebok Stadium, Bolton, before 27,884 fans.

The Third Test, again without Morley, was drawn 23-23 at Vicarage Road, Watford. Few of the 13,278 supporters could have been blamed for pondering on whether Great Britain could have won the Series if Morley's imposing presence had been available in all three games.

Adrian Morley's next season at Leeds, the 1999 campaign, included the high point of a winning appearance in the Challenge Cup Final at Wembley. The second row was in the side that beat St Helens 24-16 at Headingley in the fifth round, albeit being obliged to limp off early with a leg injury. He was, however, back to fitness for the run-in, and for the decider, against a London Broncos outfit that had Virgin entrepreneur Richard Branson as the club's colourful owner.

Leeds won the game – the last Rugby League match to be played at the old Wembley, which was to be rebuilt, until 2007 – 52-16, but the scoreline didn't tell the full tale of a contest that, at a certain stage, could so easily have gone the Broncos' way.

London, who had lost one of their founding supporters from their days as Fulham on the morning of the game, Bob Evans passing away hours before his favourites' biggest day, stunned the majority of the 73,242 crowd by blasting into a 10-0 lead with tries by winger Martin Offiah and Robbie Simpson. And with former Wigan and Great Britain scrum-half Shaun Edwards at his most committed, defying a broken thumb to play in pursuit of a tenth winners' medal, the Broncos had Leeds on the back foot.

Although Rhinos winger Leroy Rivett collected the Lance Todd Trophy as man of the match for his four tries in Leeds' successful rally, there were many who felt that scrum-half Ryan Sheridan had equal claim to the accolade. Sheridan prevented the Broncos from extending their lead by pulling off a superb cover tackle on Edwards, who had looked a certain scorer after having popped up in support of a break by Aussie prop Steel Retchless. And he prevented another likely score by cleverly reading a kick-through by London stand-off Karle Hammond when none of his team-mates had spotted the danger. The scrum-half also made a break in the same passage of play that led to a match-turning try; Leeds, thanks to Sheridan, went on to win the game in what turned out to be a canter, after Broncos centre Greg Fleming had crossed, with winger Rob Smyth converting, to put the southerners 16-12 up. A controversial penalty awarded by Castleford referee Russell Smith, who judged that Rivett had been impeded in chasing his kick, gave Rhinos prop Barrie McDermott the chance to crash over. That proved to be the turning point in a game in which Leeds fullback Iestyn Harris scored 20 of his side's points with a try and eight goals, and Australian centre Brad Godden also crossed, together with substitute Marcus St Hilaire and winger Francis Cummins. Morley had played a full, solid part in the success, and continued in the kind of form that led to him being rated as one of the best forwards in the world.

A 13-4 victory for Leeds at Wigan in June 1999 illustrated his importance to the side, his powerhouse tackle on the Warriors' tough-as-teak centre Gary Connolly leading to the former St Helens ace retiring from the fray, clutching an ice pack. 'He's had a shower, but he doesn't know where he is', said Warriors coach John Monie later.

By July, there were developments at Headingley that were to lead to a change of direction in Adrian Morley's career, Leeds coach

Graham Murray signed up to coach Sydney Roosters on a three-year deal from 2000.

Morley, meanwhile, after having missed out on the 1998 Test Series against New Zealand, was back in the Great Britain squad for the 1999 Tri-Series Down Under. The Lions got off to a dreadful start with a 42-6 hammering at the hands of Australia at Suncorp Stadium, Brisbane before a crowd of only 12,511, many perhaps being put off by the prospect of a one-sided game; although the Kangaroos were held to 10-6 at the interval.

Veteran journalist Ray French, himself a former Great Britain international, had harsh words to say in his report on a game in which the Lions had suffered their highest-ever defeat Down Under, before the lowest-ever crowd. Highlighting the game's politics as the root of the problem, he also criticised confusion in the British camp over the use of the recently introduced unlimited interchange rule, questioning why St Helens hooker Kieron Cunningham was brought off just as he was beginning to test the Kangaroos at the rucks, and why his club team-mate Sean Long was withdrawn four times and re-introduced on three occasions, spending no more than 30 minutes on the pitch. He also queried why Morley, who he described as the 'game's outstanding forward', was brought off.

Lions coach Andy Goodway said:

I don't like this interchange rule but we do, at the moment, have to play to it and use it. If we take out the first half, which was reasonably good, and take out the chances squandered then we do have something on which to build for next week in New Zealand.

He added,

It's not so much a physical problem as a mental problem with the players. The game in Australia is so intense at club level, and much quicker. Quite simply, whoever got that first try in the second half was going to win.

Morley, meanwhile, after announcing that he intended to play for Wales in the 2000 World Cup, alongside his brother Chris (another product of the Eccles club) switched allegiance to England after learning that there would be no turning back if he opted for the red shirt over the white, and having also pondered over the wisdom of missing out on the chance of playing in what would be a historic

World Cup opener against Australia at Twickenham. At the age of 22, he said:

> I love playing Test rugby, it's the pinnacle of anyone's career. We competed against Australia for a good hour at Brisbane, until we collapsed in the final quarter. We have proved ourselves in the past, and I'm sure we can do so in the future.

The packman went into the 2000 Challenge Cup Final at Murrayfield, Edinburgh – the first to be played away from Wembley during the rebuilding of the national stadium – under pressure as a player who had already been sent off five times in his career, and who the pundits felt could be targeted by Bradford in a bid to cause him to lose his cool. He admitted, on the eve of the game:

> I have just come back from a ban and there is no way I'm going to spoil the chances of my team. It will be tough for me because I do tend to get pumped up more than most before big games. I have an aggressive style and every coach I have worked with has said they do not want me to lose that part of my game. But I admit there is a problem I am working on.

Morley had no problems with his approach on the day, but there was disappointment in a 24-18 defeat in which Marcus St Hilaire and Andy Hay scored tries for Leeds, with Iestyn Harris kicking five goals; Michael Withers (2), Nathan McAvoy and Stuart Fielden replied for the Bulls and Henry Paul kicked four goals.

It was to be Morley's last season at Headingley, as Sydney Roosters came up with a deal that Leeds Rhinos simply could not match.

Adrian Morley took a while to settle, establishing himself during the 2001 season as he got to grips with the Australian club game. Having gone through his settling-in period, the Manchester lad was a pivotal figure, leading from the front, as the Roosters ended a barren 27-year period in 2002 by lifting their first Premiership since 1975. Sydney secured glory, after a fine campaign, with a 30-8 success over New Zealand Warriors at the Telstra Stadium; the club's twelfth title, going back to the Roosters' previous incarnation as Eastern Suburbs.

The following year, Sydney Roosters were back in the limelight, Morley operating in the second-row in the side's Grand Final defeat at the hands of Penrith Panthers. Along the way, Morley scored a try in the 38-0 win over St Helens in the 2003 World Club Challenge, before nearly 20,000 folk at Bolton.

Returning to England following the incident involving Corey Hughes, Morley joined Bradford Bulls for a short spell, helping them win the 2005 Super League Grand Final against his old team, Leeds. He played two games, plus another four as a substitute, for the Odsal outfit and, in picking up a winner's ring, became the first Englishman to succeed in both the English and Australian Grand Finals, and in a Challenge Cup Final.

He moved on to Warrington prior to the 2007 season, on a four-year contract, and helped the side to reach the Challenge Cup Finals in 2009 and 2010, winning both, thanks also in part to the decision to appoint Tony Smith as Head Coach. He made his Warrington debut at Wigan on 9 February 2007 but lasted only 37 minutes after an accidental clash of heads with Wigan's Eamon O'Carroll which resulted in Morley having surgery on a fractured eye socket.

Five games later, he made his home debut against Hull KR, but a similar incident after only 16 minutes left him with a displaced fracture of the left cheekbone. Despite that unfortunate start, he quickly became a central figure with Warrington, assuming the captaincy and leading from the front. His leadership skills were eulogised by team-mate Lee Briers who, after the victory in the 2009 Challenge Cup Final, said, 'I take my hat off to Mozza. He suggested to me right at the end that I should lift the trophy with him, and it's a fantastic gesture from a fantastic bloke.'

20

Tony Smith

IN September 2008 Warrington Wolves were, it would be fair to say, seen as being in something of a sorry state. 'Solid Giants Shock Shaky Wolves', proclaimed the headline in *Rugby Leaguer & League Express* following Warrington's 38-20 home defeat at the hands of Huddersfield, and disgruntled fans at the Halliwell Jones Stadium on that first Saturday evening of the month made their feelings plain over a reverse that cast doubt over whether the Wolves – who had gone into the contest targeting fourth place in the table, but were left languishing in sixth spot, just making the cut – could make any impact at all on the Championship play-offs.

Warrington had, admittedly, been without several players. Louis Anderson, Vinnie Anderson, Chris Bridge, Paul Johnson and Stuart Reardon were all the victims of long-term injuries, while key halfback Lee Briers was a continuing doubt and, in the Huddersfield game, further knocks to Adrian Morley (stomach muscle), Rob Parker (ankle) and Paul Rauhihi (back) added to the Wolves' woes.

Coach James Lowes, an upbeat character as a wonderful halfback or hooker with Hunslet, Leeds Rhinos, Bradford Bulls and Great Britain, was typically defiant and admitted:

> It was a shocking game. We were poor throughout and I'm not very happy at all. We worked hard to get into fourth spot and it was in our hands, but we failed to produce. We've got to get this out of our system.

He added,

> Harsh words will be said and we'll get on with the play-offs. We've a tough game next week.

Lowes was correct. Seven days later, Warrington were put to the sword at Catalans Dragons in the first round of the play-offs, losing 46-8 against a team that had won only one of its previous six games.

The French outfit were magnificent, but the Wolves were woeful and, even allowing for their injury problems, it was becoming clear that something deeper was amiss.

Meanwhile, England coach Tony Smith confirmed at the turn of the month that when his contract expired at the end of 2009 he would be seeking a return to the domestic game. At that stage the Australian-born Smith was unlikely to have had Warrington in his sights, but it's highly probable that the Wolves had made more than a pencilled note regarding the future availability of a man who, only two days after that defeat at the hands of Huddersfield, had become a naturalised British subject as affirmation of his commitment to the England cause.

Arriving in England as a relative unknown in 2000 to coach Huddersfield-Sheffield Giants Smith, who had had a somewhat unproductive spell as a halfback at Workington Town in the mid-nineties – affected by an Achilles injury and not helped, in his estimation at least, that the flat the Cumbrian outfit had arranged for him and his wife was situated above a fish and chip shop – was otherwise best known, if at all, as the kid brother of the charismatic Brian Smith, who had made a big impression as a coach with Bradford Bulls and Hull FC. Quietly, modestly and without undue ceremony, Tony Smith made a huge impression on the British game, firstly with Huddersfield-Sheffield Giants and secondly with Leeds Rhinos, who he guided to their first championship, in 2004, for 32 years.

Smith revealed in *Rugby Leaguer & League Express*, in the autumn of 2008:

> I haven't missed club coaching so far, but I can see that I will probably go back to that level of coaching again. I have a desire to get back into it at some point, but it won't be before my England contract is up. Then I'll have to see if there are any jobs available.

Events moved rather more quickly than that. *The Rugby Leaguer & League Express* of 9 March 2009 trumpeted on its front page 'Wolves show improvement under Smith' after having proclaimed, seven days earlier, 'Lowes on thin ice after latest defeat'.

The 48-22 reverse at Wakefield Trinity Wildcats had proved to be the catalyst for change and Raymond Fletcher said, in his match report:

The pressure on Warrington Wolves coach James Lowes increased with this eighth successive defeat, especially when club owner Simon Moran entered the post-match press conference to ask what he had said. He must have been surprised to hear that Lowes had praised a defence that had conceded eight tries.

Lowes was rated, elsewhere in that issue, as the 1/3 favourite to become the first Super League coach of the season to lose his job. Bookmakers are rarely wrong although they would perhaps have been entitled to cavil at paying out on any bets when, within a week, Smith emerged from nowhere to take on the role at the Halliwell Jones Stadium of head of coaching and rugby, with Lowes effectively acting as his deputy as 'first team coach'.

Smith was unable to get the Wolves off to a winning start, even against a visiting Rhinos outfit that, as the former Leeds boss, he knew a great deal about, and one which lacked six regulars. But there were, for all that, immediate signs of improvement, Warrington battling back from 12-0 down after only six minutes to level matters at 14-14 midway through the second period through tries by stand-off Briers, substitute hooker Mickey Higham and winger Chris Hicks, who landed one goal. Leeds, though, secured victory with a try by stand-off Danny McGuire nine minutes from time; loose forward Kevin Sinfield, who had crossed in the early blast together with second row Carl Ablett, added his fourth goal.

Smith said:

> I thought the game was there to win, but I was encouraged by many things. The spirit's good for a team that has lost three games (in 2009), and the defence against a team like Leeds was good, but there were far too many errors. It was a tough week, though, for these players and I thought they handled it pretty well. Had we executed better we could have had three or four more tries. My role is to help them learn to do that, and I'm encouraged. It takes time to build understanding for them to get where I'm coming from, and the reverse. We're not quite on that roll yet but we will be; it will turn.

Smith was as good as his word – and before the end of that very season. The Wolves consolidated in Super League, not making the play-offs but, after those opening defeats, at least finishing with a respectable record, closing only a couple of points shy of the top eight. By that stage the Warrington public had more than been won over to

Smith's approach. From a position of little hope, with a battle against relegation seemingly destined to be their main preoccupation, the Wolves were transformed into a side that won the Challenge Cup for the first time in 35 years.

The win over Huddersfield at Wembley in 2009 was followed by a success over Leeds in 2010 and, while the Wolves were unable to reach Wembley the following season, there was satisfaction of another sort through finishing top of the Super League table. Smith and his players were lauded, generally, as the best side in the competition, heading the final table with 44 points from 22 victories in their 27 games, a point ahead of Wigan Warriors.

The play-off system of settling the championship came in, however, for strong criticism of a kind that echoed the complaints of those made in 1972-73 (when Dewsbury won the title from eighth spot) when fifth place Leeds battled their way through the elimination and qualification process to prevail at Old Trafford. Warrington, to general consternation, didn't even make it that far, hammering Huddersfield 47-0 in the opening round before losing 26-24 at home to Leeds in the sudden-death semi-final, slipping out to a late penalty by Kevin Sinfield. The saving grace was that Leeds' committed and thoughtful coach Brian McDermott, who had been subjected to unfair criticism when his injury-hit side had faltered in midseason, had been vindicated. Defeat, however, was still hard to swallow for Wolves' players, fans, and for Tony Smith, who simply said:

> We did some very good things, but at times we needed to be the next team to score, and that didn't happen. We paid a dear price for that, but we'll also learn some lessons. They're bitter and hard lessons to learn, but we needed to be better.

That ability to offer an honest appraisal was a characteristic that had been evident over a decade earlier, when Smith had been the subject of some negative publicity when he was announced as Head Coach of Huddersfield-Sheffield Giants (so named because of a controversial merger of one of the code's most famous names and the, in comparative terms, fledgling outfit that had won the Challenge Cup in sensational fashion less than two years earlier, having toppled hot favourites Wigan at Wembley).

His appointment, in August 2000 on a contract lasting 30 months, meant that there was not a single English coach left in the elite

British domestic competition. The Giants' chairman Ken Davy was unrepentant, and told the *Rugby Leaguer*:

> We had a number of high quality applicants from Britain and overseas and we put over a dozen candidates through a gruelling two hours interview process. Ours is the toughest job in Super League and we wanted a person with the ability to take Huddersfield-Sheffield forwards with some degree of courage and confidence in his ability. We are an ambitious club and I do feel that Tony Smith proved to be the best candidate.

He continued,

> I am sure that the Giants can never be accused of not promoting British coaches. Since Darryl Van de Velde left of his own accord to coach a Super League club, we have had Garry Schofield, Mal Reilly and John Kear in charge at the McAlpine Stadium. And we have met with very little success I'm afraid.

Smith, 33, had beaten off other challengers despite having had relatively little coaching experience, having been assistant to his brother Brian at Parramatta Eels and, prior to that, to Rod Reddy at Adelaide Rams. As a player he had, before his ill-fated spell at Workington Town, starred at halfback for Illawarra Steelers and St George, featuring for the latter side in the Grand Finals of 1992 and 1993. He insisted, in an early illustration of the cool, calculated and analytical approach that was to serve him in good stead throughout his coaching career:

> I am not into arguments over nationality; that's for the media. I flew over to Huddersfield at my own expense to press my claims, face to face, with the club's officials. I wanted the job and I've every confidence in myself that I can do the job well.

He added,

> I have researched the Giants thoroughly and I have arrived early in order to cast an eye over the players ahead of next season. I have no intentions of doing anything regarding possible recruitment until I have studied all the videos of past games and watched the remaining fixtures of the season. Every player must be given the chance to impress and if, after that, we need to bring in other players then I'm

sure we will do that. I have no intention of playing in a British style, or in an Australian style. I will play a style of rugby that suits my players and their strengths. I possibly have the same passion for League as my brother, Brian, but I don't have the tenseness I've seen in him during a match. I think I'm a little more relaxed, certainly at this early stage of my coaching career.

A little over a year later, Tony Smith found himself the coach of a side that had been relegated from Super League. Huddersfield Giants – they had reverted to their former name a month after Smith was appointed – finished bottom, with six wins and a draw from their 28 games, a point adrift of a Wakefield Trinity Wildcats outfit that had had a couple of points deducted. The Giants had, however, won four of their last six league games and, as such, were viewed as hot favourites to win the 2002 Northern Ford Premiership.

Smith, again illustrating the approach that would help him, within a couple of seasons, steer Leeds Rhinos to their first championship in three decades, become coach of the England side, and then take Warrington Wolves to successive Challenge Cup triumphs, plus a League Leaders' award, said:

> It doesn't really matter what the bookies say. It's nice to be thought of but we haven't kicked a ball yet this year. We are new guys to the competition and we are not going to listen to any of that sort of stuff. We are simply going to go out there and do our business each week. It's a cliché, but that's the truth of it. We don't have any problems getting that message through to the players. We have a lot to prove – we've gone through a pretty tough season. People talk to me about having to overcome complacency – these boys haven't had the wins to overcome any complacency yet. We have to build our season up, match by match. We learned a lot from last season. When you stop learning you give up. It was a steep learning curve for me, as a young coach, but at the same time we were very pleased with our season. Some of the things that happened were out of our control. That happens sometimes, but that's sport. But I think I'm a better coach for the experience than when I first started out, and I hope I keep improving next year.

Smith duly guided the Giants to promotion in 2002, and the side consolidated in Super League the following year, winning 11 and drawing one of 28 games to close in tenth spot, two positions clear of the relegation berth; despite a shattering defeat in the early stages of the campaign at Hunslet Hawks, of the bottom section, in the Challenge Cup, when the team sorely missed the likes of Papua New Guinea international Stanley Gene and Great Britain back row man Steve McNamara.

That proved to be Tony Smith's last season at the McAlpine Stadium. He moved to Leeds Rhinos for the 2004 campaign, having left Huddersfield in much better shape than when he arrived, and he performed exactly the same service at Headingley.

Leeds, having not won the championship since 1972, when St Helens had been beaten in the final at Swinton, were directed to the top of the table by Smith with a record of 50 points from 24 wins and two draws in their 28 games. In what came a shade too close for comfort to being something of a harbinger of Smith's subsequent experience with Warrington in 2011, the Rhinos lost 26-12 at home to Bradford Bulls in the qualifying semi-final, the men from Odsal going straight through to the Grand Final at Old Trafford, Manchester. Leeds made certain they joined them by easing past Wigan Warriors in the elimination final, with a stunning 40-12 success.

The Rhinos, after that reverse at the hands of Bradford, won the clash that counted, delighting their supporters in the 65,547 crowd with a 16-8 verdict in which Leeds had been 10-4 up at the interval, closing with tries by hooker Matt Diskin and scrum-half Danny McGuire, with stand-off Kevin Sinfield landing four goals from as many attempts. Bradford posted touchdowns for winger Lesley Vainikolo and centre Shontayne Hape, neither of which scrum-half Paul Deacon was able to convert.

Smith said:

> People asked me if we could do it this year and the answer is yes! The play-off defeat against Bradford definitely helped us, we were delighted to earn the second chance. Jeez, we're going to come back again next year and give it a crack – we like it that much.

Leeds did return, with 65,728 fans turning up – and Bradford Bulls, who gained revenge with a 15-6 victory, also showed up in a game that turned on its head the events of the match played at Old Trafford 12 months earlier. On this occasion it was the Bulls who went in at the break ahead, 8-6 this time, and Bradford held out with tries by winger Leon Pryce and Vainikolo; Deacon, unable to hit the target in 2004, made amends with three goals and a drop goal. Leeds, meanwhile, had to settle for a McGuire try and Sinfield penalty.

It was the Rhinos' second defeat in a major domestic final that season, Leeds having lost 25-24 to Hull in the Challenge Cup Final at the Millennium Stadium, Cardiff; an occasion on which Smith suffered rare criticism, having gambled that centre Keith Senior would be able to overcome the impact of a leg injury.

Tony Smith, however, despite those disappointments, was able to reflect on a 39-32 victory at Elland Road, Leeds, over Canterbury Bulldogs in the World Club Challenge clash in February. A crowd of 37,028 – the biggest for a World Club Challenge game – witnessed a contest that owed much to Smith's input, the media generally paying due tribute to the man who had helped Leeds step up a notch.

Leeds were 26-6 ahead at the interval before holding out in the face of a strong rally by the Australian champions, who finished with two tries each by winger Hazem El Masri and centre Jamaal Lolesi, with fullback Luke Patten and loose forward Tony Grimaldi adding tries and El Masri kicking four goals. The Rhinos prevailed through tries in the opening period by centre Chev Walker, winger Mark Calderwood, scrum-half McGuire, and substitutes Willie Poching and Rob Burrow; fullback Richie Mathers and second row Jamie Jones-Buchanan added further tries on the resumption, with stand-off Sinfield totalling five goals and, crucially, landing a drop goal that helped keep Leeds out of sight.

Smith, thanks to that success and his feat in guiding the Rhinos to the other two finals on offer, was named coach of the year.

Leeds slipped out of the Challenge Cup in 2006 at the semi-final stage, missing out, ironically, to Smith's former club, Huddersfield Giants, who reached the decider for the first time in 43 years with a 30-12 success. And, in another twist, it was to be his future club Warrington that would end the Rhinos' bid for another appearance in the Grand Final with an 18-17 victory at Headingley.

Scrum-half Lee Briers, a man who would be so vital to Smith's plans within a couple of years, was Warrington's key figure, landing the drop goal – his second of the night – that put the Wolves ahead for the only time; but the time that it mattered. Briers also kicked a couple of conversions, with the tries going to winger Henry Fa'afili, substitute Michael Sullivan and loose forward Ben Westwood. Leeds scored only two tries, through scrum-half Burrow and stand-off McGuire, with loose forward Sinfield kicking four goals and a drop goal in a game that started 15 minutes late because Warrington had become ensnarled on the motorway.

With New Zealand fullback Brent Webb brought on board for the 2007 campaign, the Rhinos gave Smith a glorious finale to his time at Headingley with a stunning 33-6 win over St Helens in a one-sided Grand Final enjoyed by their own supporters, at least, in the 71,352 crowd. Leeds were only 8-6 ahead at the interval, having registered a try by Webb and two goals by Sinfield, on his way to six successes, but blasted the Saints on the resumption with two tries in two minutes for substitute Ali Lauititi and winger Scott Donald. Winger Lee Smith and prop Jamie Jones-Buchanan finished the job off, while substitute hooker James Roby crossed for St Helens and scrum-half Sean Long added the extras.

Tony Smith bade farewell to Leeds in the best possible way, with the championship trophy on the sideboard. He had already accepted the post of coach of Great Britain, leading the international side to four victories in 2007, with New Zealand accounted for in the home Test Series.

Great Britain became England in 2008 – the year in which, on 8 September, Tony Smith became a naturalised citizen of the United Kingdom in a ceremony at Huddersfield.

A month or so later, Smith and his players were put to the sword in the World Cup in Australia, amid rumours of disharmony in the camp caused by friction between Leeds Rhinos and St Helens players.

Papua New Guinea were accounted for in the opening game of the tournament, but there was very little to enthuse about thereafter. England slipped against Australia and twice – at the group and semi-final stages – to New Zealand, attracting opprobrium from a hostile press Down Under. The problems involving the squad members from the Rhinos and the Saints, while never formally confirmed, were generally believed to have been central to England's difficulties.

England's World Cup bid opened with an unconvincing 32-22 win over Papua New Guinea in Townsville. The side had trailed 16-12 at the interval but Smith insisted:

I never thought we would lose. We had only 12 sets in the opening period, and we didn't make much use of them, making a lot of errors. We played a lot more like we've trained in the second half against opponents who were much better structured defensively than we'd seen in the build-up. They scrambled well on their own line and denied us several tries, which was a bit of a surprise. We put some pressure on ourselves by taking the wrong attacking options, but to not play so well, being rusty in some areas, and still win is a great attribute; it's a good characteristic to have.

England, who had been limited to tries by wingers Adie Gardner (St Helens) and Lee Smith, of Leeds, in the first half, stepped up a gear after the break, with Smith adding two more tries and other touchdowns going to Warrington centre Martin Gleeson and Gardner; Leeds loose forward Kevin Sinfield kicked four goals. PNG, meanwhile, had led through tries by Northern Pride loose forward Rod Griffin, substitute Jason Chan (Windsor Wolves) and Norths Devils winger George Kepa; but their only further score was a late consolation touchdown by Penrith Panthers hooker Paul Alton, with Salford City Reds fullback John Wilshere kicking his third goal.

That proved to be England's only victory in the competition, with the squad never recovering from a 52-4 humiliation at the hands of Australia in the following game. England were only 12-4 down as half-time approached, St Helens hooker James Roby having crossed in reply to touchdowns by the Melbourne Storm duo of fullback Billy Slater and centre Greg Inglis.

Tries by Inglis and Gold Coast Titans second row Anthony Laffranchi, however, helped send the Kangaroos in at the break 22-4 ahead, and the Green & Golds cut loose in the second half with touchdowns for Canberra Raiders winger Joel Monaghan – who would later join Warrington – Slater and Inglis (for their hat-tricks), and Laffranchi again, with Gold Coast scrum-half Scott Prince totalling eight goals. A number of key decisions by referee Tony Archer didn't help England's cause, but there was no disguising the gulf between the sides.

Smith, who tried to be positive about England's display, was less ready to be understanding of his players when the side were beaten 36-24 at Newcastle in the next game, after having led 24-8 at one stage in the first half. The 6,000 fans who had travelled across the globe were entitled to feel let down, with Kiwi winger Manu Vatuvei of New Zealand Warriors scoring a hat-trick in the second half to add to an earlier effort, and Warriors hooker Nathan Fien also getting over the whitewash. Fullback Lance Hohaia and St George-Illawarra winger Jason Nightingale had nipped in in the first half, while South Sydney Rabbitohs substitute Issac Luke (3) and Melbourne Storm loose forward Jeremy Smith kicked the goals.

Defeat was tough to take after a 16-point lead had been established with tries by Wigan Warriors hooker Mickey Higham, Leeds Rhinos scrum-half Rob Burrow (twice) and Gleeson, with Harlequins loose forward Rob Purdham kicking each conversion. Smith, aware that England were due to face New Zealand again a few days later in the semi-final, said:

> We're all angry about it, and we need to get angrier and become more determined. But I don't think this makes it harder next week; the scoreboard will still be 0-0 when we start.

The scoreboard eventually read 32-22 in the Kiwis' favour after 80 minutes of action in a game in which New Zealand led 16-0 after 22 minutes through tries by Sydney Roosters winger Sam Perrett, fullback Hohaia, and New Zealand Warriors centre Jerome Ropati.

With only two minutes remaining, England were only six points adrift, having blasted back through Leeds Rhinos prop Jamie Peacock, Leeds stand-off Danny McGuire (twice), and Gleeson, with Burrow kicking three goals. The Kiwis, though, snuffed out the revival, a kick by Fien being palmed back by Vatuvei towards Ropati; McGuire got a hand to the ball but was unable to secure possession, New Zealand stand-off Benji Marshall, of Wests Tigers, grabbing an opportunist score. Jeremy Smith kicked three goals for New Zealand and Marshall landed one.

New Zealand went on to shock Australia with a 34-20 victory in the final. The recriminations, meanwhile, began over England's failure to live up to expectations and Smith, citing the 'negativity' of the British press, told the BBC:

> I think we did things very professionally, and that's one of the frustrations. We pushed the Kiwis in both our games. They should have had three tries disallowed in our first meeting; had those decisions gone the other way, we would have come out with a win and started to build some momentum. The difference between success and failure is pretty close, particularly when you're playing the best in the world.

He also contested reports of discord between the Leeds and St Helens contingents,

> The players were fine, they socialised in the right ways at the right times. The players were good with each other, and I can't fault them for their application off the field. There were a lot of things flying

around about us that weren't true, and that were fairly negative. I would have liked a bit more patriotism from the press, at times.

Smith, meanwhile, repudiated claims that he hadn't co-operated with the media,

> In the last week there were two occasions when I didn't return calls, one at 6.30pm and the other at 7.30pm. I was out with the staff having an evening meal. Apart from that, I was really open and accessible throughout the tournament.

Tony Smith helped steer England to the following year's Gillette Four Nations Final. The side beat France 34-12 in the tournament opener before a crowd of 11,529 – the highest attendance for a meeting between the two countries for the best part of six decades – after having trailed 12-4 at the interval. Leeds' Lee Smith, in the centre, and his club team-mate, winger Ryan Hall, grabbed tries, and there was a brace for Salford City Reds scrum-half Richie Myler. Hull winger Tom Briscoe also crossed the whitewash, and Leeds loose forward Kevin Sinfield contributed a try and five goals. France were unable to add to tries by Catalans Dragons winger Vincent Duport and hooker Kane Bentley, also of Catalans.

England looked destined for another hammering at the hands of the Kangaroos when they went in at the break at Wigan 26-0 adrift. A 23,122 crowd, however, was delighted by a rally in which Bradford Bulls loose forward Sam Burgess, Wests Tigers second row Gareth Ellis and Lee Smith crossed, with Smith and Sinfield each kicking a goal to finish at 26-16. England had left themselves with too much to do, but honour was at least satisfied in a game in which Australia and Brisbane Broncos stand-off Darren Locker equalled, with his touchdown, the record of 33 tries for the Kangaroos set by Ken Irvine. Fullback Slater bagged a brace, Inglis crossed, and there was a try for St George-Illawarra Dragons winger Brett Morris; North Queensland Cowboys scrum-half Johnathan Thurston kicked three goals.

Boosted by that display, England qualified for the final by accounting for New Zealand 20-12, before 18,390 folk at Huddersfield. Hull KR winger Peter Fox grabbed two tries, St Helens halfback Kyle Eastmond nipped over, and Sinfield added four goals. The Kiwis were left behind despite a try and two goals by Canterbury Bulldogs winger Bryson Goodwin and a touchdown to Warriors second row

Ben Matulino.

The final, against Australia at Elland Road, Leeds, was to be Tony Smith's last in charge of England, the coach announcing in the immediate aftermath of the game that he was stepping down for family reasons.

The match was very much in the balance as the hour mark approached, with England having taken a 16-14 lead with a try by Burgess which Sinfield, who had already improved Burgess's first half effort – missing an attempt after Fox scored – converted.

Australia went back in front with tries by Slater and Morris but, at only six points behind, England were firmly in contention. However, an injury to Castleford Tigers centre Michael Shenton, who was stretchered off after a collision with Kangaroo prop Ben Hannant, transformed the contest.

The Green & Golds cut loose in the last 13 minutes, easing to a 46-16 win with unanswered tries for Melbourne hooker Cameron Smith, Slater (twice, for his hat-trick) and Parramatta Eels winger Jarryd Hayne. Thurston, who had converted tries in the first half by Morris and Inglis, in addition to landing a penalty, closed with seven goals to help frustrate home fans in the 31,042 crowd. Smith said:

> I'm not sure the scoreline reflects the game. If anything, it reflects some of the special individuals Australia have. I'm proud of the effort put in by the players. Not long ago, the Kiwis built a belief that they can beat Australia, and we are building one too. We are getting there.

Smith, as it turned out, was getting to Warrington – England's loss being the Wolves' gain – and to Wembley, proving himself, unequivocally, to be one of the finest coaches of the modern era.